/PS379.H54>C1/

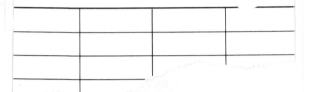

Date Due

OAKTON COMMUNITY COLLEGE
DES PLAINES, ILLINOIS 60016

In the Singer's Temple

In the
Singer's Temple

Prose Fictions of Barthelme, Gaines, Brautigan, Piercy, Kesey, and Kosinski

by Jack Hicks

67253

OAKTON COMMUNITY COLLEGE
DES PLAINES CAMPUS
1600 EAST GOLF ROAD
DES PLAINES, IL 60016

THE UNIVERSITY OF NORTH CAROLINA PRESS

CHAPEL HILL

© 1981 The University of North Carolina Press

All rights reserved

Manufactured in the United States of America

Library of Congress Cataloging in Publication Data

Hicks, Jack.
In the singer's temple.

Includes bibliographical references and index.
1. American fiction—20th century—History and
criticism. I. Title.
PS379.H54   813'.52'09   80-26074
ISBN 0-8078-1467-9
ISBN 0-8078-4096-3 pbk.
First printing, November 1981
Second printing, July 1982

Contents

Preface

I undertook *In the Singer's Temple* as a continuing interest from an earlier anthology (*Cutting Edges: Young American Fiction for the '70s*), found in its writing a larger fascination than I had planned, and labored finally to end it, as one must do with all fulfilling work that must have a life of its own. Early sections were written in Chapel Hill, North Carolina, and I am very grateful for the special counsel offered by Louis D. Rubin, Jr., and by Townsend Ludington and Christopher Brookhouse. Part of the book was drafted in Paris, and I am indebted to Michel Fabre of the Sorbonne for his observations on Afro-American fiction. Most of it was completed in Davis, California, and I am grateful to my colleagues, especially those in American literature, for their assistance: James Woodress, Michael Hoffman, and Brom Weber.

I would also like to express my thanks to the National Endowment for the Humanities, the Fulbright Commission, and the Committee for Research, University of California at Davis for their generosity in permitting me expanses of time in which to read and write.

There are many friends and students, too numerous to list, and I have appreciated their patience and support. A great deal of cooperation was offered, but the book is finally mine, and I am wholly responsible for whatever virtues or defects the reader encounters on his way.

I would like to dedicate this book to the memory of my mother, Pearl Elizabeth Hicks, who was there as long as she was here, but not quite long enough to have seen *In the Singer's Temple* in print.

JACK HICKS
University of California, Davis

In the Singer's Temple

A god can do it. But tell me, how can a man
follow his slender road through the strings?
A man is split. And where two roads intersect
inside us, no one has built the Singer's Temple.

Writing poetry, as we learn from you, is not desiring,
not wanting something that can never be achieved.
To write poetry is to be alive. For a god that's easy.
When, however, are we really alive? And when does he

turn the earth and the stars so they face us?
Yes, you are young, and you love, and the voice
forces your mouth open—that is lovely, but learn

to forget that breaking into song. It goes again.
Real singing is a different movement of air.
Air moving around nothing. A breathing in a god. A wind.

Sonnets to Orpheus, III
by Rainer Maria Rilke
(translated by Robert Bly)

One

Introduction: In the Singer's Temple

I take my title from Robert Bly's versions of Rilke's *Sonnets to Orpheus*, and I find it significant that two poets remarked for their modernity concern themselves with one of the oldest stories in the world, that of Orpheus, singer of such marvels as to sway oaks and pines, shy wild beasts to his side, repel Ciconian spears. But my Orpheus is first muted, a listener: to his lover's mortal cries, the rustlings of leaves, the warnings of underworld shades, and, finally, to the "silence, silence" of Rilke's first sonnet. "Real singing," we are told, can only come from silence, a sense of void out of which all sounds, tales, and actions issue. First quiet, attentive, our doomed singer can then heal the world again with his stories, build that singer's temple "deep inside the ears" of his rapt audiences. It is—always—a structure held in the mind, but no less real than stone or brick. And as Rilke's return to the ancient English lyric and Bly's cycling of modern German suggest, old tales do not die but are brought back to life constantly by powerful, transforming acts of the imagination.[1]

This study is a modest temple, an attempt to celebrate and clarify the many voices that "intersect inside us" in recent American fiction. It comes from my own listening and occasional comment to American prose narrative over the last decade or so. I should explain that, with Orpheus, I share a taste for youth: I am not at all interested in wailing the death of the novel or the last rales of print nor do I lament the passing of the age of the titans Faulkner, Fitzgerald, and Hemingway. I am concerned with the rich and diverse voices of contemporary American fiction, the confluence and separation of many young songs, and I am convinced that a new generation of priests and gods —for those who need them—will make themselves manifest from the chorus. If the trope of the singer in his temple seems a measure august for America in 1980, I suggest figures closer to our temper, say, that of a guide easing us through Henry James's House of Fiction or the mayor of Donald Barthelme's "muck of mucks" hurrying us through the metafictional neighborhoods of The City.

The basic premises underlying *In the Singer's Temple* are several. First, I assume that the dominant mode of American fiction has historically been realism—direct, essentially mimetic representation —and that this has been the case well into the twentieth century. Further, until the last few decades, there has existed a direct, almost reflexive relationship between the "facts" of national and individual life and fiction as a modified recording instrument. This has been especially evident in hard times, when we seem particularly to doubt national and personal centers and to worry that we are not one country but many factions. Fiction has often served as a good, readable barometer to national crisis, and the literature of the 1930s shows our almost chauvinistic self-absorption. An enormous literature of documentation was left behind, "speaking *of* the nation at large *to* the nation at large," as Harvey Swados suggests.[2] Titles tell the story: *USA, My America, The American Jitters, The Road: In Search of America, America Was Promises, An American Exodus.* It was in every sense an age of ritual national pulse taking, as if our writers worked in hope of reading our own more personal conditions in the rhythms and fevers of social collapse.

Intellectuals and would-be proletariat, many went on the road to chart the real national course and in so doing lay bare their own identities: John Dos Passos and Theodore Dreiser to Kentucky, John Steinbeck to California, Mary Heaton Vorse to wherever workers struck and fought for life. Among the directly brutalized, some— like Tom Kromer, as detailed in the grimmest of lumpenproletariat novel-chronicles, *Waiting For Nothing*—went on the road with neither choice nor destination. What you see really is what you get, and

Kromer, whose sole book was inscribed "To Jolene, Who turned off the gas," drifted long enough to get his scabid fill, vanishing from sight in 1936.[3]

More recently, in the last decades we have again been faced with national crises, a rain of them since the Bay of Pigs invasion in 1961. The rate of cultural change and a spate of massive social dislocations have both been formidable: at least four major assassinations; peaceful and violent racial agitation; ghetto insurrection and white repression; the profound alienation of many of the young from even sympathetic members of older generations; the seeming inability of political, educational, and social institutions to recognize, much less repair, the many tears in the social fabric; and widespread government inefficiency and corruption. All this plus Southeast Asia, Watergate, and profound energetic and economic quandaries. And yet very little of the fiction written over the last twenty years works with these profound social and political realities as material. And virtually no fiction by those most profoundly affected, the young, has engaged this body of experience directly, an exception being the phenomenon of drug use. It is as if most of a generation has been "in the pudding together," in Tom Wolfe's phrase, unwilling or unable to refract its own most public experiences into literary form.[4]

If we consider the events that mark off "the experience of a generation" in the recent past, the fictional lag of the last decades becomes more distinct. Writers active in World War I, the war to end all wars, wrote quickly and directly out of their own experience and of its human and social consequences. The same was true of the 1920s, as we hurried toward the Crash. And the literature of the depression period, as I have suggested, shows an almost reflexive response to daily events in those ragged times. This inescapable sense of history grinding through the husks of daily life is the source of strength (and weakness as well) of 1930s writing. But sometime during or after World War II, a break between the facts of public experience and their fictional uses as raw material becomes apparent.

Judging by the paucity of American fiction that treats such phenomena as the war itself, concentration camps and genocide, our firebombing of certain European cities, and the atomic bomb, we must pretty well agree with Wylie Sypher and conclude that "we have almost no literature of modern frightfulness because the artist was overborne by the calamity. We have lived through giant disasters, but they do not seem to be ours. To write about them would be a romantic luxury; we are struck dumb before such catastrophes."[5]

Critics of recent American fiction have echoed Sypher in greater particulars during the last decade. Raymond Olderman opens his *Beyond the Wasteland: A Study of the American Novel in the Nineteen-Sixties* with the observation extended: "The facts of contemporary experience are constantly beyond belief. . . . the unbelievability of events is no longer reserved for large world affairs. We have moved beyond the enormities of Buchenwald and Auschwitz and Hiroshima to the experience of the fantastic within what should be the firm shape of everyday reality."[6] As a consequence of "the explosion of the ordinary by the fabulous," Olderman notes that "the dominant pattern in the novel of the sixties continues the movement away from the realistic novel and toward a contemporary version of romance."[7] Building from Robert Scholes's recent work, *The Fabulators*,[8] Olderman cites not only a disinterest in the more mundane social and political events of our time as material, but a move away from the techniques of social realism toward black humor, romance, fable, and allegory.

Scholes and Olderman are correct, particularly when one realizes that the sterner realities of the period are quickly uprooted and made metaphoric, purified of their more documentary significances. Thus John Hawkes, Joseph Heller, and Jerzy Kosinski refine and extend international warfare as a metaphor for psychic struggle in *The Cannibal*, *Catch-22*, and *The Painted Bird*. The rampant hysteria of McCarthyism in the American 1950s symbolizes a darker, more pagan ritual than the political fact in Robert Coover's *The Public Burning*. For William Burroughs, the problem of opiate addiction comes to represent man's slavery to flesh, language, and society, and even as politically committed a writer as Sol Yurick shows urban insurrection as a psychological representation, just as much as it is a social and political event. On the West Coast, recent novelists as diverse as James D. Houston, Thomas Sanchez, and Diane Johnson manifest greater interest in the familiar exigencies of natural tectonic disaster, native American genocide, and underground warfare as extended metaphors for psychic dislocation rather than documentable facts.[9]

Indeed, the little fiction that does deal with social dislocation has been by older, more established writers. And while men like Joseph Heller, Jerzy Kosinski, and Kurt Vonnegut work at the peripheries of World War II, I can think only of Norman Mailer, who has always taken the world for his battlefield, Sol Yurick, in his remarkable novel *The Bag*, E. L. Doctorow (*The Book of Daniel*), and Robert Stone (*Dog Soldiers*), who work seriously with the more recent public realities of our time. Even Mailer's recent work has moved from creation or recreation of a fiction to the plumbing of actual events to yield up cultural secrets (Pentagon demonstrations, 1968 conventions, American moon shots, Gary Gilmore). Or he plumbs nothing, exposing the sheer barren bulk of our national "triumphs," as in *Of a Fire on the Moon*, especially in recording six successive pages of wire-serviced news releases and long snatches of "conversation" between Houston and the astronauts.[10] It is as if silence and despair are the only possible metaphysical comments before such a hollow, weighted event.

I agree at least partially with Alvin Toffler in *Future Shock* (however sweeping his thesis) that the magnitude and rate of change has created, however temporarily, a society unable to cope psychically— "the confused, the violent, the apathetic."[11] Through his lens, I find it scarcely odd that the young, earliest victims of future shock, choose neither to treat it nor to project its causes in their fiction. A fruitful image is that of the individual trapped in the crudest of diving bells under tons of water, crushed or certainly impacted a bit, who has become very introspective. We come through a time when young writing has all but denied itself the luxury of fictionalizing, of fabulating. Writers young and old take themselves directly as their major characters and work their own interiors—in confessions, analysis, fantasy—as subject matter. But the most powerful writing of recent years has been nonfiction: energized biography, as in rightly skewed Vietnam reports like Michael Herr's *Dispatches* and in accounts such as *The Autobiography of Malcolm X* and *Soul on Ice*; bastard journalism, as in Tom Wolfe's *The Electric Kool-Aid Acid Test*, Carlos Castaneda's five Don Juan chronicles, and Mailer's fictionalized chronicles; and confessionals such as Joan Didion's *The White Album*. Philip Roth kidnaps the cast of Nixon and company for *Our Gang* and even Ken Kesey turns to shredded memoirs and reflections in his ragbag *Kesey's*

Garage Sale.[12] For all their success and power, these books constitute a literature of doubt, hopefully a brief fictional moratorium. The popularity of nonfiction, with both writers and readers, suggests a broad lack of belief in the imagination's ability or need to transmute social reality to any higher form. In his recent anthology, *The New Journalism*, editor Tom Wolfe documents the case for recent nonfiction, and adds in his own abrasive, partisan fashion:

> By the Sixties, about the time I came to New York, the most serious, ambitious and, presumably, talented novelists had abandoned the richest terrain of the novel; namely, society, the social tableau, manners and morals, the whole business of "the way we live now," in Trollope's phrase. . . . That was marvelous for journalists—I can tell you that. The Sixties was one of the most extraordinary decades in American history in terms of manners and morals. Manners and morals *were* the history of the Sixties. A hundred years from now when the historians write about the 1960's in America . . . they won't write about it as the decade of the war in Vietnam or of space exploration or of political assassinations, but as the decade when manners and morals, styles of living, attitudes toward the world changed the country more crucially than any political events. . . . This whole side of American life that gushed forth when postwar American affluence finally blew the lid off—all this novelists simply turned away from, gave up by default. That left a huge gap in American letters, a gap big enough to drive an ungainly Reo rig like the New Journalism through.[13]

Of the fiction that has been written over the last decade or so, especially among the young and the consciously avant-garde, the direction continues inward, toward more personal experience and subjective modes of perception. The journey inward, ordered by the existentialists, is virtually a forced march now, quickened by the current, dystopian version of the American dream. The fiction that does speak of the nation at large to the nation at large and that broadcasts warnings from behind the lines is properly suspicious. An active literary "recoiling reflex" is apparent, as writers concern themselves more with threats than presences.

When there is a marked concern for social or political matters, it takes negative forms, as fear, for example. There is an apparent fear of social programming—the conscious, long-range manipulation of groups and minds—and several recent works, Ken Kesey's *One Flew Over the Cuckoo's Nest*, for instance, dwell on contemporary consciousness (the walking-around, average sort) as a form of engineered social addiction.[14] As I suggest in a later chapter, Marge Piercy's *Dance the Eagle to Sleep* offers a similar vision.[15] Taking R. D. Laing at his word, many recent writers seem to feel that one must go out of his mind to approximate sanity. Schizophrenia is a stratagem of self-protection against Kesey's Combine, and paranoia is a higher form of knowledge. Chief Bromden opens the novel with a sage observation: "They're out there."[16]

Recent works by John Barth, William Burroughs, Sol Yurick, and Thomas Pynchon are concerned with conspiracies and plots and lay bare great subterranean caves of truth, hitherto systematically withheld from us. Only a paranoid can fully savor Robert Stone's *Hall of Mirrors* as it unravels a frighteningly complex right-wing conspiracy.[17] And Pynchon's *V.* compels one to mimic Herbert Stencil's search until even his dreams compose endless flights of V-forms. Maybe they are out there.

But far more often, there is a pronounced lack of interest in fictionally rendering, by social realism or other modes, any sort of social or political concerns. Marge Piercy, a Marxist-feminist who works as one of our most socially engaged writers, writes recently that "economy is the bone, politics is the flesh."[18] And Rudolph Wurlitzer goes even further in his Beckettesque fiction *Flats*, urging on us the "politics of displacement," adding, "that strategy toward the collective voice is only another shuck. That reaching out, as if for collaboration, is only delay."[19] A basic premise of socially engaged fiction, that heightened awareness can move us toward political action, has been all but abandoned, and Raymond Olderman's explanation seems appropriate: "The older device of simply shocking a reader into awareness of his sins is unproductive—if social value and reform are to be criteria—because it only pushes us deeper into a closed cycle: guilt—inaction—atrocity—guilt."[20]

In place of our relation to any exterior worlds and institutions, a fictional interest in human consciousness has become especially dominant in recent American fiction. The varieties and extremities of human and artistic visions, how social forces mold consciousness and how it may be liberated—these are matters of major interest to younger writers and their readers. The recent waves of "speculative fiction" (science fiction) such as *Childhood's End*, *Stranger in a Strange Land*, and Ursula LeGuin's work and of "pop fiction" such as Hesse's and Tolkien's works demonstrate this, as do the attentions paid "head" nonfiction like Carlos Castaneda's five Don Juan chronicles and Tom Wolfe's *Kool-Aid Acid Test*. And the basic appeal of our most popular writers, Richard Brautigan and Kurt Vonnegut, is the way in which they can realize, verbally, not only their own distinct fictional worlds, but offer unique modes of perceiving and responding to them. In short, their gifts are for offering wholly created *sensibilities* and for depicting attractive, sustaining states of consciousness. It is no accident that both Brautigan and Vonnegut are especially attracted to children, harmless eccentrics, naïfs, mildly insane characters—divine idiots all but immune to the chaos and hostility of the modern world. They are by no means isolated in their interest in the minds and rendered worlds of the innocent. More established writers such as John Updike and Joyce Carol Oates also dwell on the bittersweet landscapes of child and adolescent minds. Perhaps Castaneda's *brujo* points the way in urging travel "only on the paths that have heart, on any path that may have heart." His spirit prevails, that there might yet be magic down some path, and for fiction writers, an interest in "non-ordinary reality," in the timeless, placeless outposts of human consciousness, seems apparent.[21]

Among black writers, the interest in consciousness reveals itself in a curious and growing awareness of the uses of history and literature to provide human models. At the lowest level, one might note the many children's books and black histories and biographies published recently, directed mainly at black grade-school audiences. More directly, the proper literary use of history was the basis for the protracted quarrels following William Styron's *The Confessions of Nat Turner*.[22] And both Imamu Baraka (LeRoi Jones) and Ishmael Reed see themselves metaphorically as black magicians breaking old spells and casting new ones. As Reed observes, "Manipulation of the word has always been related to the manipulation of nature. One utters a few words and stones roll aside, the dead are raised and river beds emptied."[23]

The interest in consciousness also manifests itself in the creation of black myth-figures. John A. Williams' hero Captain Blackman, from his recent novel of that title, successfully creates a black culture hero, a soldier whose experiences are a composite of wars from the Revolution to Viet Nam.[24] A general interest in character *types*, especially for purposes of satire and ridicule, also indicates an awareness of literary images and heroes as they develop and reinforce attitudes. Reed's *Yellow Back Radio Broke-Down* is a good case in point, as he remakes the basic Western in a more self-conscious, distorted manner, filling it with white-pansy villains, children's crusades, and black heroes.[25] And literary styles are a basic concern to black writers, not only because they seek appropriate modes for new experiences but because a style is a projection of consciousness, a means of making substantial an entire vision of what is, has been, or could be. Baraka, for example, writes of his need for languages and structures that do not delimit existence but instead allow him to record "life and its many registrations." He turns to black music, particularly John Coltrane, to develop a "chromatic style," a stylistic equivalent of Coltrane's sheets of separated chords. "He sees chords as kinetic splinters of melody rather than generalized blocks of sound, and attacks each chord and its overtones, separating it, sucking out even the most minute musical potential."[26] Oral and musical borrowings are also frequent elsewhere. On a different track, William Melvin Kelley attempts some neo-Joycean toolings of language appropriate for realms of Afro-American experience in *Dunfords Travels Everywheres*.[27]

A social development accompanying the rise of black and other ethnic sensibilities, the growth of the women's movement has been responsible for a tide of recent fiction by females, many writing with an incipient feminist consciousness. Although early books by Erica Jong, Alix Kates Shulman, and, more recently, Marilyn French found large popular audiences, continuing excellent work from older writers like Grace Paley and Tillie Olsen (a feminist heroine of the 1970s) assures that women's fiction will develop much further. I find recent work by Rita Mae Brown, Maxine Hong Kingston, Alice Walker, and Rosellen

Brown to be among the most substantial written by young American women. Marge Piercy and Diane Johnson continue to build deserved national reputations and Margaret Atwood, who writes across the border in Quebec, has gained an international reputation on three excellent novels: *Surfacing, The Edible Woman,* and *Lady Oracle.*[28]

A broad strain in recent American fiction denies fixed styles and forms, as if closed genres and modes of realism (short story, novel, sustained discourse) are rigid cultural projections of a totalitarian mind. Although senior writers as dissimilar as Saul Bellow and Norman Mailer continue to view the individual self—and fictions that originate in but finally transcend the self—as the only possible bulwark against cultural breakdown, many young writers find even that station denied. As different as they seem, Mailer's Rojack and Bellow's Sammler both retreat to the isolated experiences of isolated men and both see a strong self, or progression of selves, as an aesthetic island from which to fight a holding action. But younger writers such as Rudolph Wurlitzer, Donald Barthelme, Ronald Sukenick, and Richard Brautigan seem to regard even that first-person certainty as an improbable convenience. Wurlitzer, in particular in *Nog* and *Flats*, depicts a muddled world in which discrete identities have collapsed.[29] The "hero" of *Nog*, the central fluid as the title suggests, flows between three selves. In more active moments, he extends his formal studies of beaches and waters, traveling from port to port with a rubber sideshow octopus. His greatest bliss is to sit motionless as an ocean plays over him, an ecstasy unbearably doubled when he reaches the midpoint of the Panama Canal (where two oceans meet) at the climax of the novel. The metaphor of Nog's existence offers a fluid, often blurred style and mode of narration.

Elsewhere, in the works of Barthelme, Sukenick, and Brautigan, there is an even greater turn toward fragmentation to truncated, discontinuous, often thoroughly impressionistic forms. Brautigan's *Revenge of the Lawn* offers sixty-two fictions spread lavishly over one hundred seventy pages, including "Lint," which reads in full:

> I'm haunted a little this evening by feelings that have no
> vocabulary and events that should be explained in dimensions
> of lint rather than words.

I've been examining half-scraps of my childhood. They are
pieces of distant life that have no form or meaning. They are
things that just happened like lint.[30]

Barthelme habitually works in several styles and parodies of styles
simultaneously. He advises us often that "fragments are the only form
I trust," asserting half comically, "It's my hope that these . . . souve-
nirs . . . will someday merge, blur—cohere is the word, maybe—into
something meaningful. A grand word, meaningful. What do I look
for? A work of art, I'll not accept anything less."[31]

Just as Ken Kesey's McMurphy challenges Big Nurse's "United
Front" with a run of orchestrated chaos (laughter, sex, spontaneity),
we can see the same game responses among younger writers. Liberation generally appears first as a series of negative gestures or rejec-
tions and can hardly be expected to please those whose first priority is
ORDER (read familiarity or habit), literary or political. Thus the
fiction of the 1960s and 1970s incorporates collage techniques, random disorder, sudden stylistic shifts and exaggerations, even self-
parody. As Richard Gilman notes of Barthelme's work, "We perceive
in fragments, live in fragments, are no doubt dying by fragments;
should we not, then, write in fragments, thereby emphasizing the
juxtapositions, the stranger disjunctions, that are a part of everyday
experience of modern life?"[32]

Out of these patterns, an overall movement becomes clear. Young
American writers of the 1960s and 1970s were absorbed in their own
personal and subcultural experiences. This, I suggest, is an indication,
at least in part, of the dissolution of the American cultural mainstream, the presence of which created and sustained Hemingway,
Faulkner, and other major modern novelists. Since World War II, the
process of cultural splintering has accelerated enormously and whatever broad national culture there was has now splintered into a series
of distinct subcultures—ethnic, racial, philosophical, and artistic.

In contemporary American literary circles, each group tends to
develop its own champions, distinct subject matters and preferred
styles, aesthetics, even, in some instances, its own means of publishing
and distributing manuscripts. Conflicts are frequent. The most obvious flashpoints occur during the granting of literary awards and

monies, as in the National Book Awards of 1971 and 1972. During the 1971 nominations, a bitter and open feud was waged between advocates of Mona Van Duyn and Gregory Corso, both vying for the poetry award. A year later, a series of brush quarrels raged over an award made to the "nonbook" *Whole Earth Catalog* and its California creators.

This cultural fragmentation has had an adverse effect on the publishing of fiction, particularly that written by young or experimental writers. Faced with the loss of a broad central reading public, highly centralized publishing houses note that first novels almost invariably take a loss—perhaps one in twenty makes a substantial profit. Publishing houses are no longer the patrons of the arts they once were. Their function as components of large, interlocking communications conglomerates and the pressures of the free market economy conspire to make fiction a bad risk. Many editors and publishers frankly admit interest only in fiction books with "futures" (translated: works with obvious book club, paperback, or film prospects). The once familiar evolution from hardcover to paperback to film has often been reversed and, since *Jaws*, it is not uncommon to find "novels" developed after the success of a film. The result of all this is that the tail very often wags the dog, because publishers are in the position not merely of accepting or rejecting fiction but of encouraging and commissioning potentially lucrative work over more innovative or unfamiliar writing. In this development, stylistic and narrative innovation are discouraged in favor of more straightforward fiction. Collections of short fiction attract almost no interest (how can you make a movie from a ten-page story?) and the success of young masters of the genre such as Leonard Michaels or Raymond Carver is rare. Immediacy is a prime virtue, as are its companion qualities of a strong story line, cinematic central characters, engaging material. Thrillers and mystery novels, for one example, have become very popular in the last five years, and woe betide the young novelist who runs against the escapist tide.

But the decline of the broad national cultural base and the publishing industry it supported has had unforeseen positive influence as well. Feeling themselves at the cruel mercies of New York, computer studies, and publishing fads, minority groups have begun to develop their own journals, publishing houses, and distribution networks.

Women's publishing collectives have become familiar and welcome, making less commercial, more controversial writing available. Thus, for the first time, with the advent of ventures such as Dudley Randall's Broadside Press, black writers can publish with a black house, for a black audience, and be available to formerly isolated regions of black readership. A recent pamphlet of poems by Don L. Lee has sold twenty thousand copies to date; such impressive sales have been accomplished without ads and puffs in *Publisher's Weekly*, friendly reviews by partisans in the New York book pages and reviews, or the financial support of book clubs.[33] Randall's venture is one of many. Further evidence that he has helped create new black reading audiences and new black talent, as well, is suggested by the success of his recent large-market anthology, *The Black Poets*.[34]

Along the same lines, but in a far more sophisticated manner, the publishing ventures of the multiethnic minority community of writers on the West Coast have grown prominent. Ishmael Reed and a large, growing circle of Afro-American, American Indian, Asian-American, and Chicano artists have created and supported an excellent journal of Third World writing—*Yardbird*, continued as *Y'Bird*. Reed's publishing activities, mainly under the Reed, Cannon, and Johnson imprint, have been significant in retrieving and introducing writing by men and women once unknown or ignored.[35]

A similar offshoot has been the growth of national paperback reviews like *New American Review* (renamed *American Review* until its recent demise). Although many similar reviews survived only three or four issues at most, *American Review* flourished under editor Ted Solotaroff's guidance, continuing intermittently through twenty issues, regularly introducing young talent in each number, and doing as much as any other single organ to sustain a readership for contemporary writing. The conveniences of a tabloid format are shown in appearances of *Fiction* and *The American Poetry Review*.[36] Early in 1972, *Fiction* made an initial impressive showing. Issuing from editor Mark Mirsky and a loosely organized national writers' collective, it opened around a spate of manifestos. Mirsky insisted that "there is not a single publication of any significant circulation in America that is devoted to good fiction," and further, "writers must take matters into their own hands and search out the audience they believe is there. By going outside the marketplace (none of us at *Fiction*, writers or artists or editors, have been paid), without grants or foundations, we have begun. As the Chairman says, seize the day."[37] That his fellow writers agreed with his conclusions is evident: the first several issues included work volunteered by Donald Barthelme, Anthony Burgess, John Hawkes, John Barth, and Samuel Beckett. Remarkably, readers responded by buying out twenty thousand copies on the East Coast and plans were quickly set for a West Coast supplement.

But the best instance of adversity turned to benefit has been that of the Fiction Collective, a New York–Colorado-based group disheartened by the harsh economic realities of corporate publishing. Directed initially by novelists Peter Spielberg and Jonathan Baumbach in 1974, the Collective has expanded its editorial board and list to twenty-six writers (mainly innovative), a compendium of young talent including Mark Mirsky, Mimi Albert, Jerry Bumpus, Steve Katz, and Clarence Major. The Collective now functions much as *New Directions* did in its shaping years of the late 1940s and early 1950s.

Pooling authority and editorial resources, the Fiction Collective has offered unpublished writers a vehicle for their work. Perhaps their best-known author, novelist and academic Ron Sukenick, indicates the basis for their growth and survival: "The publishing industry has been increasingly forced by inflation, profit demands and the logic of its inefficiencies toward the immediate large audience; while serious fiction, in its slow discourse with the culture, most often finds its initial public among the happy few. But even serving the happy few has become nearly impossible for innovative writers once published by a large house. Risky novels are rarely published unless they promise movie sales. You can simply forget about short fiction."[38] The incongruity of the situation appalls the audience of French intellectuals Sukenick addresses. Known internationally to students of serious fiction, he explains why, after five successful books, large publishing houses are uninterested in three recent manuscripts. "Few publishers are willing to support the careers of promising talent. Faulkner, for example, published a handful of unsuccessful novels early in his career. I don't think he would have been published today."[39]

My final premise is that, for better or for worse, the breakup of American culture, seen particularly in its literary reflexes, is an inescapable fact. "The puzzle of the-one-and-the-many," as Ralph Ellison terms it, the eternal dialectic between mass national identity and regional, ethnic, or subcultural self-definition, is presently being won by the latter. Further, what we now see are a series of overlapping literary subcultures, especially among younger writers and their audiences. Each subculture has a distinct readership receptive to particular modes and topics in fiction; each is finally working toward a unique literary reflex and relation to culture and, in some cases, is developing independent means of publishing and distributing that literature.

In the Singer's Temple is my attempt to hear those varied voices and note the dominant chords in contemporary American fiction, mainly those sounded in novels and short stories of the 1960s and 1970s. The discussions that follow are both selective and representative: selective, in that I work centrally with fictions by six American writers; and representative in the sense that their works bring to life the concerns and substances of the most prominent strains of American prose narrative of the last several decades. In each instance, my critical emphases—textual, historical, cultural, generic—seek to vivify the characteristics of the broader strain and the individual work. Specifically, I consider metafiction—the story of postmodern consciousness—as exemplified by the fiction of Donald Barthelme; the Afro-American fiction of social and historical imagination, as evidenced in prose works by Ernest J. Gaines; countercultural fiction—the varieties of dreaming ourselves out of this binding world—demonstrated in single works by Marge Piercy, Richard Brautigan, and Ken Kesey. I then close with a long chapter on the romance of public and private terrors, the novels of Jerzy Kosinski.

Two

Metafiction and Donald Barthelme

While public America battled outside in the late 1960s and early 1970s—on urban streets and university swards, at the steps of the Pentagon and the foot of the White House, in Miami and Southeast Asia—the private life of American fiction moved further than ever into the interior, there to become less concerned with art as a mimetic reflex, more taken with literature as a linguistic construct tracing the play of the psyche, more enchanted with the creation of alternate worlds, fictional cities, and lunar landscapes. We can see several distinct developments in the fiction of the 1960s: On one hand, we can note a marked interest in large, eclectic, fantastic books like John Barth's *The Sot-Weed Factor* and *Giles Goat-Boy*, Joseph Heller's *Catch-22*, Thomas Pynchon's *V.*, Sol Yurick's *The Bag*, and William Gaddis's *The Recognitions*.

But I address myself to an opposing stream of avant-garde fiction, one turned loose by the American publication of the first volume of *Ficciones* by the Argentine Jorge Luis Borges in 1964. With Borges's *Labyrinths*, we can fix the beginning of interest in short, highly self-conscious, philosophically concerned fiction, a strain of writing termed *metafiction* by William Gass and Robert Scholes. It is fitting that a group of essays by a philosopher turned litterateur, William Gass, should serve as a manifesto and an apologia for the new fiction. His essays in *Fiction and the Figures of Life* (1970), particularly "Philosophy and the Form of Fiction," offer still another rejection of the varieties of mimetic fiction. Continuing his thinking in *The World Within the Word* (1978), Gass dismisses concepts of fiction as a means of viewing social reality (from naturalism to the fabular), those which use writing as a lens to direct our gaze back to the substantial world. In these two seminal works he is insistent, urging instead a sense of fictional worlds as additions to reality, as fields of experience independent of those already familiar to us, with little or no redeeming social significance. The first critic to use the term *metafiction*, Gass tentatively and suggestively traces the outlines of this emerging body of writing:

> The use of philosophical ideas in the construction of fictional works—in a very self-conscious and critical way, I mean—has been hastened by the growing conviction that not only do these ideas often represent conceptual systems of considerable complexity, they have the further advantage of being almost wholly irrelevant as accounts of the real world. They are, that is, to a great degree *fictional* already, and ripe for fun and games. Then, too, the novelist now better understands his medium; he is ceasing to pretend that his business is to render the world; he knows, more often not, that his business is to *make* one, and to make one from the only medium of which he is a master—language. And there are even more radical developments.
>
> There are metatheorems in mathematics and logic, ethics has its linguistic oversoul, everywhere lingos to converse about lingos are being contrived, and the case is no different in the novel. I don't merely mean those drearily predictable pieces about writers who are writing about what they are writing, but those, like some of the work of Borges, Barth, and Flann O'Brien, for example, in which the forms of fiction serve as material upon which further forms can be imposed. Indeed, many of the so-called antinovels are really metafictions.[1]

They are metafictions in a dual sense: as metaphysical fiction, the prime interest of which is in a world of ideas; and *meta*-fiction, a literature extended beyond its former possibilities, transcending an essentially mimetic status. Borges provided early instances, but he is simply one expression of a broad international impulse. Recently there has been a sense, in America and abroad, of being weighted down by the immensity of our collective past, and, even more, of being almost powerless to respond to the devastations of post-1945 experience. Again, Wylie Sypher observes rightly that Americans lack a contemporary literature of frightfulness. He reasons that "we have lived through giant disasters, but they do not seem to be ours. To write about them would be a romantic luxury; we are struck dumb before such catastrophes."[2]

Younger writers, particularly, seem to have difficulty in conceiving of themselves as part of any viable past or body of traditions and have increasingly felt themselves "heaped," in Richard Poirier's words, "by history, by literature, by the accumulations of myth and allusions, by technologies, cant styles, articulated modes of being which are the world's semblance of logic, its pretense to solidity, its projection of nature. . . . They are [all] a part of the 'heap' which befuddles every effort to locate a stabilizing reality."[3] Recent writers as diverse as William Burroughs, Thomas Pynchon, Imamu Baraka (LeRoi Jones), and Norman Mailer share this sense of having come to a complex of cultural dead ends, but it is especially powerful for those working within the imaginary limits of metafiction. John Barth's first three novels all close on notes of having exhausted the logical possibilities out of which life and art can grow. But only in his most recent works, the collections *Lost in the Funhouse* (1970) and *Chimera* (1972) and the novel *Letters* (1979), does he permit the full, weighted fruits of metaphysical doubt to ripen, threatening the existence of literature itself. Writing on Borges's work in "The Literature of Exhaustion," Barth poses the problem and one solution:

> No one has claim to originality in literature; all writers are more or less faithful amanuenses of the spirit, translators and annotators of preexisting archetypes. Thus his inclination to write brief comments on imaginary books: for one to attempt to add overtly to the sum of "original" literature by even so much as a conventional short story, not to mention a novel, would be too presumptuous if it weren't part of a lively, passionately metaphysical vision, and slyly employed against itself precisely to make a new and original literature. Borges defines the Baroque

as "that style which deliberately exhausts (or tries to exhaust) its possibilities and borders upon its own caricature." While his own work is *not* Baroque, except intellectually (the Baroque was never so terse, laconic, economical), it suggests the view that intellectual and literary history has been Baroque, and has pretty well exhausted the possibilities of novelty. His *ficciones* are not only footnotes to imaginary texts, but postscripts to the real corpus of literature.[4]

Thus metafiction may be profitably seen as a series of searches for a way out of a cultural labyrinth.

Let us think of metafiction as a great city without permanent citizens, a place to dream for a time. Its visitors, who strain within the walls, are multinational and include the Argentine master, the Italian Italo Calvino, the Irishman Flann O'Brien, and, of course, Americans such as John Barth, Donald Barthelme, William Gass, Robert Coover. Some less lauded, younger Americans have created work that shares many of the same characteristics: Ronald Sukenick, Ishmael Reed, Steve Katz, Leonard Michaels. While our visitors work longer forms— indeed, Barth's *Giles Goat-Boy* and Coover's *The Public Burning* seem to subject the novel to intolerable stresses—their imaginations have turned to shorter works published in collections: Barth's *Lost in the Funhouse* and *Chimera*, Calvino's *t zero* and *Cosmi-Comics*, Coover's *Pricksongs and Descants*, Gass's *In the Heart of the Heart of the Country*, Barthelme's five collections beginning with *Come Back, Dr. Caligari*, the younger Michaels's *Going Places* and *I Would Have Saved Them If I Could*, and Sukenick's *Death of the Novel and Other Stories* and forthcoming *Endless Short Story*.[5]

These writers by no means comprise a conscious school but nonetheless show clear similarities of execution and interest. Metafiction does not accept the world "out there" as a referent for its own existence but works, instead, from second-order literary and intellectual materials. Coover, for example, combines and compresses a series of fairy tales and American folk stories in his work (from Hansel and Gretel to the baby-sitter to Lucky Pierre). Calvino takes a single scientific hypothesis or speculation as the germ for each fantastic fiction in *t zero*. Barth's *Chimera* consists of three exotically recast Greek and

Oriental tales. In his fictions Ishmael Reed makes no attempt to disguise his historical detective work as part of the text; indeed, he insists that we see it. Like his hoodoo detective Papa La Bas, Reed seeks to recreate and reimagine a submerged culture, an entire mode of perceiving existence, and, to that end, *Mumbo Jumbo* is a metafiction of research linking the cult of Osiris in ancient Egypt with the rise of jazz in early twentieth-century America. Lest we miss his message, the novel ends with a bibliography of more than a hundred items. Throughout his work, an artful quilt of serious thought and popular culture—the speculations of Poulet, Kierkegaard, Gabriel Marcel appear with the presences of Batman, Robert F. Kennedy, Snow White —is the unlikely basis for Donald Barthelme's world.

Metafictionists tend to regard everything about them as man-created, as fiction: the language systems that enfold us, the labyrinths of conceptual systems (social, psychological, philosophical) that impinge on our inner lives, the artistic structures that remove existence even further from itself. They often share Barth's sense of exhausted forms and languages, of the paradoxical necessity and impossibility of fresh utterance. They handle the substances of fiction as heavy industry does scrap steel: the red enameled skin of my fine new Oldsmobile hides many other lives—the case of an ancient Frigidaire, the wheel brace of a DC-3, ten coat hangers, shell casings from a recent war, a case of spent Pabst cans. Thus old forms are plastic, recyclable, and can be bent and torn and reassembled. William Burroughs's use of the "cut-up" is one expression, but it is much more conscious and less left to chance among metafictionists. Barth recasts ancient myths, tales, and stories-within-stories of Oedipus, Menelaus, Echo, Captain John Smith. Ishmael Reed redrafts slave narratives, "yellow back" pulps, the detective story. At the American gas station, Coover has fantasies of the teenage baby-sitter and the infamous Lucky Pierre. Barthelme turns myth and tale inside out in *Snow White* and *The Dead Father* and tinkers endlessly with the form of the story as the "subject" of his fictions. "The Dolt," for example, examines the paradox of "beginnings, middles and ends" in the fictions of the short story and human life.

Language itself must be made new, and the metafictionists are some of the most inventive stylists writing in the United States today. The robust, mock-Jacobean language of Barth's *The Sot-Weed Factor* is an endless joy. William Gass offers us the richest of poetic prose in *Omensetter's Luck* and the meditative *On Being Blue*. And the language of his masterful "In the Heart of the Heart of the Country," that snowy tale of loss in Indiana, approaches George Poulet's ideal of a style "artless enough to espouse each change . . . of the heart."[6] Consider this sentence from Barthelme's "The Indian Uprising," a kind of linguistic allegory about the "war" between civilized and primitive consciousness: "Red men in waves like people scattering in a square startled by something tragic or a sudden, loud noise accumulated against the barricades we made of window dummies, thoughtfully planned job descriptions (including scales for the orderly progress of colors), wine in demi-johns, and robes."[7] This also approaches, as we see later in greater detail, Poulet's ideal living, gliding language that simultaneously creates and destroys expectations (note the inversion "in waves like people"), wrenching language free from habitual meaning without quite casting it into nonsense.

We should note that metafiction is utterly, perhaps maddeningly, self-conscious, both in its awareness of a place in literary history and its self-acknowledged presence as a linguistic structure, an artifice, an object of words. Barth writes often of the presumption of writing without a sense that it has all been done before, and Robert Scholes notes how our visitors employ myth and archetype in a very new way:

> Once so much is known *about* myths and archetypes, they can no longer be used innocently. Even their connection to the unconscious finally becomes attenuated as the mythic materials are used more consciously. . . . Thus the really perceptive writer is not merely conscious that he is using mythic materials: He is conscious that he is using them consciously. He *knows*, finally, that he is allegorizing. Such a writer, aware of the nature of categories, is not likely to believe that his own mythic lenses really capture the truth. Thus his use of myth will inevitably partake of the comic.[8]

Metafiction is also self-conscious in that the text itself is a consciousness aware of itself, insisting upon its own fictive nature. Thus Barthelme's characters, as well as those of Flann O'Brien, discuss the very works they inhabit. Barthelme's stories frequently invoke other written and graphic materials (in footnotes and direct impressions), and thinkers and artists as well, to gloss the text as we read it. Too, metafiction devours and subsumes criticism; it is as fully self-reflective as any postmodern mode of thought or art must be. In a more satirical vein, Ishmael Reed responds to Irving Howe's past and future criticisms by writing him into *Yellow Back Radio Broke-Down*. "What's your beef with me Bo Shmo," Reed writes in defense of his form. "What if I write circuses? No one says a novel has to be one thing. It can be anything it wants to be, a vaudeville show, the six o'clock news, the mumblings of wild men saddled by demons."[9] It can be not merely criticism, but those styles of teaching that reduce literary experience to subject matter. Barthelme and Sukenick short-circuit the process by including "tests" within their fictions, as in Sukenick's "The Birds": "Part II *Essay* (90 points). This story is 'entirely without design, precedent or orderly planning, created bit by bit on sheer impulse, a natural artist's instinct, and the fantasy of the moment.' Why do you think the police don't like that? Discuss."[10]

Metafiction is self-conscious, too, in its sense of existence as a physical text or a language construct and as a thing or an object in the material world. Barth opens *Lost in the Funhouse* with a Möbius strip, to be cut out and assembled. The fictions of Coover, Reed, Barthelme, Katz, and Sukenick make use of collage and pastiche techniques, are laced with typographics and engravings, are often broken or truncated assemblages, and stress their presences in the world as artifacts. Sukenick's "The Birds" refers to its metaphoric similarities to Simon Rodia's Watts Towers in Los Angeles. And Barthelme writes, in a significant early essay on modern art and writing, "The question so often asked of modern painting, 'What is it?' contains more than the dull skepticism of the man who is not going to have the wool pulled over his eyes. It speaks of fundamental placement in the world in relation to the work, that of a voyager in the world coming upon a strange object."[11] Objects like rocks or stones are fictional kingdoms as well and we should observe a remarkable similarity of inversion: these writers' fictive realms all occur in language as physical structures, fortresses created by human consciousness resting at its own center. Barth's Funhouse, Sukenick's Tower, Gass's "heart of the heart of the country," Coover's menacing fairy-tale land behind "The Door," Borges's Tlön, Barthelme's City—all are carefully limned physical worlds, the prime realities of which exist only in the imagination, as fiction.

Needless to say, such a fiction requires a very attentive reader. There are certainly those who agree with John Gardner's remark in his recent treatise *On Moral Fiction*:

> Fiction as pure language (texture over structure) is *in*. It is one common manifestation of what is being called "post-modernism." At bottom the mistake is a matter of morality, at least in the sense that it shows, on the writer's part, a lack of concern. To people who care about events and ideas and thus, necessarily, about the clear and efficient statement of both, linguistic opacity suggests indifference to the needs and wishes of the reader and to whatever ideas may be buried under all that brush. And since one reason we read fiction is our hope that we will be moved by it, finding characters we can enjoy and sympathize with, an academic striving for opacity suggests, if not misanthropy, a perversity or shallowness that no reader would tolerate except if he is one of those poor milktoast innocents who timidly accept violation of their feelings from a habit of supposing they must be missing something, or one of those arrogant donzels who chuckle at things obscure because their enjoyment proves to them that they are not like lesser mortals. Where language is of primary concern to the writer, communication is necessarily secondary.[12]

Gardner's wrath seems misplaced to me, for, as Barthelme suggests, metafiction may be an invitation to the reader to "reconstruct the work by his active participation, by approaching the object, tapping it, shaking it, holding it to his ear to hear the roaring within."[13] Alain Robbe-Grillet's comment that the author of open-ended fictions "proclaims his absolute need of the reader's cooperations, an active, conscious, *creative* assistance," offers the reader a more significant role than that of passive consumer.[14] And Gass's praise of "the recreative power of the skillful reader," is in no sense an indication of indifference to the reader.[15] On the contrary, Robbe-Grillet appeals for an involved reader, one "no longer willing to receive ready-made a world completed, full, closed upon itself, but on the contrary to participate in a creation, to invent in his turn the work—and the world—and thus to invent his own life."[16]

Donald Barthelme's position among metafictionists is significant. From his earliest work, *Come Back, Dr. Caligari* (1964), he has been regarded as a major innovative talent, drawing comparisons with Kafka and Nathanael West. His vision is comic and intensely ironic—the tragedy of contemporary urban life is so great that comedians can best evoke it for us—and his interests are more directly social than those of others laboring within the walls of metafiction. His eight fictional books fall conveniently into two groups. *Caligari* and *Snow White* (1967) examine man's place or lack of place in the postmodern world and trace imaginative versions of ways in which external reality "heaps" man, rendering him powerless and helpless. Barthelme's interest here is in how metaphysical crises take social forms, and his emphasis is on artful destruction, on dismantling the received "hierarchical structures" that "heap" writer and reader without offering solace or comfort. His is a literary attempt to undo the given material world, more particularly the stranglehold that mimetic art fixes on the imagination and its literary projections. *Unspeakable Practices, Unnatural Acts* (1968) and *City Life* (1970) comprise a second group. In these works, the emphasis is on liberation and creative exuberance, as if the imagination has freed itself, canceled that which lies outside itself, and is free at last to project its own world. Barthelme's more recent fiction works, *Sadness* (1972), *The Dead Father* (1975), *Amateurs* (1976), and *Great Days* (1979), I regard as continuing these two tendencies in his writing.[17]

The intellectual center from which Barthelme writes is remarkably diverse, but he owes a special debt to the French phenomenologists and derivative philosophies, especially Gabriel Marcel and Georges Poulet. From Marcel, Barthelme appropriates the sense that the metaphysical crises of our time are rooted in the curse of consciousness—rational, waking, intellective consciousness. Marcel poses two modes of consciousness: 'having' and 'being.' 'Having' is a self-destructive mode of existence, a condition in which one's analytical consciousness attempts to subsume and cannibalize the entire world, emptying out meaning, draining off value, leaving only a hollow at the center of existence, the self, and the world. The more one searches for the sources of his despair, the further he is driven from himself, abstracted, cut off from being. The keys to 'having' are "problems," "objectification," "roles," "I-It," all of which imply a fixed, knowable external reality that is ordered and possessed by consciousness. As a remedy, Marcel urges a mode of 'being,' an acceptance of the mystery of existence, a return by leap of faith to some notion of incarnation and spirit-in-flesh, a sense of the simple, awesome sacredness of human communality. What this amounts to is a suspension of the war within consciousness, waged by one aspect against another.[18]

The spirit of Marcel pervades Barthelme's first two books, but his later works owe much more to the French "critics of consciousness," the phenomenologists, in particular George Poulet. Much metafiction incorporates its own most appropriate criticisms and it comes as no surprise that Poulet's mode of thought is important in Barthelme's fiction. His writings are directly appropriated in several works, and Poulet's sense of a writer's body of work as a sustained expression or act of complex consciousness is a fruitful approach to Donald Barthelme's writings. To Poulet and his fellows, literature is a projection of human consciousness, an extended series of linguistic gestures best examined as a series of tracings of the consciousness in which it originates. His approach in *The Interior Distance* is to conceive of modern consciousness as "discovering itself," as moving somehow out of inertia, nonexistence, and unity in the void into an awareness of or awe at its own existence: Adam falling into the State. From the start, this consciousness considers itself, the phantasm of its own existence, and projects what it sees into verbal forms and literary structures. Thus there is forever a space, an "interior distance," between the process of thought and its expression in images and words.[19] The primary reality one seeks in the luxury of mere 'being' is denied from the start as consciousness turns on itself, regarding and doubting itself. This is the tension from which much of Donald Barthelme's writing originates—in the dialectic between literature as a subjective action or process of creation (in Poulet's resonant phrase, "the invisible face of the moon") and literature as a sequence of finished, objective works, the destroyed landscape of reified existence. The distinction is basically between literature as a reflection of personality and consciousness and literature as an objectively rendered means of transcending consciousness or personality.

Mercifully, Barthelme's treatment of consciousness and the burden of it are not as solemn as Poulet's; perhaps the times are so grave that comedy is the most appropriate response, as Nabokov's jugglers and Beckett's clowns suggest, and this is certainly true of Barthelme's work. The great drama of consciousness is not so majestic to Barthelme, and in his best work there is an almost desperate amusement that makes man's sorry state bearable. In his later work, his amusement takes playful shapes, as "light-mindedness" and "brain damage," a properly paradoxical malaise we can never fully comprehend: "Skiing along on the soft surface of brain damage, never to sink, because we don't understand the danger. . . ."[20]

The dominant strain in his first two collections, then, is that of suspicion and doubt. Consciousness seems to emerge, to regard the social terrain and its relation to it, and to see everywhere the overwhelming facts of anxiety, dread, and emptiness in their social aspects. The created, historical world seems oppressive, a prison, and human consciousness chases the thread inward; finally doubting its own images of an outside world, its own verbal structures and their right to exist. Thus every perception rendered in these works is undercut, each character holds within himself his own opposite, and even the certainty of one style projected through a single sentence is rejected. Richard Gilman makes some appropriate comments on the skeptical vision behind these fictions and on the "new reality" it defines:

> In the most summary way this new reality can be described as being open-ended, provisional, characterized by suspended judgments, by disbelief in hierarchies, by mistrust of solutions, denouements and completions, by self-consciousness issuing in tremendous earnestness but also in far-ranging mockery, by emphasis on the flesh to the anachronization of the spirit, by a wealth of possibility whose individual possibilities tend to cancel one another out, by unfreedom felt as freedom and the reverse, by cults of youth, sex, change, noise and chemically induced

"truth." It is also a reality harboring a radical mistrust of language, writing, fiction, the imagination.[21]

Come Back, Dr. Caligari (1964) is Barthelme's earliest and most mimetic work. Although the fourteen stories are his most accessible, they are not, in any sense, conventional. The impress behind these consciousnesses is firm, a classic sense of existentialism. The television hostess of "Who Am I?" sums up for us: "People, today, we feel, are hidden away inside themselves, alienated, desperate, living in anguish, despair and bad faith. Why have we been thrown here and abandoned? Man stands alone in a featureless, anonymous landscape, in fear and trembling unto death. God is dead. Nothingness everywhere. Dread. Estrangement. Finitude" (174). But this is a television commentator, and whatever wisdom was once held in those hollowed phrases is gone, reducing them to the level of national cliché. As we are told elsewhere, "everybody knows the language" (176). This is Barthelme's own contemporary twist, to reveal meaninglessness and futility as terrible as ever, but comic and threatening by turn, never allowing the condition a straightforward solemnity that once so unsettled us.

Nor are the characters of *Come Back, Dr. Caligari* given the possibility of self-created, meaningful action that generally permits existential characters safe passage. We see the same disasters on every street corner. As the title suggests, both a clear sense of past and a coherent vision of any future are denied his people. They live in an eternal, foolish, heart-rending present, posed in static isolation like furniture, wrenched from binding, familiar relationships with a larger society, from those with narrow circles of family and friends, and finally from their own human natures.

If these are social fictions, hothouses of postmodern urban despair and futility, the sorrows therein are more than a little wilted. A basic fictional situation is repeated; more than half the stories dwell on aborted attempts to convey a sense of meaning or belief from one person or group to another. I. A. L. Burlington, in "Hiding Man," makes a sort of wayfarer's confession to a stranger as the two sit in an abandoned marathon movie theater. The owner of the radio station in "The Big Broadcast of 1938" takes up his air time with a balance of repeated playings of "The Star-Spangled Banner" and peculiar Beckett-like monologues directed at his former wife and their idyllic past. "Marie, Marie, Hold On Tight," depicts Henry Mackie's vain attempts to protest "the human condition" by picketing churches and public gatherings. His leaflet reads, "We are simply opposed to the ruthless way in which the human condition has been imposed on organisms which have done nothing to deserve it and are unable to escape it. *Why does it have to be that way?*" (118). Edward and Carl of "Margins" try to "communicate across a vast gulf of ignorance and darkness" and fail, finally able to discuss only the nonmessage "secrets" held in the margins and handwritings on the latter's sandwich board (141–46).

It all takes a peculiar and uneven bite. There is an underlying sense of treachery and deception throughout these fictions, as if the characters themselves suspect something going on beneath and behind their own brittle surfaces. Nameless forces seem to be spreading menace and despair, draining off value and distinction, plundering whatever dignity and emotion that remain. It becomes obvious that a sort of cosmic trick works through all these fictions, for if they do indeed articulate our "inability to communicate," they parody it as well. Former spokesmen for existentialism, gathered from all the post–World War II books and movies Barthelme can recall, weary and noble Sisyphuses every one, gather in these fictions in business suits, simultaneously lamenting and mocking "the human condition." The fictional scenarios in which they appear are exhausted, too familiar for authentic reactions, by now set pieces for stock responses. They include: two strangers hurled together by fate in an abandoned theater, exchanging life's secrets; the violent and comic human condition manifesting itself as an urban citizen's scuffle with a group that pickets a church to protest "the human condition"; a disc jockey who can communicate only while broadcasting; love notes between a man and woman that take form as a flurry of personal checks. Absurdity itself has become absurd in these stories, and the individual's rejection of society for the "isolated experiences of isolated men" emerges from the depths as a national ethic.[22]

As I suggested earlier, the influence of Gabriel Marcel is considerable in *Come Back, Dr. Caligari.* The characters here stand around discussing the sources and influences of their own fictional beings and most often their talk indirectly honors Marcel. Much of the parody and satire rests on his vision of modern man cut off from 'being,' wholeness, and basic humanity by the very consciousness that identifies his "dis-ease." In the analytic, possessive, abstracting mode of consciousness that reveals his problem, man is even further abstracted from any sort of immanent state.

A helpful comparison can be found in the work of Walker Percy, a southern contemporary of Barthelme's who admits a considerable debt to Marcel. In Percy's *The Last Gentleman* (1966), Sutter Vaught, his pornographer-pathologist-philosopher, finds that even recording the details of his research in a casebook puts the possibility of ever explaining the mystery of postcoital triste suicide at one greater remove.[23] In Barthelme's work, this doubt by consciousness of its *own* powers to ease its own agony has a much more profound effect on the forms of fiction that embody it. If one suspects that human consciousness can only make matters worse, can one value any of the projects of human consciousness—history, art, society itself? However comic, this is a corrosive vision—creating itself and distrusting itself at every turn, recognizing the structures of an external world as the projections of earlier, binding consciousnesses and even as projections of its own powers, and then seeking to annihilate them so that it might live alone, at ease for once.

Thus these parodies, burlesques, satires, and ironic figures have social functions; they are serious comic expressions of metaphysical crisis as it expresses itself in social situations. We should notice that whatever hierarchies do "certify" existence in *Come Back, Dr. Caligari* inevitably humiliate people, providing neither solace nor illumination. The elementary school that the Gulliver-like narrator of "Me and Miss Mandible" attends seems remarkably cruel to him. Those "problem children" who resist the institution sense that it perpetuates an incredible charade, the lie that everything can be known and explained through some logical process. The narrator concludes that, in spite of the efforts of educational engineers, "everything that is either interesting or lifelike in the classroom proceeds from what they would probably call interpersonal relations" (104). Mass media extend "the human condition" in every direction, and it is clear that the social dislocations so prevalent here mask a much deeper crisis, in art and in life. As Robert Scholes writes,

> In the world of existence we see how social and political modes of behavior lose their vitality in time as they persist to a point where instead of connecting man to the roots of his being, they cut him off from this deep reality. All revolutionary crises, including the present one, can be seen as caused by the profound malaise that attacks men when the forces of human behavior lose touch with the essence of human nature. It is similar with fiction. Forms atrophy and lose touch with the vital ideas of fiction. Originality in fiction, rightly understood, is the successful attempt to find new forms that are capable of tapping once again the sources of fictional vitality.[24]

Barthelme's characters are ludicrous to begin with, but the means they choose to express what little "essence of human nature" they have left distort them even more. The radio announcer of "The Big Broadcast of 1938" makes a running series of impassioned pleas to his former wife but only to her as she exists in fantasized memories. Successful in wooing her, faced with her presence once again, he regards her as a sort of smelly, extinct specimen: "Martha, old skin, why can't you let the old days die? That were the days of anger, passion, and dignity, but are now, in the light of present standards, practices, and attitudes, days that are done?" (80). Such scenes are suffused with the ludicrous oaklike dignity reminiscent of Samuel Beckett's fiction, where an intentional woodenness of tone and rhythm seems to seal man helplessly inside his environment. Even moments between friends suddenly become violent, incongruous: "But that situation dear to him as it was helped him not a bit in this situation. And that memory memorable as it was did not prevent friends of the family from stopping the car under a tree, and beating Bloomsbury in the face first with a brandy bottle, then with the tire iron, until at length the hidden feeling emerged, in the form of salt from the eyes and black blood from the ears, and from his mouth, all sorts of words ("For I'm the Boy," 63)."

Static, isolated as they are, most of Barthelme's characters share a single quality, their "objectness." As they seem to lose energy and

32

emotion, the objects around them, the landscape itself, come alive. They are prisoners of the physical worlds they inhabit and exist finally as things, as phenomena to which surreal events happen. Objects become animated, merely silly, as in "Florence Green Is 81," in which the gazpacho at a dinner party "sways from side to side with a secret Heinz trembling movement" (9); or they become threatening, as in a later story when a parachutist mocks Cincinnati beneath him as he leaps, only to find himself suspended, as "frostily the silent city approached his feet" (136). Or they may turn suddenly and absolutely violent, rupturing whatever thin membrane of realism ever did exist: "He strode over to the piano. He took a good grip on its black varnishedness. He began to trundle it across the room and, after a slight hesitation, it struck him dead" (22).

For the most part, the characters of *Come Back, Dr. Caligari* are unable to live in the eternal present that existentialism supposes, and they take no solace in the active, fluid, exuberant concept of identity that attends it. As the title of the collection suggests, many look backward to a nostalgic past or forward to an illusory, golden future. But from the few characters that do possess autonomy comes a glimpse of human and artistic liberation. Protean men, Robert Jay Lifton would call them, and they recapture the spotlight, reinvesting their lives with purpose, intensity, and human relationships, however momentarily. Consider the earliest example, that of The Joker, in "The Joker's Greatest Triumph." The Joker is the first of a series of comic figures borrowed from recent politics and popular culture; they seem to fascinate Barthelme and provoke him to recreate them in his fictions in their essential forms, according to a principle of scattered particles in momentary, active suspension. In this version of "Batman," the man himself and friend Frederic are cruising—in every camp sense of the word—in the Batcar, fitted out as a portable bar on wheels. Batman predictably interrupts the Joker's jewel theft, a thoroughly banal and tiresome story line. The fiction up to this point is mildly funny, a sequence of limping, camping parody and cliché. Suddenly, Batman is knocked unconscious, and The Joker peers under his mask, learning "the caped crusader's true identity." As they drive "seriously" back, Batman is even more ludicrous: "Great Scott! If he reveals it to the whole world it will mean the end of my career as a crime-fighter! Well, it's a problem" (156). Characteristically, the sole moment of intensity is Bruce Wayne's "analysis" of The Joker:

> "Consider him at any level of conduct," Bruce said slowly, "in the home, on the street, in interpersonal relations, in jail—always there is an extraordinary contradiction. He is dirty and compulsively neat, aloof and desperately gregarious, enthusiastic and sullen, generous and stingy, a snappy dresser and a scarecrow, a gentleman and a boor, given to extremes of happiness and despair, singularly well able to apply himself and capable of frittering away a lifetime in trivial pursuits, decorous and unseemly, kind and cruel, tolerant yet open to the most outrageous varieties of bigotry, a great friend and an implacable enemy, a lover and an abominator of women, sweet-spoken and foulmouthed, a rake and a puritan, swelling with hubris and haunted by inferiority, outcast and social climber, felon and philanthropist, barbarian and patron of the arts, enamored of novelty and solidly conservative, philosopher and fool, Republican and Democrat, large of soul and unbearably petty, distant and brimming with friendly impulses, an inveterate liar and astonishingly strict with petty cash, adventurous and timid, imaginative and stolid, malignly destructive and a planter of trees on Arbor Day —I tell you frankly, the man is a mess." [157]

Now this is the sort of energy, liberating and comic, found in the very best of metafiction, especially in John Barth's *Lost in the Funhouse* and *Chimera*, works by a writer sharing Barthelme's love of language. Coming from the mouth of a Batman-gone-Rotarian, the statement seems even more foolish and properly bristles with excesses, all of which are carefully combed and balanced. Barthelme offers us very few surfaces on which to rest and get a fix on all this, and he moves immediately to undercut his only impassioned comment: "That's extremely well-said Bruce," Frederic stated. "I think you've given really a very thoughtful analysis." "I was just paraphrasing what Mark Schorer said about Sinclair Lewis," Bruce replied (157). Within his fictional world, The Joker represents an impulse toward spontaneous life that is at once social and artistic. He is a criminal, but the essence of his criminality—focused disorder—is necessary, the sole alterna-

34

tive to the state of "objecthood" that threatens everyone in *Come Back, Dr. Caligari*. Here, as elsewhere, Barthelme regards literature as a single hierarchical system within a vastly oppressive mega-hierarchy. The act of writing is a projection of human consciousness; what is needed is a form of literature that releases consciousness from the burden of the past and from its own self-destructive tendencies. Richard Poirier's prefatory remarks to *The Performing Self* are thoroughly appropriate:

> Writing is a form of energy not accountable to the orderings anyone makes of it and specifically not accountable to the liberal humanitarian values most readers want to find there. Such an idea of literature excites a blind and instinctive resistance in most quarters, and for good reason. It makes literature not a source of comfort and order, but rather, of often dislocating, disturbing impulses. Energy which cannot arrange itself within the existing order of things, and the consequent fear of it which takes the form of repressive analysis—these are what makes the literary and academic issues I shall be discussing inseparable from larger cultural and political ones.[25]

The final fiction of the collection provides another, more extensive instance of this energetic, self-creating figure. In "A Shower of Gold," Peterson accepts two hundred dollars to appear on "Who Am I?," a national television show that uses private detectives, interrogation, and polygraphs to expose instances of "BAD FAITH" and in so doing psychically annihilates the lucky contestant. Peterson watches as two contestants are humiliated and destroyed. As an artist and a human, he is unable to live in this Kafkaesque world and chooses to live and create himself in self-defense, dwelling constantly in the present. *Come Back, Dr. Caligari* ends, significantly, with his monologue:

> I was wrong, Peterson thought, the world is absurd. The absurdity is punishing me for not believing in it. I affirm the absurdity. On the other hand, absurdity itself is absurd. Before the emcee could ask the first question, Peterson began to talk. . . . "In this kind of world," Peterson said, "absurd if you will, possibilities nevertheless proliferate and escalate all around us and there are

opportunities for beginning again. I am a minor artist and my dealer won't even display my work if he can help it but minor is as minor does and lightning may strike even yet. Don't be reconciled. Turn off your television sets," Peterson said, "cash in your life insurance, indulge in a mindless optimism. Visit girls at dusk. Play the guitar. How can you be alienated without first having been connected? Think back and remember how it was." A man on the floor in front of Peterson was waving a piece of cardboard on which something threatening was written but Peterson ignored him and concentrated on the camera with the little red light. The little red light jumped from camera to camera in an attempt to throw him off balance but Peterson was too smart for it and followed wherever it went. "My mother was a royal virgin," Peterson said, "and my father a shower of gold. My childhood was pastoral and energetic and rich in experiences which developed character. As a young man I was noble in reason, infinite in faculty, in form express and admirable, and in apprehension. . . ." Peterson went on and on and although he was, in a sense, lying, in a sense he was not. [183]

Like Sisyphus, Peterson enters the world of myth by placing himself there. Note the formulaic "My mother was a royal virgin . . . my father was a shower of gold." But unless he follows this course by choice, by choosing at every instant (a logical impossibility), Peterson will find himself trapped by the very structures that gave him new life —the case of all characters in *Snow White*. Barthelme has a special fascination with mythic figures from folklore, popular culture, and contemporary public life. What he sees in each case is the only possibility for artistic and social existence. To live freely, as a work of art or a man, one must create himself constantly. Properly metafictional, Barthelme allows Robert F. Kennedy to sum up his own significance for us in "Robert Kennedy Saved From Drowning." Reaching into his own heart, Kennedy dredges up Georges Poulet, almost directly from "Marivaux" in *The Interior Distance*:

"For Poulet, it is not enough to speak of *seizing the moment*. It is rather a question of, and I quote, 'recognizing in the instant which lives and dies, which surges out of nothingness and which ends in dream, an intensity and depth of significance which ordinarily attaches only to the whole of existence.'

"What Poulet is describing is neither an ethic nor a prescription but rather what he has discovered in the work of Marivaux. . . .

"The Marivaudian being is, according to Poulet, a pastless futureless man, born anew at every instant. The instants are points which organize themselves in a line, but what is important is the instant, not the line. The Marivaudian being has in a sense no history. Nothing follows from what has gone before. He is constantly surprised. He cannot predict his own reaction to events. He is constantly being *overtaken* by events. A condition of breathlessness and dazzlement surrounds him. In consequence he exists in a certain freshness which seems, if I may say so, very desirable." [44]

Another basic quality that metafiction possesses is the way in which worlds encapsulate worlds, so that an event or comment made on one level seems to flash through to work on other levels. The materials seem to resonate and meaning often seems to be multiple. The examples of The Joker, Peterson, and Robert Kennedy do just that. They are all instances of this "Marivaudian being," a powerful presence in Barthelme's mind. The passage from "Robert Kennedy Saved From Drowning," for example, is a guide to the mythic and historical figures Barthelme recreates and to their cultural roles; it is a description and prescription for an entire artistic attitude (life may well be an art form here) and illustrates the approach to style and structure throughout his own work. The "Marivaudian being" is foremost a principle, a vision of existence created by consciousness as an *active expression* of its own contradictory processes. While this being may take shape as a character in a fiction or a man in a life, he can also appear in more extensive forms. As Barthelme seems to refine his basic interests, the Marivaudian being increasingly appears in the barest workings of consciousness; it then moves away from characters in social contexts toward liberated creators and, finally, away from character at all toward a purer landscape of consciousness in *City Life*. If indeed there are only instants that make up an eternal present, how can one retain the pretense of any sort of fixity in fiction? How can one maintain a story, compel a character to live through such a thing, sustain even a single style through a single sentence?

Now these considerations are neither original nor unique in Barthelme; as he suggests, they are virtually public knowledge. What *is* original is the use he makes of this body of ideas. A sense of the eternal present, of defining one's existence in every act, lives at the heart of most varieties of modern existentialism. Norman Mailer has taken such ideas seriously because they suggest a mode of conduct through modern life. Notice the emphasis they take in "The White Negro":

> It is on this bleak scene that a phenomenon has appeared: the American existentialist—the hipster, the man who knows that if our collective condition is to live with instant death by atomic war, relatively quick death by the State as *l'univers concentrationnaire*, or with a slow death by conformity with every creative and rebellious instinct stifled (at what damage to the mind and the heart and the liver and the nerves no research foundation for cancer will discover in a hurry), if the fate of twentieth century man is to live with death from adolescence to premature senescence, why then the only life-giving answer is to accept the terms of death, to live with death as immediate danger, to divorce oneself from society, to exist without roots, to set out on that uncharted journey into the rebellious imperatives of the self. In short, whether life is criminal or not, the decision is to encourage the psychopath in oneself, to explore that domain of experience where security is boredom and therefore sickness, and one exists in the present, in that enormous present which is without past or future, memory or planned intention, the life where a man must go until he is beat, where he must gamble with his energies through all those small or large crises of courage and unforeseen situations which beset his day. . . . The element which is disturbing, nightmarish perhaps, is that incompatibles have come to bed, the inner life and the violent life, the orgy and the dream of love, the desire to murder and the desire to create, a dialectical conception of existence with a lust for power, a dark, romantic, and yet undeniably dynamic view of existence, for it sees every

man and woman as moving individually through each moment of life forward into growth or backward into death.[26]

This is a very revealing passage, and it tells us very much about the intentions behind much of Mailer's own public conduct: his insistence on entering perilous situations—public and private—in which he undertakes the impossible (running for mayor of New York, for example) or in which he alienates whatever persons, audiences, groups are at hand so that he might win them back with passionate argument. One might well note his various joustings with Women's Liberation figures during recent television shows and public lectures. But it tells us even more about Norman Mailer's fictional heroes, distillations like Stephen Rojack in *An American Dream*, and the dynamic source of energy that compels them to action.

Compare Mailer's statement with one on the same ideas made by Alain Robbe-Grillet, spokesman for the French "New Novel" and "New Cinema." His *Notes For a New Novel* is a manifesto, a series of essays in defense of pure literary and cinematic art, an argument for "new forms of the novel, forms capable of expressing (or of creating) new relations between man and the world, to all those who have determined to invent the novel, in other words, to invent man."[27] Robbe-Grillet continues:

It is not rare, as a matter of fact, in these modern novels, to encounter a description that starts from nothing; it does not afford, first of all, a general view, it seems to derive from a tiny fragment without importance—what most resembles a *point*— starting from which it invents lines, planes, an architecture; and such description particularly seems to be inventing its objects when it suddenly contradicts, repeats, corrects itself, bifurcates, etc. Yet we begin to glimpse something, and we suppose that this something will now become clearer. But the lines of the drawing accumulate, grow heavier, cancel one another out, shift, so that the image is jeopardized as it is created. A few paragraphs more and, when the description comes to an end, we realize that it has left nothing behind it: it has instituted a double movement of creation and destruction which, moreover, we also find in the book on all levels and in particular in its total structure—whence the *disappointment* inherent in many works of today.[28]

And later, in defending his work and that of his contemporaries, he might well be speaking directly of Donald Barthelme's fiction:

These descriptions whose movement destroys all confidence in the things described, these heroes without naturalness as without identity, this present which constantly invents itself, as though in the course of the very writing, which repeats, doubles, modifies, denies itself, without ever accumulating in order to constitute a past—hence a "story," a "history" in the traditional sense of the word—all this can only invite the reader (or the spectator) to another mode of participation than the one to which he was accustomed. If he is sometimes led to condemn the works of his time, that is, those which most directly address him, if he even complains of being deliberately abandoned, held off, disdained by the authors, this is solely because he persists in seeking a kind of communication which has long since ceased to be the one which is proposed to him. For, far from neglecting him the author today proclaims his absolute need of the reader's cooperation, an active, conscious, *creative* assistance. What he asks of him is no longer to receive ready-made a world completed, full, closed upon itself, but on the contrary to participate in a creation, to invent in his turn the work—and the world—and thus to learn to invent his own life.[29]

The significant differences between these two uses of the same concepts—an eternal and timeless now and how art and life function within it—lie mainly in the differences between two streams of existentialism. Mailer is familiar with an earlier (1940–50) group of thinkers, Jean Malaquais for one, who are much more political and psychological in orientation. The stream that runs through Robbe-Grillet and his contemporaries is more strictly philosophical, with an interest in the phenomenon of human consciousness, in what it is and how it may be diverted. This stream is much more a mode of vision, a way of "re-seeing" that which is around us, than a series of notes on how to make one's way in the social world. It is this second stream of ideas, nourishing both Robbe-Grillet and Poulet, that informs Barthelme's work and poses an ideal toward which to write.

This sense of constant change as the only order, the "Marivaudian essence" that Poulet speaks of, especially fascinates Barthelme. And when Robbe-Grillet writes of the "double movement of creation and destruction . . . we find in the book on all levels and in particular in its total structure,"[30] he refers to a kind of art that absorbs its ideological matrix thoroughly. Barthelme is engaged in the kind of writing in which philosophical premises penetrate every structural level: the sentence, the paragraph, the short fiction, and in his only sustained long fictions, *Snow White* and *The Dead Father*. The emphasis in his early work, though, is "destructive," as consciousness undercuts and doubts whatever structures have come before it, either historically or through habit. The Marivaudian being as a primarily destructive premise takes clearest shape, that is, the most transparent, in Barthelme's "The Viennese Opera Ball."

Metafictionists regard everything about themselves as fictions: the language systems that enfold us, the labyrinths of conceptual systems —psychological, social, philosophical—that impinge on our realities, the artistic structures that remove existence even further from itself. William Gass has a vision of what would happen if we could undo it all: "Imagine for a moment what would happen if the television paled, the radio fell silent, the press did not release. Imagine all the clubs and courses closed, magazines unmailed, guitars unplugged, pools, rinks, gyms, courts, stadia shut up. Suppose that publishers were to issue no more dick, prick, and booby books; movies were banned along with gambling, liquor and narcotics; and men were suddenly and irrevocably alone with themselves. . . . alone only with love to be made, thought, sense, and dreadful life."[31] Imagine another possibility: what if that sort of freedom were so strong that it could only be absorbed gradually and what if consciousness could prepare itself for freedom only by destroying that which restricted. Suppose existence could be dismantled, unscrewed, panel by panel, and reassembled elsewhere in newer, composite, superfutile, metafictional shapes? This is what is imagined for us in "The Viennese Opera Ball."

The story provides its own schema: "Within the plane of each individual work—experienced apart from a series—he presents one with a similar set of one-at-a-time experiences each contained within its own compartment, and read in a certain order, up or down, or across" (91). The fiction is made up of a series of distinct voices that fade in and out of hearing as one circulates through an evening at the Viennese Opera Ball. Each of these voices works off a single plane of existence, has its own special language and subject matter, and intersects with other voices from time to time. The first monologue we overhear issues apparently from a doctor, as he discusses therapeutic abortion. This is interrupted by an anthropological summary of the revenge practices of primitive tribes, and this, in turn, by a fashion magazine summary of the discovery of a popular model. By the end of the piece, at least ten distinct voices and conversations have had our ears, most several times, interrupting each other at an increasingly rapid rate. Although each monologue is only a fragment, there appears to be a steady increase in semantic entropy—even "compartments" within fragments—and meaning falls inevitably into contradiction and absurdity. The medical monologue, for example, maintains a steady level of diction and tone but errs, one might say, in judgment: "I mean, the doctor resumed, we should study each patient thoroughly and empty the uterus before she has retinitis; before jaundice has shown there is marked liver damage; before she has polyneuritis; before she has toxic myocarditis; before her brain is degenerated" (86).

Medical, anthropological, fashion, technical, architectural, and business jargons assault us; monologues seem to usurp each other, bleeding through two or three levels of meaning at once:

> Carola Mitt met Isabella Albonico at the Viennese Opera Ball. Isabella Albonico, Italian by temperament as well as by birth (twenty-four years ago, in Florence), began modeling in Europe when she was fifteen, arrived in New York four years ago. Brown-haired and brown-eyed, she has had covers on *Vogue, Harper's Bazaar* and *Life*, makes $60 an hour, and has won, she says, "a reputation for being allergic to being pummeled around under the lights. Nobody touches me." I entirely endorse these opinions, said a man standing nearby, and would only add that the

wife can do much to avert that fatal marital *ennui* by independent interests which she persuades him to share. For instance, an interesting book, or journey, or lecture or concert, experienced, enjoyed and described by her, with sympathy and humor, may often be a talisman to divert his mind from work and worry, and all the irritations arising therefrom. But, of course, he, on his side, must be able to appreciate her appreciation and her conversation. The stimuli to the penile nerves may differ in degrees of intensity and shades of quality; and there are corresponding diversities in the sensations of pleasure they bestow. It is of much importance in determining these sensations whether the stimuli are localized mainly in the frenulum preputti or the posterior rim of the glans. *Art* rather than *sheer force* should prevail. (There is an authentic case on record in which the attendant braced himself and pulled so hard that, when the forceps slipped off, he fell out of an open window onto the street below and sustained a skull fracture, while the patient remained undelivered.) The Jumbo Tree, 254 feet high, is named from the odd-shaped growths at the base resembling the heads of an elephant, a monkey and a bison. Isabella told Carola that she "would like most of all to be a movie star." [88]

The technique may be compared to that of William Burroughs's "cut-ups," in which he cuts up several different texts and randomly reassembles them, asserting that new meanings and nuances emerge randomly out of the chaos. But Barthelme works differently. He leaves far less to chance than Burroughs, providing recurring links between the various monologues—several deal with procreation and destruction, for example. Barthelme also returns frequently to the fact that all this occurs at the Viennese Opera Ball, asserting the element of artifice in his fiction ("Morehead Patterson, however, did not attend the Viennese Opera Ball," [90]).

The emphasis in *Come Back, Dr. Caligari* is the creation of a new world, but this is impossible until ties to old ones have been severed. Lest any new structure immediately entrap the very consciousness that created it, it must be negated and parodied at once. Robbe-Grillet's "double movement of creation and destruction" is a functional principle here, and the fiction exists, however paradoxically, as it repeatedly destroys itself. For any sort of "Marivaudian being" at all to be born, the world that comes before him must be destroyed or at least cleared away. Thus the interest through several of the monologues in abortion, the willful termination of a creative act. This theme is mirrored on a structural level as a fiction or a life is created as we participate in it and simultaneously destroyed. Whatever magic threatens to take us in, make us believe in this alternate fictional reality, must be exposed and undone. The function of the repeated self-commentary is just that, to assert the element of deception, of artifice, in the world that struggles to be created. This is also the function of the "white noise" in the story, which appears in the form of other communications, books, or narratives commenting on themselves. We are offered an alphabetical list of some one hundred words (from *sailing* to *syphilis*) at one point, part of an appendix to another work, and occasional fragments of stray narratives from other worlds at several intervals: "Far off at Barlow Ranger Station, as the dawn was breaking, Bart slept dreamlessly at last" (91). Entropy develops within the system and within the "compartments" of the system (the monologues) it is pronounced. Language deteriorates into jargon, argot, or bodies of cliché and platitude, and semantic meaning trails off inevitably into exaggeration and absurdity. One has the sense of humans trapped inside of language, which in turn is trapped inside phenomena, history, all of what has gone before.

We emerge from *Come Back, Dr. Caligari* pointed inward. While these are Barthelme's most mimetic and social works, dealing with man in some relation to a larger group, it is clear that the interest in man is a diminishing one. The urgent absurdity of consciousness simultaneously creating and destroying its own collective history is defined even more in *Snow White*, in which the social matrix is all but disposed of.

In *Dr. Caligari* he accepted patterns and types from recent existential art to parody and satirize both the writing and the states it sought to vivify. In *Snow White*, Barthelme accepts an entire structure—a sequence of significance, characters, a familiar oral tale—as if to signify the impossibility of primary creation. The folk tale here is a bag in which the characters feel themselves trapped, an imposition by literary history on consciousness. Even handed to us through Walt Disney's mind, the fairy tale retained a vestige of truths from past ages—the eruption of the supernatural or magical into daily life or the movement of archetypal, unconscious forces through ritual patterns. But if Disney cartooned the truths in delivering them to us, Barthelme extends the process even further, giving them the status of an adult, angst-ridden soap opera, as if the magical is most impossible when it is most desperately needed. The tale is thoroughly contemporary, utterly self-conscious, and retold in the strange corporate point of view ("we") of the seven dwarfs, although we are allowed access to Snow White's mind, as well as to the minds of the supporting cast.

The premises of the fairy tale are inverted on every level. The ritual, magical, unconscious, timeless qualities one expects are not to be found here. Rescued from the forest by the dwarfs, Snow White joins their household as mistress and housekeeper and is anything but asexual. The dwarfs, led by Bill, are scarcely magical "little people." They "produce," work at modernized jobs. They are a roving, flexible labor gang, working mainly at washing office buildings and manufacturing Chinese baby food. But they have also invented a line of plastic buffalo humps and are not above moonlighting, committing at least one apartment robbery as we watch.

There is loss everywhere on the landscape because everyone is aware of what he *should* be doing, what behavior is appropriate for his respective role in this folk tale, but unable to carry it out. The leader, Bill, is the first to be cursed with self-consciousness and he withdraws from the family, bored, unwilling and unable to carry on. The dwarfs, in turn, spend a great deal of time discussing their plight: "Snow White has added a dimension of confusion and misery to our lives. Whereas once we were simple bourgeois who knew what to do, now we are complex bourgeois who are at a loss. We do not like this complexity" (88). Snow White spends her time as a semiliberated female, reading *Liberation* magazine and admiring her body, but most of all waiting endlessly for her prince. The prince, however, is equally helpless. Paul, the eighteenth in a series of rescuing princes, has decided to enter a monastery. There is a witch, Jane Villiers L'Isle d'Adam, who is equally self-informed, and a villain, Hogo, who spends his time reading war atrocity magazines and pondering the banality of evil. By the beginning of the final part, the dwarfs are unable to stand the burden any longer and each escapes to his favorite drinking place and personal hideaway. Edward, perhaps the most modern of all his fellows, hides under the local boardwalk, easing his mind behind "nine mantras and three bottles of insect repellant" (142). But the action rolls along, as Hogo and Jane conspire to eliminate their counterparts. Hogo mails the dwarfs a large amount of money and then reports them to the Internal Revenue Service for tax evasion. Jane tries to poison Snow White with a deadly vodka Gibson. Bill is arrested for being publically drunken (Hogo's money suspiciously on his person), having hurled two six-packs of Miller's High Life through a Volkswagen windshield. As in all poisoned kingdoms, law and order become important; Barthelme calls in the police and the courts to forcibly restore order and to provide a denouement for the fiction. The courts convene and Bill is brought to trial, during which he is found guilty of letting the fires go out under the baby food vats and of general leadership failure. The final actions are thoroughly incongruous: Bill is finally hanged for failure; Paul accidentally quaffs the poisoned drink destined for Snow White's lips; Hogo moves into the family and stimulates morale and production. Snow White pines to death on Paul's grave and, at the book's end, removes herself from all human contact; she rises forever into the sky, properly "virginized" and "apotheosized."

Barthelme wrings a good deal of comedy from the demented proceedings, but he has a more serious purpose. His inversion or eversion—turning the myth inside out—allows myth to perform a function that is precisely the opposite of its normal function. Myths, especially those embodied in folk tales, have traditionally told us that we are part of a great story, that there is a great continuity in all things. Robert Scholes suggests a polar opposition between the mythic view and "the philosophical view of life," which tells us that "every man is unique, alone, poised over chaos."[32] Like Camus in his use of the myth of Sisyphus, Barthelme seeks a myth that makes eternal crisis a universal state for all men, but, since myth is part of the great historical baggage that restricts consciousness, he uses myth more to contradict itself, to express its traditional opposites: self-consciousness, anxiety, temporality, helplessness, futility. Scholes is accurate in noting that this use of myth is a recent development, quite different than former uses, even by Joyce and Eliot:

> Once so much is known *about* myths and archetypes, they can no longer be used innocently. Even their connection to the unconscious finally becomes attenuated as the mythic materials are used more consciously. All symbols become allegorical to the extent that we understand them. Thus the really perceptive writer is not merely conscious that he is using mythic materials: He is conscious that he is using them consciously. He knows, *finally*, that he is allegorizing. Such a writer, aware of the nature of categories, is not likely to believe that his own mythic lenses really capture the truth. Thus his use of myth will inevitably partake of the comic.[33]

Thus he makes of the myth of Snow White a bag in which it has trapped itself. Within the bag, Barthelme's characters seek to undo the universe that gives them existence. Their dominant modes of expression are retraction and negation. The fallen leader Bill has a preference for the palinode as a literary form, as if one could make it all go away by reversing the film: "I would wish to retract everything, if I could. . . . I would retract the green sea, and the brown fish in it" (13). Later, as we tour the plastic buffalo hump works, one of the dwarfs describes his world for us, in which everything is waste. The dwarfs aspire to a position on "the leading edge of this trash phenomenon, the everted sphere of the future" (97). And there is a constant undercurrent of helplessness, of being in the orbits of another's power. The evil Jane Villiers L'Isle d'Adam makes an oblique commentary on the theme in an anonymous hate letter:

> DEAR MR. QUISTGAARD:
> Although you do not know me my name is Jane. I have seized your name from the telephone book in an attempt to enmesh you in my concerns. . . . You and I, Mr. Quistgaard, are not in the same universe of discourse. . . . Now it may have appeared to you, that the universe of discourse in which you existed, and puttered about, was in all ways adequate and satisfactory. It may never have crossed your mind to think that other universes of

discourse distinct from your own existed, with people in them, discoursing. You may have, in a commonsense way, regarded your own u. of d. as a plenum, filled to the brim with discourse. . . . But I say unto you, Mr. Quistgaard, that even a plenum can leak. Even a plenum, *cher maitre*, can be penetrated. New things can rush into your plenum displacing old things, things that were formerly there. . . . The moment I inject discourse from my u. of d. into your u. of d., the yourness of yours is diluted. The more I inject, the more you dilute. Soon you will be presiding over an empty plenum, or rather, since that is a contradiction in terms, over a former plenum, in terms of yourness. You are, essentially, in my power. [45–46]

Snow White is offered to us from the other side of the mirror, carries no magic with her, and yearns for a prince "or something else" to redeem her world. She is an interesting reversal of the original fabular figure. Oppressed as she feels by her worldly existence, she has a special loathing for mimetic art, for what she has been and what she is. One of her greatest fears is that of mirrors, for it was in a witch's mirror that she was cast in a mythic shape. Later, in an incident entitled "The Irruption of the Magical in the Life of Snow White," we are given another comic instance of a world attitude that seems to press everyone down, that of a physical world bent on purging its own complementary, metaphysical aspect:

Snow White knows a singing bone. The singing bone has told her various stories which have left her troubled and confused: of a bear transformed into a king's son, or an immense treasure at the bottom of a brook, of a crystal casket in which there is a cap that makes the wearer invisible. This must not continue. The behavior of the bone is unacceptable. The bone must be persuaded to confine itself to events and effects susceptible of confirmation by the instrumentarium of the physical sciences. Someone must reason with the bone. [70]

Indeed, Snow White is finally a long, animated comic discourse on retraction, an attempt by consciousness to cancel out an entire world and the accompanying literary modes that threaten it. In choosing a fantastic situation—the fable of Snow White and the Seven Dwarfs—Barthelme frees himself from mimetic considerations even more than in *Come Back, Dr. Caligari*. Much of the comedy issues from the incongruity of fairy-tale figures redrawn as contemporary and banal puppets, but Barthelme's interest is much less in making statements about "our time" than in making a detailed fiction in which the only interest of consciousness in an external world is in the ways in which the two impinge. Thus there is no need to distinguish between the dwarfs; part of the horror is the single deafening voice to consciousness, so the corporate "we" point of view is appropriate. And it is also appropriate that the characters exist almost as choral voices within which the words themselves weigh down consciousness. Snow White, typically, yearns, "Oh I wish there were some words in the world that were not the words I always hear" (6).

Palinodes, retractions, eversions, mirrorings, irruptions, "emptied" plenums: these are all tracings of a wish to negate external reality rather than copy it, of a desire by consciousness on at least five occasions for "something better." Barthelme is very much one with his avant-garde fellows here: in William Burroughs's apocalyptic fantasies time is on film, able to be reversed; and in Samuel Beckett's absolutely minimal fictions—most minimally his mimes—there is an accord with the premise of *Snow White*, that "the main theme that runs through my brain is that what is, is insufficient" (135).

In Barthelme's third and fourth works, *Unspeakable Practices, Unnatural Acts* (1968) and *City Life* (1970), there is a clear shift of emphasis. There is little of the need to negate all that has issued from this or previous consciousness, as there is in *Come Back, Dr. Caligari* and *Snow White*, little of the manic undercutting and parodying of verbal structures and their sway over us, little of the need to break language and structural forms loose from their social moorings. The consciousness at work in Barthelme's first two books senses itself trapped inside its own creations, imprisoned by its own attempts at creation. On the level of language, for example, there are only sublanguages—argots, jargons, bodies of clichés and platitudes—that have been emptied of meaning, drained of whatever power they once

49

possessed. There remain only skeletons, residues of meaning caked inside each cliché, each turn of phrase, each slice of jargon, and these have power only in their ability to parody themselves, as they do in the radical juxtapositions of "The Viennese Opera Ball."

The lamentations of powerlessness and helplessness and the muffled sobbing that recurs in *Snow White*, as well as the gravely manic humor, are not so dominant in *Unspeakable Practices, Unnatural Acts* and *City Life*. The spirit of Marcel that dominates earlier work, yields to a second cast of mind, nearer to Georges Poulet. Poulet's "Marivaudian being," as I have suggested, is an appealing principle to Barthelme, and he works with him on several simultaneous levels. But the quality of self-cancellation and futility that so pervades Barthelme's early books is not found here. His field of vision widens to encompass consciousness in the process of creating itself and its own larger world, and he works away from the sense of exhaustion and paralysis toward a sense that consciousness can exist only in the forms it permits itself. In Robbe-Grillet's terms, there is a greater interest in creation than destruction.

For the most part, these fictions are more fantastic and more fabular; almost all are spun out of the minds of equally fantastic creators, dreamers, artists. "The Balloon," for example, works with the appearance of a huge, surreal balloon that suddenly appears in the city sky; as the narrator tells us, it is his own self-inflated, literal-allegorical "spontaneous autobiographical disclosure" (21). "This Newspaper Here" is unfolded powerfully and eccentrically by the crazy old editor. (Or is he crazy? It seems to be Barthelme's ideal work of art, adjusting itself in new and powerful configurations through each reader's mind. As the editor describes it: "My newspaper warm at the edges fade in fade out a tissue of hints whispers glimpses uncertainties, zoom in zoom out" [30].)

The Marivaudian being, almost an impossible ideal within the confines of early works, is prominent here. Within the world of *Unspeakable Practices, Unnatural Acts*, he is a dominant image, a positive metaphor for life and art as impossible acts of creation. "Robert Kennedy," for example, is "saved from drowning," saved from helplessness before the overwhelming flux and tedium of a modern world, simply by acting:

"Sometimes I can't seem to do anything. The work is there, piled up, it seems to me an insurmountable obstacle, really out of reach. . . . I am thinking of something else, I can't seem to get the gist of it, it seems meaningless, devoid of interest, not having to do with human affairs, drained of life. Then, in an hour, or even a moment, everything changes suddenly: I realize I only have to do it, hurl myself into the midst of it, proceed mechanically, the first thing and then the second thing, that it is simply a matter of moving from one step to the next, plowing through it. I become interested, I become excited, I work very fast, things fall into place, I am exhilarated, amazed that these things could ever have seemed dead to me." [35–36]

And Barthelme saves Kennedy from drowning, from nonbeing, by creating him (or rather by allowing him to be created), an abstraction taking more literal shape near the fiction's end, as the narrator tosses the drowning Kennedy a rope.

It is the Marivaudian being's energy that propels these little fictional galaxies, gives them birth in the individual self-creations of Barthelme's gallery of artists. Because he lives "in the instant which lives and dies, which surges out of nothingness and ends in a dream," we see the centers of consciousness in these fictions threatened with destruction, the response to which danger is to incorporate chaos as part of their natures, to assert disorder as an aspect of being. There is an interest throughout *Unspeakable Practices, Unnatural Acts* in "coming through," of the movement of consciousness from one state to another. After the concern with abortion in *Come Back, Dr. Caligari*, it is difficult not to see the recurrence of literal and metaphoric birth out of nothingness, as in "Robert Kennedy Saved from Drowning," and the final remarkable story, "See the Moon?" The drift of consciousness between dreaming and waking states is also focal, as in "A Few Moments of Sleeping and Waking." Throughout, there is an abiding interest in ways in which consciousness, an order in itself, issues from apparent fluxity and chaos—an impossibility, a miracle —and must return somehow to chaos in order to be reborn. This can take playful forms, as in "Alice," an erotic fantasy with a peculiar birth: "twirling around on my piano stool my head begins to swim my head begins to swim twirling around on my piano stool twirling around on my piano stool a dizzy spell eventuates twirling around on my piano stool I begin to feel dizzy twirling around on my piano stool" (115).

One has doubts, to be sure, when reading this collection, but they are not so much doubts about the possibility of fiction or about its legitimacy but concerns of a different sort. "The Dolt" is about Edgar, preparing once again to take his National Writers' Examination. Edgar has failed before, and has special difficulty with "the written part." He proceeds to read his latest effort to his wife. It is a beguiling, epic story set in a medieval kingdom, a tale, as Edgar advises his wife, "so old it's new" (59). The tale within the larger story begins at the end, that is to say, on the tragedy of Baron A——,

> "who was in the service of young Friedrich II of Prussia. The Baron, a man of uncommon ability, is chiefly remembered for his notorious and inexplicable blunder at the Battle of Kolin: by withdrawing the column under his command at a crucial moment in the fighting, he earned for himself the greatest part of the blame for Friedrich's defeat. . . . Now as it happened, the chateau in which Madame A—— was sheltering lay not far from the battlefield; in fact, the removal of her husband's corpse placed the chateau itself in the gravest of danger; and at the moment Madame A—— learned, from a Captain Orsini, of her husband's death by his own hand, she was also told that a detachment of pandours, the brutal and much-feared Hungarian light irregular cavalry, was hammering at the chateau gates." [62]

Edgar's tale is a tour de force; its effect does not originate in what is said, in a body of fact or detail, but rather in what is left unsaid. His interest is in what a mind can create from almost nothing, in the tensions consciousness works and compels itself to act upon. The Baron kills himself, fearing the worst between his beautiful wife and the handsome Orsini. "In truth," Edgar writes, "his knowledge of their intercourse, which he had imagined had ripened far beyond the point it had actually reached, had flung him headlong into a horrible crime. . . . the exposure of the lovers, whom he had caused to be together there, to the blood-lust of the pandours" (62–63).

The auto-destructive element in these fictions is separated from the creative impulse and isolated as simply another mode of thinking—invariably factual and objective, altogether peripheral to the magical effect of the fiction on the reader. Edgar's wife, for example, listens to his story, interrupting repeatedly for "factual clarifications." She is a former hooker, and Barthelme shades her in as a sort of literary whore whose very attitude prohibits understanding. She is purely analytical, practical, and critical and wants Edgar to pass the National Examination as one might hurdle his bar exam or final Ph.D. orals: "With a certificate he could write for all the important and great periodicals, and there would be some money in the house for a change instead of what they got from his brother and the Unemployment" (59).

A crisis ensues near the fiction's end, as Edgar uncertainly confesses that the story may be "structurally flawed." His story has an end and a beginning, but tragically he admits to the lack of a middle. The middle, of course, is powerful by its absence, offering a note of speculation; but, for that matter, the end and beginning are at the beginning and end, respectively. Barbara cannot allow this: "The possibility of a semiprofessional apartment, which she had entertained briefly, was falling out of her head with this news, that there was no middle" (63).

But Barthelme's characters make the same discoveries as John Barth's cosmopsis-ridden paralytics, namely, that most of the dimensions of emotional lives (and of fictions of this sort) are not categorical or quantifiable. The logic of what to do, of how or why to act, of beginning-middle-end, these cannot account for the secrets of the mind or its artistic projections or for any sort of creative act. Barthelme makes the point deftly, in multiples in "The Dolt": " 'Something has to happen between them, Inge and what's his name,' she went on. 'Otherwise there's no story.' Looking at her he thought: she is still streety although wearing her household gear. Their child, though, was a perfect love, however, and couldn't be told from the children of success" (63).

The self-destructive aspect of consciousness, then, splinters off as a series of characters in *Unspeakable Practices, Unnatural Acts*. Barthelme's protagonists are dreamers and fantasizers, and they are opposed almost dialectically by characters seeking to conquer the world with logic, to factualize it, as exemplified by Edgar's wife in "The Dolt." Barthelme's interests manifest themselves in other recurring patterns. If consciousness seems free to grow for the first time in these fictions, it also seems free to die. The ideal existence is a succession of instants, each within its own present, but these instants seem destined to describe a line. If one lives creatively, this line will be nothing more than an "extended instant," but more often the fate of the narrators is to fall into history. Thus there is an interest in the relationship to one's past—more an interest in sequence, in duration, the way in which a mind or life flows, than in history. This is expressed by the frequent concern with the relationships between children and parents, especially fathers and sons. "The Dolt," "A Picture History of the War," and "See the Moon?" all work directly out of paternal situations. Children represent rescue and regeneration in these fictions. It is as if the process of literal and metaphoric aging, of becoming a creature threatened with history, suggests a decline toward matter and fixed form, an inevitable slide toward entropy that wrings magic and spirit, leaving ossified matter behind. Youth, birth, gestures of creation are inseparable here; they are manifestations of a concept voiced best in "A Picture History of the War," that "in a viable constitution, every excess of power should structurally generate its own antidote" (135).

Thus children, primitives, and savages appear in these fictions as ineffable, contradictory *presences*—fluid, menacing, yet charged with tension, magic, and *possibility*. They are almost opposites of the wooden, one-dimensional figures in *Come Back, Dr. Caligari* and the semianimated cartoons of *Snow White*. As the narrator of "See the Moon?" admits, "When a child is born, the locus of one's hopes . . . shifts, slightly. Not altogether, not all at once. But you feel it, this displacement. You speak up, strike attitudes, like the mother of a tiny Lollobrigida. Drunk with possibility once more" (164). If this appears sentimental, we should note that the unborn child will be named Gog. Children serve a particular function within the tissue of events in each fiction, almost always threatening whatever old people are at hand, plunging the fiction back into the realm of the fantastic. It is as if parents and adults block the flow of consciousness, deflect it into static forms: memory, reminiscence, futurity. "The Dolt" ends:

> At that moment the son manque entered the room. The son manque was eight feet tall and wore a serape woven out of two hundred transistor radios, all turned on and tuned to different stations. Just by looking at him you could hear Portland and Nogales, Mexico.
> "No grass in the house?"
> Barbara got the grass which was kept in one of those little yellow and red metal canisters made for sending film back to Eastman Kodak. Edgar tried to think of a way to badmouth this immense son leaning over him like a large blaring building. But he couldn't think of anything. Thinking of anything was beyond him. I sympathize. I myself have these problems. Endings are elusive, middles are nowhere to be found, but worst of all, is to begin, to begin, to begin. [65]

Another aspect of the strain of liberation that runs through these fictions is Barthelme's treatment of processes, particularly social processes. A strong interest in self-creating men surfaces in these pages, and most of the fictions issue in the consciousnesses of men who create themselves in the telling of their fantastic tales. There is a corollary interest in men such as "Robert Kennedy" who are related to large groups, who have power over the lives of groups. Barthelme also scrutinizes large social processes themselves. As his fictions become more free and open, less social and representative, they become curiously more stylized, purer in form, almost abstractly architectural in effect.

"Robert Kennedy Saved from Drowning" is composed of a series of panels—brief commentaries on his life from those who work around him interspersed with his own self-commentaries. The effect, finally, is an instance of literary cubism, as if one had arranged a series of plane surfaces in a rough circle, giving life to a vacant space by virtue of boundaries that define it. His being in this sense is nothing more than an area in which something may go on, a freed space, like John

Cage's *4'33"*, which defines a period of unattended silence so that sound might profitably occur within it.

Fixed social processes such as war and institutional religion are of interest because they provide a kind of rigidity against which consciousness defines itself, like the banks of a levee. The stories treating social processes or institutions seem at once to detach the process, isolating it from its conventional social underpinnings but also pulling it open and giving it more fragmentary character. "Fragments," our narrator tells his foetal pride, Gog, in a strangely resonant statement, "are the only forms I trust" (164).

"The Indian Uprising," by illustration, is an updated war story, a cowboy-and-Indian saga as an ill-defined guerilla action. Even something as monstrously present as war—with its baggages of attack and retreat, of heroes and villains, quantifiable kills and captures—is deceptive. Narrated by a white man, this is a surreal tale of Indian attack on a city held by whites. An apparent "victory" blurs into "defeat" in this least familiar of wars. Though the fairy tale was a rigid structure, a dead weight, in *Snow White*, the cowboy-and-Indian war story is used in a nearly opposite manner. The element of play is strong, as there is only movement here; people emerge, merge, vanish, change sides and shapes. The distinctions between character and landscape break down. The language, ossified panels of cliché and jargon suitable only for stacking and smashing together in *Come Back, Dr. Caligari*, is a plastic expression of consciousness itself. Poulet has noted the great difficulty in finding a living, gliding language, and his conclusion is an ideal toward which Barthelme writes: "How else except by inventing a language artless enough to express every transport, supple enough to espouse each change, a language which would be susceptible of detecting the briefest cries and the most modulated transitions? A language which by its spontaneity *would actually be* all the variations of the heart."[34] The style of "The Indian Uprising" is remarkably flexible; note how it embodies the streaming of character and landscape: "Red men in waves like people scattering in a square startled by something tragic or a sudden, loud noise accumulated against the barricades we had made of window dummies, thoughtfully planned job descriptions (including scales for the orderly progress of other colors), wine in demi-johns, and robes" (4). This is mimetic fiction of a different order. It alludes not to external social reality but only to the play of consciousness itself, which it expresses as accurately as possible. It contains received structures—a familiar war story—but uses them, as Poirier writes of Faulkner, "the way a child might need a jungle gym: as a support for exuberant, beautiful, and testing flights."[35]

This is mimetic fiction with almost no sustained social interest; it has little interest in casting light back on an external world. It flows in a dream, shifts and evolves according to the pulse of consciousness from which it stems, and gives us a sense of the substance of thought as fluid and protean, moving in and out of landscapes and characters as if they were simply temporary conveniences or molds to be occupied and abandoned. Miss R., for example, has been the narrator's teacher in the arts of life and war. But near the end, she reveals herself as an Indian agent, and captures him. He strips as ordered, surrendering his white flesh to the liberation of rain and color: "I removed my belt and shoelaces and looked (rain shattering from a great height the prospects of silence and clear, neat rows of houses in the sub-divisions) into their savage black eyes, paint, feathers, beads" (11).

If the fictional world of *Unspeakable Practices, Unnatural Acts* does approach, in a curious and comic way, a pure fiction of consciousness, it is largely because of Barthelme's remarkably kinetic style. Language is no longer repressive but expressive, offering shapes and creative tensions within which to work: the skin of a balloon and the sliding lexical surfaces of a newspaper. It is a prison only to consciousnesses that conceive of it that way; for example, in "A Picture History of the War" General Kellerman complains to his son that "there are worms in words." He is old and rigid and language hardens around him like a shell: "Why does language subvert me, subvert my seniority, my medals, my oldness, whenever it gets a chance? What does language have against me—me that has been good to it, respecting its little peculiarities and nicilosities, for sixty years. What do 'years' have against me? Why have they stuck stones in my kidneys, devalued my tumulosity, retracted my hair? Where does 'hair' go when it dies?" (135). But for the living, language is nearly consciousness; as the working mind describes itself, "Strings of language extend in every direction to bind the world into a rushing ribald whole" (10).

The disease plaguing the narrator of "See the Moon?," we are informed, is a "frightful illness of the mind, light-mindedness" (152). He conducts "lunar hostility studies," and seeks to prove that the moon and all that it stands for hates us. The most basic function of the moon is to shine, simply to exist, but man seems invariably to humanize it, to make it an extension or symbol of some aspect of his world, or otherwise to seek mastery or possession. The notion is expressed obliquely, as the narrator recalls the view from a Tampa porch: "And at night the moon graphed by the screen wire, if you squint. The Sea of Tranquility occupying square 47 through 108" (152). The moon, even at this late date, continues to shine. Consider the evidence of its hostility, the danger of exposure to moonlight: the foetus Gog must be protected, lest "harsh moonlight falls on his new soft head" (165). Otherwise, he too will be seized by "light-mindedness."

The narrator not only serves as a "Distant Early Warning System" for Gog but prefigures the characterization of consciousness in *City Life* as well. Although the narrator's reports are tentative, "pieced together from the reports of travellers" (164), Barthelme's personae exhibit greater certainty in *City Life*. The moon suggests not only an external natural world that man seeks to dominate but man's own internal phenomenological nature as well. The moon's revenge, the defensive response of one aspect of consciousness toward another, takes definite shape in "Brain Damage" in *City Life*. There is no escaping it:

> Oh there's brain damage in the east, and brain damage in the west, and upstairs there's brain damage, and downstairs there's brain damage, and in my lady's parlor—brain damage. . . . There's brain damage on the horizon, a great big blubbery cloud of it coming this way—And you can hide under the bed but brain damage is under the bed, and you can hide in the universities but they are the very seat and source of brain damage. . . . Brain damage caused by art. I could describe it better if I weren't afflicted with it. This is the country of brain damage, this is the map of brain damage, these are the rivers of brain damage, and see, those lighted-up places are the airports of brain damage, where the damaged pilots land the big, damaged ships. . . . And

there is brain damage in Arizona, and brain damage in Maine, and the little towns in Idaho are in the grip of it, and my blue heaven is black with it, brain damage covering everything like an unbreakable lease—Skiing along the soft surface of brain damage, never to sink, because we don't understand the danger. [146]

This "brain damage," which represents a semicomic view of the curse of consciousness so terrible in *Snow White*, also appears as a more specific malady in "Kierkegaard Unfair to Schlegel." During a series of routines with "Q," "A" recalls living for a time in a ranch house filled with games and play equipment. "A" recalls having joked about the house, that the toys represented a particular way of dealing with boredom: "I might have said, for instance, that the remedy is worse than the disease. Or quoted Nietzsche to the effect that the thought of suicide is a great consolation and had helped him through many a bad night. Either of these perfectly good jokes would do to annihilate the situation of being uncomfortable in the house. The shuffleboard sticks, the barbells of all kinds—my joke has, in effect, thrown them out of the world. An amazing magical power!" (87).

What follows is a summary of Kierkegaard's argument against Friedrich Schlegel's novel *Lucinde*. Since it indicates Barthelme's own metaphysical interests and underscores his basic ironic technique, the passage is an excellent entry to *City Life*:

> Schlegel had written a book, a novel, called *Lucinde*. Kierke-
> gaard is very hard on Schlegel and *Lucinde*. Kierkegaard
> characterizes this novel of Schlegel's as quote poetical unquote
> page 308. By which he means to suggest that Schlegel has con-
> structed an actuality which is superior to the historical actuality
> and a substitute for it. By negating the historical actuality poetry
> quote opens up a higher actuality, expands and transfigures the
> imperfect into the perfect, and thereby softens and mitigates that
> deep pain which would darken and obscure all things unquote
> page 312. That's beautiful. Now this would seem to be a victory
> of Schlegel, and indeed Kierkegaard says, is not a victory over the
> world but a reconciliation with the world. And it is soon dis-

covered that although poetry is a kind of reconciliation, the distance between the new actuality, higher and more perfect than the historical actuality, and the historical actuality, lower and more imperfect than the new actuality, produces not a reconciliation but animosity. Quote so that it often becomes no reconciliation at all but rather animosity unquote same page. What began as a victory eventuates in animosity. [89]

One does indeed become "drunk with freedom, lighter and lighter," as "A" suggests, and this is especially true of Barthelme's most recent fiction. We should note that Kierkegaard criticizes Schlegel not for "depriving" the physical world of its reality but for not mastering his own ironic vision. As Edith Kern suggests, "The ironist can speak subjectively and yet, as the poet, can hide behind the mask of a pseudonym or a fictional character. He can resort to the realm of the possible, the aesthetic, and, while inhabiting it in many guises, can remain authentic only as long as he masters irony and avoids living 'completely hypothetically and subjunctively.' "[36] What this implies is an almost dialectical examination of relationships between things—be they inanimate objects, people, natural phenomena, human relations—and their "meanings" or some abstract construction translating them to verbal or visual terms. Between the phenomenon and its translation a tension arises, the vital element in all art ("poetry" in Kierkegaard's terms) that is at least a temporary resolution of man to actuality. Kierkegaard felt that resolution between existence and essence lay finally in making a leap of religious faith and saw his goal in writing as somehow discovering "how to become a Christian."[37] But for Barthelme, for whom such faith is a lost luxury, there remains only the lower-order magic of creation. "What do I look for?" a persona asks, "A work of art, I'll not accept anything less" (156).

Like his fellow metafictionists, Barthelme evokes his own imaginary city in *City Life*, not so much a geographical entity as an interior place, an arena dreamed by the mind for its own amusements. Barthelme's city is a public metaphor for a very private world like Barth's Funhouse; Italo Calvino's multi-worlds converging in the mind of his single narrator, old Qfwfq; Gass's "heart of the heart of the country";

and the master Borges's incredible Tlön. Consciousness has pruned its interests even more severely in this collection, where the protean manic world of *Unspeakable Practices, Unnatural Acts* yields to a series of classic, almost old-world fictions. A static, sculptural quality pervades these fictions and they are bound in ancient, timeless circumstances: in ballrooms, museums, opera houses, formal sitting rooms, at polished antique writer's desks.

We should notice several things initially. The creative narrators—dreamers, fabulators, writers, storytellers—who dominate *Unspeakable Practices, Unnatural Acts* vanish in *City Life.* There is only the dreamed world in its concrete aspect and its narrators are nameless, stateless functionaries who work almost as direct reflexes of consciousness itself. They are tour guides leading us through great physical edifices, recording responses as they go through Paraguay, The City, ancient opera houses, even through the shell of a sentence as it hardens around them. Notice also that Barthelme's interest in a series of characters in dramatic relation is minimal. The movement since *Come Back, Dr. Caligari* is clear. In that first volume he felt the need to create characters, if only to parody themselves and their fictive existences; in *Snow White*, he turns a series of familiar mythic characters inside out; in *Unspeakable Practices, Unnatural Acts*, his interest is solely in fabulators who fantasize themselves and a larger world into being; by *City Life*, Barthelme feels little need to dress his thoughts in anthropomorphic guises. He gives shape only to ghostly guides and the landscapes before them and to "characters" beyond that are secondary, fleeting phantasms in the guide's mind. When they are directly rendered, as in "Q" and "A" of "The Explanation," they exist only as voices in a dialectic inquiry.

More important, though, is the peculiar abstract, almost sculptural, quality of these fictions, because Barthelme uses architectural structures and massive natural phenomena as landscapes of consciousness and nearly unmediated dialectical inquiry at the surface in most of them. In addition, the fictions themselves tend to resemble the visual arts, a direction marked in "See the Moon?". There Barthelme works disparate materials in suspension around an emotional core (the lunar cycle), and the result is a poetic collage. The narrator of "See the Moon?" addresses his unborn son Gog, hoping that his own words and life will, like a collage on the wall before him, "someday merge, blur—cohere is the word, maybe—into something meaningful" (152).

With several of the French New Novelists, Barthelme shares an unspoken urge to liberate objects, to relocate things in their purest, nonhumanized states. An equally probable influence is that of contemporary arts and artists. A former museum director, Barthelme maintains friendships with a wide circle of New York artists. And like the art of Andy Warhol, Claes Oldenberg, and Robert Rauschenberg, his work moves increasingly toward mixed media forms. All are aware that represented objects may not only be "pure," as in Warhol's infamous Campbell Soup cans, but also can provoke surprising emotional responses, can be silly and even menacing, as in Oldenberg's expanded and stuffed vinyl cigarette butts, light switches, and french fries. The gigantic replica of Tolstoy's coat in "At the Tolstoy Museum" and the varieties of dogs and dog-lore in "The Falling Dog" suggest an interest in "object-hood." We should note further that the only artist in this collection is the sculptor of "The Falling Dog" and that a major part of his fiction is a collage—a spool of dog images, puns, references that a dog falling on him from an apartment window has inspired.

The static quality is evident at once on the dust jacket of *City Life*. What little physical movement depicted in these fictions is ritual, frozen, caught-in-the-act, as the jacket engraving of an old man and young woman dancing suggests. There is a basic distinction, though, between the two sorts of abstraction that Barthelme works with and the very different effects they have on the reader. Some of the fictions are virtual chamber pieces, fictional tableaux of consciousness within which we are presented with a set of objects or a problem of finite series of possibilities. "View of My Father Weeping" is technically adept but severely limited, a tale in which we see two contradictory simultaneous events revealed—views of the narrator's father under the wheels of a carriage posed against images of his father sitting in bed weeping. Barthelme seems to be relying far too heavily on a *representational* fiction of consciousness; in this story he simply offers us a set of two contradictory possibilities occurring in the same instant of time and space, as if a simple depiction of paradox automatically evokes a sense of awe and wonder. The fiction is skeletal, an almost naturalistic expression of a sequence of possibilities. In "Bone Bubbles," the mind seems to yield even more to the "objectness" of things, to their material presences. This story is a series of fifteen dense spheres of "cut-up" descriptions of actions, people, and historical events. As the title indicates, rigorous compression occurs, but no tension is created—the bubbles never reach the surface—and the fiction offers little beyond its own portentously avant-garde presence.

"Paraguay" works on a much larger scale but suffers a similar lifelessness. Consciousness creates for itself some sort of country, above all concrete and particular, but if human consciousness is a grand theme and an eternal miracle, a styrofoam scale model is not necessarily going to be fascinating. Barthelme labors to create the impression that this landscape is a marvel, a direct projection of a state of mind in terms of a nation. It is not the familiar Paraguay, "not the Paraguay that exists on our maps. It is not found on the continent, South America; it is not a political sub-division of that continent, with a population of 2,161,000 and a capital city named Asuncion. This Paraguay exists elsewhere" (20). Our entry to this mental kingdom is a classic element of travelogue, an account of treacherous journeys over mountains and plains. A history of disaster makes us wary, and a sense of ritual sanctifies the passage: "At the summit there is a cairn on which each man threw a stone, and here it is customary to give payment to the coolies. I paid each man his agreed-upon wage, and, alone, began the descent. Ahead was Paraguay" (20). What follows is a depiction of physical and psychological manifestations of a mass consciousness, merged in a single silent landscape. "Such is the smoothness of surfaces in Paraguay that anything not smooth is valuable" (25). But the effect is not so much awe-inspiring as boring; this landscape is too substantial to suggest a presence of the marvelous. Like the mysterious red snow that encrusts it, this Paraguay finally proclaims itself "a mystery, but one there was no point in solving—an ongoing low-grade mystery" (27).

Although human consciousness may well be a fascinating subject for study, direct mimetic fictional representations of its processes are likely to be uninspiring. Once one refines away characters, even those incessantly self-destructive figures in Barthelme's earlier work, and then disposes of energizing narrators who create selves and worlds, the resonance or tension that Barthelme's best creations contain is difficult to create or sustain. If nothing else, there must be a dialectic of voices on tape, as in several of John Barth's fictions in *Lost in the Funhouse*. But the skeletal nature of the materials makes any sort of tension difficult to generate; thus metafictions are by their natures short and break off repeatedly, shifting attentions repeatedly within their own limited structures; in this sense the notion of a novel as a more extended form is virtually a logical impossibility. Metafictions may also develop into a series of voices-within-voices-within-voices, eight in all, as in John Barth's maddening tour de force, "The Mene-laiad."[38] If there is any clear relationship between a fictive world's capacity to suggest the marvelous and its representational, pictorial qualities (detail, documentation, length), it is probably inverse. The less offered, the better, in such fictions. Jorge Luis Borges, after all, takes only nineteen pages to describe the nature and discovery of the world of Tlön; and beyond that, takes merely a page to offer us a vision of infinity in "The Aleph."[39] As in most abstract art forms, the demands placed on metafiction by its own nature are considerable. As consciousness refines its interests, as it abandons conventional fictional trappings, its effect on the reader is more difficult to justify and sustain, as Barth found in *Lost in the Funhouse*. With that collection he painted himself into a personal corner and escaped in time-honored fashion through tale spinning and fabulation, as evidenced in his recent *Chimera* and the massive work-in-progress, his own version of *One Thousand and One Nights*.

A second group of fictions in *City Life* is more successful and more absorbing for the reader; these fictions tend to be static but in a very different way. In this group Barthelme focuses on pictorial qualities, especially on the manipulation of visual abstractions such as old wood-cuts and faked engravings. Barthelme plays with mixed media here by using large abstract blocks of black surface in "The Explanation" and "Kierkegaard Unfair to Schlegel," collages of antique etchings and engravings in "City Life" and "At the Tolstoy Museum," and complex "image games" in "The Falling Dog."

The primary feature of these fictions is that Barthelme finds an adequate means of *symbolizing* the dialectical process within consciousness instead of simply *representing* it. Because there is also an abstract quality in these fictions, they are neither dead nor rigid. In "Falling Dog," which is, significantly, the single work in the volume about an artist or creator—a sculptor—the workings of consciousness are not presented as tableaux portraying a fixed series of possibilities or a single smooth surface. A dog falls from a third-story window; this event is undeniable and absurd, but the fiction is composed around the shuttle of the sculptor's mind as it searches for significance. What we have, finally, is a fiction not only stylized and abstract but also resonant and open-ended. A collage of the possible in its most playful state follows:

dirty and clean dogs
ultra-clean dogs, laboratory animals
thrown or flung dogs
in series, Indian file

an exploded view of the Falling Dog:
head, heart, liver, lights

to the dogs
putting on the dog:
I am telling him something which isn't true

and we are both falling

dog tags!
but forget puns. Cloth falling dogs, the
gingham dog and the etc., etc. Pieces
of cloth dogs falling. Or quarter-inch
plywood in layers, the layers separated
by an inch or two of airspace. Like old
triple-wing aircraft.

dog-ear (pages falling with corners bent back)

Tray: cafeteria trays of some obnoxious brown plastic
But enough puns

Groups of tiny hummingbird-sized falling dogs.
Massed in upper corners of a room with high ceilings,

14–17 foot
in rows, in ranks, in their backs
·   ·   ·   ·   ·   ·   ·   ·   ·   ·   ·
(flights? sheets?)
of falling dogs, flat falling dogs like sails
Day-Glo dogs falling

am I being sufficiently skeptical?
try it out

die like a
dog-eat-dog
proud as a dog in shoes
dogfight
doggerel
dogmatic [35–36]

    This extract presents an evocative, open-ended series of images depicting the creative processes of the sculptor's mind. "Paraguay" and "View of My Father Weeping," on the other hand, seek to directly represent a limited series of possibilities, suggesting that whatever aspect of process consciousness follows is over before the fiction reaches paper. Barthelme is especially concerned with the pictorial quality that words have, the images they create. He concerns himself with ways that the sculptor mentally shapes his material and examines the material even as it assumes concrete form. The most provocative fiction in *City Life* is Barthelme's "At the Tolstoy Museum," which opens with this forbidding engraving of the master of realism (Fig. 1). The museum itself is an appropriate salute to Leo Tolstoy, exhaustive in the sorts and volume of materials related to its subject. There are 30,000 pictures of him and 640,086 pages (Jubilee edition) of his work; visitors feel his eyes, at least 60,000 of them, trained on them constantly. The effect is monstrously oppressive, a fact seen most vividly in its strange architecture:

    The Tolstoy Museum is made of stone—many stones, cunningly wrought. Viewed from the street, it has the aspect of three stacked boxes: the first level is, say, the size of a shoebox, the second level the size of a case of whiskey, and the third level the

Fig. 1. Drawings from "At the Tolstoy Museum" from *City Life* by Donald Barthelme. Copyright © 1969, 1970 by Donald Barthelme. Reprinted by permission of Farrar, Straus and Giroux, Inc.

size of a box that contained a new overcoat. The amazing cantilever of the third floor has been much talked about. The glass
floor there allows one to look straight down and provides a
"floating" feeling. The entire building, viewed from the street,
suggests that it is about to fall on you. [45]

"At the Tolstoy Museum we sat and wept," is the note the verbal
part of the fiction opens with; from then on, weeping and sadness
prevail. The guards, for instance, carry buckets filled with stacks of
clean white handkerchiefs. But though the narrator weeps at the
outset, his reaction is immediately suspect and undercut. In the second sentence, the weeping is "ironized," cut loose from its normal
meaning by a peculiar description: "paper streams came out of our
eyes" (43). Thereafter, he takes pains to indicate his own ambivalence
to the threat the museum poses to his fellow visitors. Concerning the
effect of Tolstoy's stern gaze, the narrator speaks only of the effect on
others, an important means of distancing: "It is like, people say,
committing a small crime and being discovered at it by your father,
who stands in four doorways, looking at you" (45).

Note again that the description of the museum provides two perspectives at once. From outside, the stone building is utterly menacing; but inside, within this vast orchestrated phenomenon, the
peculiar cantilever gives one the sense of floating, of being free. The
narrator's final remarks are even more significant, faced as he is with
the monstrous presence of Tolstoy, "Some people wanted him to go
away, but other people were glad to have him. . . . I haven't made up
my mind." But an instant or so later, after "several hazes" pass over
his eyes, he decides to stay—as well he might, having neutralized the
threat of the museum on his own mind: "Perhaps something vivifying
will happen to me here" (49).

The significance of perspective and narrative levels is strengthened
by a tale-within-a-tale that the narrator recounts reading in the museum. Borgesian in mirroring and clarity, it is a tale told by Tolstoy
about a bishop aboard a ship who hears of three devout hermits living
on a nearby island. The bishop diverts the ship to meet the hermits
and is startled to hear their only prayer: "Three of You, three of us,
have mercy on us." This strikes him as an improper prayer, and he

laboriously instructs them in the Lord's Prayer and sails off. After night falls, the bishop sits on deck pondering his strange experience, and a light catches his eye, one "cast by the three hermits floating over the water, hand in hand, without moving their feet" (47). They have forgotten their prayer and implore him to reinstruct them, but the bishop refuses, crossing himself and adding, "It is not for me to teach you. Pray for us sinners!" The bishop bows and the three return to their island. Thus the framed tale concludes.

The importance of perspective, suggested in the preceding and following descriptions of the museum and its effect on visitors, is highlighted by the parable of the hermits and confirmed by the sequence of development of the nine visual elements within the fiction. The tale opens with the great head of Tolstoy peering at us; the head is repeated on the next page with a small Napoleonic view added in a lower corner. The third cut follows a brief list of Tolstoy's idiosyncrasies—that his name means "fat" in Russian, that his mother knew no bad words, that he was once bitten in the face by a bear, became a vegetarian in 1885, and occasionally "bowed backward" to make himself interesting. These details lighten the press of the master on the consciousness offering all this, but the etching that follows them heightens the note of absurdity that has crept in (Fig. 2).

Immediately following Tolstoy's coat is an engraving of Tolstoy as a child, diminishing his presence even more. Cut five (page 46) shows him posed beside a huge, old-fashioned bicycle and cut six, "Tiger hunt, Siberia," is more exaggerated, showing "him" in a group of seven soldiers posing with their tiger. A reduced version of the great head opening the story has been pasted on the shoulders of one of the figures in the portrait. The seventh illustration follows the parable of the hermits and is essentially a perspective study of a pavilion. In the eighth cut "Tolstoy" is a tiny figure singled out by a black arrow, inspecting the rubble of a formerly great building. The engraving is a kind of silent self-testimony to the way in which the consciousness of the narrator has undone the psychic paralysis induced by Tolstoy, his museum, and his historical realism. The process depicted in "At the Tolstoy Museum" is described in "Kierkegaard Unfair to Schlegel": "By negating the historical actuality poetry opens up a higher actuality, expands and transfigures the imperfect into the perfect, and

Tolstoy's coat

Fig. 2. Drawings from "At the Tolstoy Museum" from *City Life* by Donald Barthelme. Copyright © 1969, 1970 by Donald Barthelme. Reprinted by permission of Farrar, Straus and Giroux, Inc.

thereby softens and mitigates the deep pain which would darken and obscure all things" (89). Barthelme's final illustration offers mute certitude of what has gone on in the fiction. The reduced negative of the intentionally faded head is a new demythologized version of the head with which the story begins. Here, recessed in a horizontal perspective study, it no longer threatens (Fig. 3).

Although there is a certainty, an insistent visual and physical presence in the trappings of Barthelme's consciousness in these fictions, this presence is only a way of being for a time, with little solace offered once the landscape has been imagined, the illustrations made, the structures built. "Sentence," a tour de force that grows through eight pages, holds a prison in the title's pun and, for all the freedom found in creating it, we should be glad it too will vanish, "a disappointment, to be sure, but it reminds us that the sentence itself is a man-made object, not the one we wanted of course, but still a con-

Museum plaza with monumental head (Closed Mondays)

Fig. 3. Drawings from "At the Tolstoy Museum" from *City Life* by Donald Barthelme. Copyright © 1969, 1970 by Donald Barthelme. Reprinted by permission of Farrar, Straus and Giroux, Inc.

struction of man, a structure to be treasured for its weakness, as opposed to the strength of stones" (114).

The City is a place of the mind, that much is made particularly clear when we are about to leave *City Life*. It is muddy, a muck, it "heaves and palpitates. It is multi-dimensional and has a mayor. To describe it takes many hundreds of thousands of words. Our muck is only a part of a much greater muck—the nation state—which is itself the creation of that muck of mucks, human consciousness" (166–67). However immense its presence, The City will thankfully vanish. Near the end of "City Life," everyone in The City watches the same movie; Ramona, in turn, thinks about the citizens and orchestrates their many existences in her mind. They in turn, under her consideration, regard the narrator, who is, as directly as possible, Donald Barthelme. Although he may seem to create this fictional world and to project the entire City, The City also shapes him in its own dreams and allows him to live in its own illusion:

> —Upon me, their glance has fallen. The engendering force, was, perhaps, the fused glance of them all. From the millions of units crawling about on the surface of the city, their wavering desirous eye selected me. The pupil enlarged to admit more light: more me. They began dancing little dances of suggestion and fear. These dances constitute an invitation of unmistakable import—an invitation which, if accepted, leads one down many muddy roads. I accepted. What was the alternative? [167–68]

Barthelme's fourth collection of stories, *Sadness* (1972), gathers sixteen fictions, many of which concern themselves with metaphors and motifs of changes or shifts—in urban domestic life; in our habitual expectations of each other; in restricting social roles; in formerly "fixed" philosophical, artistic, political, and religious configurations of power and authority—and how they nourish and terrify us. *Sadness* again reverberates with the voices of Marcel and Poulet, and "Critique de la Vie Quotidienne," one of a handful of the author's most accomplished fictions, represents the tenor of the collection nicely.

The tale does well as a fiction of social history, because it deals with the dissolution of a family, a development not endemic to New York, the late 1960s, or Donald Barthelme. The carefully controlled tone of the piece and the quality of the narrator's voice and perception raise it above the level of just another story about marital failure. Recounted quickly in seven unnumbered sections, the tale dwells on the narrator's estranged wife and child; the three made a rosy circle that he was compelled to violate. In retrospect, he can discern only ghosts in the circle, "traces but only traces. Vestiges. Hints of a formerly intact mystery never to be returned to its original wholeness" (12). He recalls an incessant disappointment in married life, as if the realities of husbanding and parenting could never approach the great expectations surrounding those American institutions. "Our evenings lacked promise," he tells us. "The world in the evening seems fraught with the absence of promise, if you are a married man. There is nothing to do but go home and drink your nine drinks and forget about it" (4).

The tone throughout is a fine blend of mordancy and nostalgia, and beneath the comic absurdity of daily life that Barthelme sees so clearly—as if urban family life were conducted in a deranged hive by colonies of inept bees—runs a vein of frustration and destruction that suggests once again the keenly felt oppression of human institutions. The husband, depressed by a free-floating sense of "not-enoughness" rampant in his life, drinks his evenings away until "my hostility came roaring out of its cave like a jet-assisted banshee" (10). He gathers up the detritus of hostile acts from his marriage, in gestures great and small, and we gradually realize that his bitterness is not merely about marriage but about the continual disappointment with the unfulfilled promises of American life: the loss of young hope, the failure of marriage to fit neatly into a new GE all-electric kitchen, the boredom with his narrow roles as provider and husband, the total emptiness of urban American domestic life. None of these is erased by an awareness that "there are wretches worse off than you, people whose trepanations have not been successful, girls who have not been invited to the sexual revolution, priests still frocked" (7).

The child in this story does not represent any sort of potentiality or magic possibility as it does elsewhere in Barthelme's fiction; it exists here as a series of whining demands, a fixed and inescapable sentence to a dreary life. Nor does Wanda fulfill her promise as the centerpiece of domestic life. They must be left behind.

If the simple weight of unfulfilled promise in life forces the narrator to flee his marital life, there is no guarantee in Barthelme's vision that things can be altered for the better by dissolution. There is every suggestion that the great yawning need on the narrator's part may be impossible to satisfy. Wanda and the husband finally drink amicably at the close of the brief tale, when they meet for the first time after separation. As they hoist toasts to survival itself, she becomes angry at his morose considerations of "what-went-wrong." "You are touring the ruins," she drunkenly cries and attempts to "ventilate [him] then, with the horse pistol." Ever unsuccessful, she is dispatched weeping in a cab. The story closes on a sardonic chord in a parody of happy endings, as many in *Sadness* do. Wanda's new life takes her to Nanterre as a student in Marxist sociology studying with the very author of *Critique de la Vie Quotidienne* (a promise of a new cycle?). The child is being cared for in a utopian, highly streamlined Piagetian nursery school. And the husband, mournfully recounting all of this, has his hopes and anodynes: "And I, I have my J & B . . . case after case, year in and year out, and there is, I am told, no immediate danger of a dearth" (13). He speaks as if, however comic, the entire inescapable complex of emotions coalesces in a paralyzed, bemused sadness at the institutional and psychic failure of American city life.

The Dead Father (1975), Barthelme's second novel, is a fantastic mythic compendium of the paternal role and image; here the father is perceived as oppressive and destructive, an impulse depicted in every way by the black images of "Tolstoy" in "At the Tolstoy Museum." The D. F., Julie, Thomas, and Edmund set out on a quest, the end of which will be to lay the patriarch finally to rest. As in *Snow White*, the author uses the baggy shapes of the novel as an occasion for many subjects and literary styles. But the focus is inevitably on the fused suggestions of paternal authority, kingly certitude, masculine protection and aggression, historical achievement and male fiat that hurry them all toward the novel's last word and the overwhelming father's rightful end: "Bulldozers" (177).

The Dead Father is an excellent instance of metafiction drawn out to the proportions of the novel (a turnabout, for several of Barthelme's Edward and Pia stories in earlier volumes are resurrected from a failed novel). In metafictional terms, it is of special interest because it manifests the prevalent self-conciousness of the form. As Scholes notes in his text on metafiction, the highly self-conscious use of materials traditionally associated with the unconscious—myth and archetype in particular—will inevitably partake of the comic.[40] *The Dead Father* is certainly dependent on the touch of a writer highly conscious of the father in his many mythic, psychological, historical, and literary guises. Of greatest interest to us is Barthelme's virtuosic technique in the novel, for beyond the inevitable cleverness in manipulating styles of discourse and description, the incessant sequences of lists, the familiar incongruity of contemporary brand names and popular ideas taken on an ancient journey, the constant struggle between male and female for dominion, beyond these customary elements in Barthelme's work, *The Dead Father* breaks new ground.

First, we should note that much of the novel is developed in dialogue unbroken by quotation marks and frequently unattributable to a particular speaker. For example, when Julie and Emma talk by the campfire, their conversation is woven through the larger fabric of evening voices:

To partake of this al fresco party.
Where can a body get a pop around here?
Everyone was very enthusiastic.
He is a perpetual drudge restless in his thoughts.
He's not bad looking.
The reindeer, man, and snowflakes were cut.
Tears some meat from his breast and puts it on a bun.
You're safe with me.
If this is what you believe you are wrong.
Dejected looks, flaggy beards, singing in the ears, old,
wrinkled, harsh, much troubled with wind.
Everyone is very enthusiastic.
Darkening the skies above the walkers.
Pouring over diaries and memoirs for clues to the past.
Most people conceal what they feel with great skill.
Not getting anywhere not making any progress. [155]

Barthelme's purpose in scattering such conversations throughout the novel is neither to develop character or theme, nor to move the story line along, nor to emphasize the dreamy colors of this holy quest. Such dialogues exist as much to deny the march of such logics as to advance them. The effect is not unlike the cinematic technique of taping dialogue as part of a much larger field of sound and meaning, of recording background and peripheral "noise" so faithfully that the voices of on-screen subjects may be muffled or lost. Barthelme's purpose is to establish the expectations of dialogue and then to deny them, an instance of consciousness desiring shape but resisting mediation or restriction into progressive discourse. Here, as in "City Life," the author is fascinated with the organism of consciousness made up by that "muck of mucks," the collective mind, be it in a city or around a campfire. Thus his dialogues exist not to examine the ways in which thought defines itself and refuses definition in literary models. Barthelme simultaneously erects structures of meaning and then reduces them to babble.

"A Manual for Sons," a thirty-page mock medieval conduct book at the center of *The Dead Father*, enacts metafiction's distinct sense of its artifice, of its presence as a literary form among those of the past. Much of Barthelme's sense of patriarchal weight is developed in this satire, where "fathers are like blocks of marble, giant cubes, with veins and seams, placed squarely in your path. They cannot be climbed over, neither can they be slithered past. They *are* the 'past'" (129). As much of a tour de force as Captain John Smith's secret "Diary" in *The Sot-Weed Factor*, the "Manual" also allows Barthelme fictional leave to articulate the complex burden of the need to control, quantify, accumulate, and make historic—the masculine impulse of the human mind.

At the other end of the spectrum is another parody, a two-page chapter of Joycean prose in the manner of *Finnegans Wake* in which the father's authority breaks down into the childish (senile?) babble of unimpeded consciousness. Although the "Manual for Fathers" emphasizes paternal authority and the fixity of literary structure, chapter 22 defines the breakdown of oppressive masculine consciousness by means of the preliterate rush of the mind through memory in several languages, in multiple puns and broken and fused words, in disrupted and exploded snytax, and in the almost unmediated play of sound in the aural imagination. "Endshrouded in endigmas" (172), the Great Pap flows like Molly's subconscious in *Ulysses* toward the end of his day.

The twenty fictions comprising *Amateurs* are his shortest and most accessible to date. Like *Sadness*, the author's ninth book does not take its title from a single story. That collection is named for the recurrent fog of lost hope, thwarted desire, or bad faith, for the great cloud of paralyzing sadness that looms over most of the individual fictions. In a similar way, the controlling double metaphor suggested in the title *Amateurs* relates to its contents in several ways. First, many of Barthelme's central characters are frankly amateurs in a world atomized and made abstract by technology and specialization. From the first story, "Our Work and Why We Do It," to the final one, "The End of the Mechanical Age," contemporary life has become so demanding that every aspect of existence has been given over to professionals, with their accompanying black magic of argot and instruments. Thus Barthelme's citizens, faced with an increasingly perplexing order, take on a kind of lifeboat mentality by which they become enthusiastic amateurs, all in this together, making their common way through incongruous experience and a strange and threatening cityscape. Although there are endless rules and orders for a "successful life," they are very much hidden, and his inspired seekers grope their way blindly, doers nonetheless, do-it-yourself virtuosos at the keyboards of their own individual neuroses and desires.

Unaware of quite how to proceed, Colby's friends whip up an elegant and comic lynching in "Some of Us Had Been Threatening Our Friend Colby." "The School," similarly, is run by well-meaning volunteers who watch every educational exhibit, plant and animal, shrivel to their touches and who find themselves true amateurs in explaining the vagaries of love and death to their students. "The Captured Woman" is an absurd blueprint for capturing affection and the Dean of "Porcupines at the University," in an opposing plight, is at a loss to turn back an invading herd of five thousand porcupines.

Although Barthelme's agents are active beings in the world, they are not the fantasizers, dreamers, artists, or Marivaudian creatures of *Unspeakable Practices, Unnatural Acts*. In *Amateurs* they are more pragmatic, however ludicrous the effect of their efforts. The narrator of "I Bought A Little City," for instance, recounts his purchase of Galveston, Texas, in a matter-of-fact tone parodying the get-it-done sensibility of American business. "What to Do Next" is a monologue that very practically lays out a plan for life repair, a sequence of satiric self-help instructions designed to offer "your leaning personality the definition that it lamentably lacks" (84). Considerably less anxiety and less of the tension pervasive in Barthelme's early work appear in these pages, as if a basic shift in the author's vision has taken place. The manic shifting and undercutting that characterizes stories in the first few volumes are dampened here, as if to acknowledge the complex absurdity of human existence and the need, nonetheless, to patiently slog on. "Of course it's also called 'making the best of things,'" Rebecca advises her lesbian lover in "Rebecca," "which I have always considered rather a soggy idea for the American ideal." Her mate Hilda has the last healing words, sounding a representative affirmative tone in these stories: "Soon it will be snow time. Together then as in other snow times. Drinking busthead 'round the fire. Truth is a locked room that we knock the lock off from time to time, and then board up again. Tomorrow you will hurt me, and I will inform you that you have done so, and so on and so on. To hell with it. Come, viridian friend, come and sup with me" (144).

"Rebecca" continues as the narrator pulls back from the female lovers, advising that "the story ends. It was written for several reasons. Nine of them are secrets. The tenth is that one should never cease considering human love. Which remains," he affirms, "as grisly and golden as ever, no matter what is tattooed upon the warm tympanic page" (144). Here we have the second significance of the title *Amateurs*, for many of Barthelme's tales dwell upon the root sense of the word amateur; they are fictions about those who love or admire something or someone. The most successful stories depict amateurs as both lovers and improvisers in a life without a script—"The Captured Woman," "Rebecca," "110 West Sixty-First Street," and "At the End of the Mechanical Age"—in which partners love neither wisely nor particularly well, moving through fields of "modern relationships" like speeding cars on an unlit freeway, finding and losing the trail as they go. The captured woman and her captor, Rebecca and Hilda, Paul and Eugenie, Tom and Mrs. Davis, the couples dance in their amorous comic embraces, improvising and aware that "our arrangement will automatically self-destruct, like the tinted bubble that it is. . . . They are merely flaky substitutes for the terminal experience" (181).

But love they do, and though the affirmation implicit in their repeated willingnesses to risk forays out of their tattered selves may be comforting, it does not necessarily make the best fiction. These twenty fictions lack the structural and linguistic energy of Barthelme's most significant work. There is no experimentation with typography or engraving, nor is there widespread use of literary fragmentation or collage, as in "The Falling Dog" or "Departures." The voices of Marcel and Poulet are muted in these pages and the energetic shifts between language and syntax are less pronounced. Barthelme's fiction, a representation of metafiction at its finest, is a precarious balancing between lyric poetry and narrative prose; it depends on the tension between the necessary baggage of character, plot line, sustained mood, traditional syntax, and consistence of verbal style and the correcting need to deny, modify, or escape from those holding cells. It thrives on the eternal dichotomy between fiction as artistic sublimation ruled by logic, order, and coherence, and verbal expression as the more unrestricted play of the mind, particularly in its preconscious and subconscious aspects, daubing as an idiot savant at the palette. However accessible and affirmative, *Amateurs* does not work in the artistic dialectic I described in detail earlier and, consequently, the stories often lack the richness of texture and narrative invention that characterizes Donald Barthelme's finest work.

Donald Barthelme's tenth and most recent book is delivered even further from the influences of Marcel and Poulet and is entitled, with almost unbearable irony, *Great Days*. Although many of the sixteen fictions seem concerned with "The Important Topics"—historic pivots ("Cortés and Montezuma"), political revolutions ("The Crisis"), philosophical inquiry ("The Leap"), literary history ("The Death of Edward Lear"), or folk art ("The King of Jazz"), it is quickly clear that they work mainly with the tectonic shifts in domestic relationships in the American 1970s and 1980s. It may even be tempting to read them as a series of domestic parables, as novelist Diane Johnson suggests, and Barthelme's unending penchant for metaphor (a subject is forever like or about something else: note the torrent played through a single page of "The King of Jazz") tempts us to swerve toward such a gloss. But if the fictions are honed down (ten of the sixteen are monologues or dialogues set down in European dashes instead of quotation marks), they are by no means as simple as parable or as direct in message.[41]

Barthelme assimilates the fund of our modern experiences (the disease of incessant "newness," aging and suicide, denial of admission to professional school, bodyguards, art theft, supernatural invasion), but his fictional gaze, in style and subject, is on the seriocomic and always incongruous meldings of men, women, and occasionally animals and plants—straight, gay, platonic, or parental.

The characters in these fictions temper themselves to lost youth and love, deceit, or the vagaries of friendship; they are not the resourceful scam artists found in "The Joker's Greatest Triumph" or the manic self-creators in "See The Moon?". Neither is the tone suffused with the mourning and paralysis that so pervade the comic facade of *Snow White.* There is little of the marital ugliness seen in earlier works like "Critique de la Vie Quotidienne," but instead characters show a willingness to confess their own parts, cut their losses, and slog on, as two friends do in "The Leap." They find morning "wine of possibility and the growing popularity of light" (145) sour to vinegar and darkness. A step becomes difficult, a leap of faith impossible on this great day:

—What?
—I can't make it.
—The leap.
  .   .   .   .   .   .
—So we'll try again? Okay?
—Okay.
—Okay?
—Okay. [152–54]

Great Days is an exploration of the narrative possibilities of monologue and dialogue. Its apposites lie in the stand-up performances of Lenny Bruce and George Carlin or in the radio plays of the 1930s and 1940s, in which background can only be spoken of or heard and characters are limited. It parallels Samuel Beckett's dramas, in which time and place are cracked away like asphalt and his speakers are buried to their necks, freed and bound to make their mad, sad metaphysical commentaries on our lives.

Thus these stories are more pruned but not as static as those in *City Life*; their narratives move forward obliquely—by pillow talk, confession shouted to Manhattan streets, interrogation, rhetorical questioning, and even candid conversation—all for the purpose of shaping a comic view of the confusions of contemporary life, a life peculiarly urban, sophisticated, and New York in reference and roots. Although Barthelme has an annoying taste for cheap endings ("The Apology" and "Tales of the Swedish Army"), he exhibits a masterly control, a balanced virtuosity in his art here; even more, he reveals a surprising human warmth beneath the perpetual irony in his auctorial voice, a quality that his readers will value more in the 1980s.

Great Days opens with "The Crisis," a brief monologue on a revolution in which the rebels, led by the narrator's lost darling, Clementine, have neither desire, nor support, nor interested opposition. The "crisis" is not a political one but simply the feeling that no one cares, that "we feel only 25 percent of what we ought to feel, according to recent findings" (6). The narrator resolves an apparently political or social stalemate in personal terms, admitting that "yes, success is everywhere. Failure is more common. Most achieve a sort of middling thing. . . . This allows, if not peace of mind, ongoing attentions to other aspects of existence" (8).

The title dialogue, "Great Days," closes the collection with a mature discourse between an unnamed male and female lover who mourn with, scheme against, envy, and comfort each other, who share successes and failures. If there is "gonna be a great day," it has either been hopelessly unfulfilled or unrecognized by this couple; if it exists, it finds them in a world set apart from decrees and parades and is made by each of them rarely, from individual effort. As one partner asserts: "Each great day is itself, with its own war machines, rattle and green lords" (171).

Barthelme's most recent bound fiction ends with a curiously mixed and open ceremony; it strikes a tentatively affirmative note, resembling a lover's vows sprung from the classic child's question: "Will you always love me?" The successive answers to the serious game are always yes and, metafictionist that he is, Barthelme snaps the trap with a bad stand-up comic's bait, as if to uncloy the proceedings, to assert that "caring" is not so simple or eternal, and simultaneously to turn our attentions back to the tales over which we have just lingered:

—Will you remember me five years from now?
—Yes, I will.
—Knock knock.
—Who's there?
—You see? [172]

Donald Barthelme's work has established him as the best of the metafictionists, both here and abroad. His work has been consistently that of one of the finest stylists in contemporary American fiction and, though *Amateurs* and *Great Days* have turned more to the prickly conditions of urban human society, his path continues to be the creation of an essentially private fiction, one that finally not only mirrors life but also expands our fund of conscious imaginative experience.

Thus we leave the City of Jacklegs in contemporary fiction and modern love and the obtuse mechanics of daily life, our perceptions altered by the metafictional workers at the perimeters. Restrained but undaunted, we bid a temporary farewell, as Barthelme writes, "until the last destruction of our art by some other art which is just as good but which, I am happy to say, has not yet been invented" ("Our Work and Why We Do It" [9]).

Three

Afro-American Fiction and Ernest Gaines

The process of cultural splintering that I described in chapter 1 is nowhere more evident than in recent Afro-American literature. Since the Supreme Court decision of 1954, Afro-Americans have been persistent in claiming the rights guaranteed them as citizens; but their gaze has turned more inward, to seek out what they have become since their white kidnappers landed the "twenty Negars" at Jamestown in 1619. What they have found in recent years has been a "double consciousness" described best some seventy-nine years ago by W. E. B. DuBois. Stark and threatening as it seemed to blacks and whites in 1903, the truth of his words now seems almost self-evident:

> After the Egyptian and Indian, the Greek and Roman, Teuton and Mongolian, the Negro is a sort of seventh son born with a veil, and gifted with second sight in this American world—a world which yields him no true self-consciousness, but only lets him see himself through the revelation of the outer world. It is a peculiar sensation, this double consciousness, the sense of always looking at one's self through the eyes of others, of measuring one's soul by the tape of a world that looks on in amused contempt and pity. One ever feels the twoness—an American, a Negro, two souls, two thoughts, two unreconciled strivings; two

warring ideals in one dark body, whose dogged strength alone keeps it from being torn asunder.[1]

DuBois's "double consciousness" lies at the heart of the American experience. At best an uneasy and shifting peace. To stress one's national and ethnic origins and culture or to conceive oneself as purely an American, cut from the ties of people and past—these are truly warring ideals, the poles of total assimilation and the supreme isolation of place, race, and class that have generated the tension defining our national struggles. DuBois himself was rent by the personal and public effort to reconcile his blackness and his Americanness—a particularly painful search in a racist culture—and the struggle continues to our day.

In the decade following his landmark *Invisible Man* (1952), Ralph Ellison addressed himself to this plight, advocating a classic "melting pot" cultural pluralism. He argued eloquently for a black literature that would "define Negro humanity" and assigned Afro-American writers the task of "contributing to the total image of the American by depicting the experience of their own groups."[2] Through his "Hidden Name and Complex Fate," particularly, Ellison dominated the black intellectual forum, defending his vision of a literature that would bring to the American cultural mainstream its own unique black language and experience:

> I also began to learn that the American novel has long concerned itself with the puzzle of the one-and-the-many: the mystery of how each of us, despite his origin in diverse regions, with our diverse racial, cultural, religious backgrounds, speaking his own diverse idiom of the American with his own accent, is, nevertheless, American. And with this concern with the implicit cultural pluralism of the country and with the composite nature of the ideal character called "the American," there goes a concern with gauging the health of the American promise, with depicting the extent to which it was being achieved, being made manifest in our daily conduct.[3]

However impassioned, such arguments for cultural pluralism generally depend on two assumptions: (1) that American culture is indeed a "melting pot," a brew of many ethnic streams working toward an overall equality and assimilation; (2) that the diverse cultural strains have essentially common origins and can be remixed in the New World. In more direct terms, this assumes that Afro-Americans and Afro-American cultures are basically compatible with the transplanted European cultures dominant in the United States; that is, they are complementary figures capable of working harmoniously in the pattern of a larger carpet. These assumptions have been seriously challenged in the last twenty years.

The rich activity of American and Third World liberation movements since the march on Washington in 1963 has helped us to reconceive the role of blacks in the New World, and from Ellison's classic cultural pluralism has evolved a distinct separatist sensibility. Black and white scholars such as Frantz Fanon, Herbert Aptheker, Winthrop Jordan, Addison Gayle, Jr., and Harold Cruse, suggested the model of a colonized people occupied by an oppressor nation as possibly appropriate for Afro-Americans, particularly those in the urban East.[4] They stressed the forcible introduction of blacks into America and the very great cultural differences between African ways and forcibly adopted European customs. In addition, such scholars have stressed that integration—both socially and culturally—has in fact implied a cannibalizing of black heritage and culture rather than an assimilation and preservation of ethnic values and forms within a larger national framework. As if to provide evidence for later black anger, sociologists like Nathan Glazer and Daniel Moynihan could state blithely in 1963 that "the Negro is only American and nothing else. He has no values and culture to guard and protect."[5] Whatever their intentions, during the mid-1960s Glazer and Moynihan enraged black and white scholars, who read in their message a foreboding of psychic and cultural genocide. Stung severely by accusations of racism, Glazer acknowledges his myopia in a corrective introduction to a later edition, "The View from 1970." Speaking of the rise in ethnic and racial pride in the late 1960s, he writes in a long, apologetic footnote to his inflammatory passage: "One passage in *Beyond the Melting Pot* has given me considerable pain, and the point I make here gives me a chance to correct it."[6]

Integration came to imply cultural imperialism to many—white over black, in Jordan's term. In its place, the varieties of black separatism became more pronounced, certainly in the decade 1965–75. What this has meant in cultural and literary terms has been an outpouring of scholarly and creative work, defining the distinctiveness of Afro-American existence: the nature of his experience as an uprooted African replanted in the United States as a chattel and how this experience is manifested in his history, institutions, psychology, language, music, and literature. More, there has been a steady growth in the black belief that dominant artistic categories and ways of judging are inappropriate because Afro-American experience has been so different from that of white America.

Certainly the pattern of history drawn in white critical response to black writing has not helped matters any, for it has insisted that black poetry, drama, or fiction should strive for our vision of the "universal." James Joyce's "transcendence" of Irish culture has been the handiest working example for this sort of argument, with unfortunate consequences for black writers whose material, sense of form, language, or social obligations have not permitted ready access to the critic. Afro-American literature has recently made greater demands on white critics, and David Littlejohn's reaction is only slightly exaggerated:

> It may one day be different, but a white American today will find it an exhausting and depressing enterprise to immerse himself for long in the recent literature of the American Negro. . . . Not all of the poems and plays and novels of the American Negro, of course, are miserably bleak—only most of them; but even the few positive works still convey heavily to a white reader the sense of the "prison," of the debasing life sentence that being a Negro can mean in America. Taken all together, the works of recent American Negro authors evoke a close, colorless, nonextensive world that the most despairing white existentialist will never know.[7]

Littlejohn's snideness is merely annoying, but his stunning ignorance of Afro-American culture—of the worlds pressing through the pages of those "miserably bleak" books he blithely waves off—is a serious matter. And so are his masked political biases, tricked out in the thin-

86

nest of aesthetic garbs. Littlejohn prefers an apolitical literature, more genial and refined, and given the history of American blacks—a legacy of kidnapping, slavery, and repression—this is an impossibility. But even liberal white scholars, those granting black writers a strong social obligation, have had difficulties with recent writing. Robert Bone's *The Negro Novel in America*, the first adequate critical survey of black American fiction, has recently come under severe attack.[8] Similarly, Irving Howe's reviews and articles have precipitated another series of angry controversies. At one time very sympathetic to proletarian fiction, the socialist Howe waged a lengthy disagreement with Ralph Ellison in the mid-1960s. In Ellison's opinion, Howe argues from the left of Littlejohn, from a conviction that "unrelieved suffering is the only 'real' Negro experience, and that the true Negro writer must be ferocious." What Ellison and fellows resent in this instance is simply another face of the prescriptive, paternalistic stance of the white critic toward black writers and their work. Ellison's tone throughout the exchange was uncharacteristically sharp, and he concludes:

> Dear Irving, I am still yakking on and there's many a thousand gone, but I assure you that no Negroes are beating down my door, putting pressure on me to join the Negro Freedom Movement, for the simple reason that they realize I am enlisted for the duration. . . . For, you see, my Negro friends recognize a certain division of labor among members of the tribe. Their demands, like that of many whites, are that I publish more novels —and here I am remiss and vulnerable perhaps. You will recall what the Talmud has to say about the trees of the forest and the making of books, etc. But then, Irving, they recognize what you have not allowed yourself to see; namely, that my reply to your essay is in itself a small though necessary action in the Negro's struggle for freedom.[9]

Following Howe's attacks on Ellison and Wright, a loud and less gentlemanly second round ensued in the late 1960s. His attacks on Ishmael Reed and Cecil Brown, mainly because of their "failure" to maintain in their work a familiar militant attitude in accepted veins of social realism, prompted Reed to write him into a novel. Reed's "hoo-doo Western," *Yellow Back Radio Broke-Down*, an all-points satirical attack on white myths and history, includes Bo Shmo and his "neo-socialist realist" gang:

> Bo Shmo was dynamic and charismatic as they say. He made a big reputation in the thirties, not having much originality, by learning to play Hoagland Howard Carmichael's "Buttermilk Sky" backwards. . . . People went for it. So sympathetic Americans sent funds to Bo Shmo which he used to build one huge neo-social realist Institution in the mountains. Wagon trains of neo-social realist composers, writers and painters could be seen winding up its path. . . . Bo Shmo did all their thinking for them. Their job was merely to fold their arms and look mean. You see Bo Shmo was a collectivist. Worked hard at it. Fifty toothbrushes cluttered his bathroom and when he walked down the street it seemed a dozen centipedes headed your way. He woke up in the mornings with crowds and went to bed with a mob. The man loved company. It seemed that he wore people under his coat although none of them would pull it for him. He resembled Harpo Marx at times, you know, the scene where Harpo has shoplifted a market and stuffed all the smoked hams under an oversized coat. He looked like that. . . . What's your beef with me Bo Shmo, what if I write circuses? No one says a novel has to be one thing. It can be anything it wants to be, a vaudeville show, the six o'clock news, the mumblings of wild men saddled by demons.[10]

A more informed and sympathetic approach was taken by Richard Gilman. Following Frantz Fanon's assertion that a colonial oppressor is powerless to judge the mode and substance of a rebellious "native art," Gilman declared a temporary moratorium of commentary on contemporary Afro-American writing. Writing in his *New Republic* column: "I am saying that I don't know what truth for black people is, that I don't wish any longer to presume to know, that I am willing to stand back and listen, *without comment*, to these new and self-justifying voices."[11]

Black writers and critics engage themselves in very different considerations. A spirited discussion of the "black aesthetic" has begun, and studies to develop a basic critical methodology appropriate to Afro-American writing are under way. As Addison Gayle writes, "unique art derived from unique cultural experiences mandates unique critical tools for evaluation." Two recent volumes of essays edited by Gayle, *The Black Aesthetic* and *Black Expression*, testify to efforts to create these tools.[12] Gayle has examined the roles assigned to black characters in American fiction, as well as the human and political functions of black character types.[13] His study of the Afro-American novel, *The Way of the New World*, though a distinctly uneven work, does succeed in establishing a rudimentary theory in literary history and criticism.[14] Carolyn F. Gerald examines the deep structure of image and myth—the learned association of black with evil, for example—and traces social biases masked in aesthetic theories.[15] Ishmael Reed and Larry Neal propose folk bases for evaluating black writing as replacements for culture-coded "white" genres like the novel.[16]

During the several generations since Ellison and Baldwin, a sizeable group, including Imamu Baraka (LeRoi Jones), Henry Dumas, William Melvin Kelley, Ishmael Reed, John A. Williams, Cecil Brown, Al Young, George Cain, Ernest Gaines, Toni Morrison, and Alice Walker, has created the most vital and socially engaged fiction of our time. It is a distortion to lump their purposes together, but it is fair to say that, whatever their stated politics, they work with a new and quietly subversive intent; that is, *in their art*, they desire nothing less than to alter literary history; to express new forms, myths, histories for Afro-American experience; and finally to bring alternative modes of perception and valuation to the dominant Western humanistic tradition.

Among these writers there are clear common interests, implicit or explicit, as to the sorts of things black fiction should do. Most generally it should: (1) grow from an historical awareness of *black* experience before and after being kidnapped to the New World and (2) absorb and extend *black* forms and languages, past and present. African culture was mainly oral, and enforced illiteracy in America restricted simple writing skills. Thus literary arts to this day retain strong oral and rhetorical influences, especially in their folk aspects: spirituals and blues music, "toasts" and "dozens" and street raps, animal fables and folk tales, the black sermon and the slave narrative. In addition, black fiction should: (3) address itself, more directly than in the past, to *black* readers and their common interests and (4) minister to the psychic and political needs of Afro-Americans, be a literature with the expressly moral function of making black lives better. A militant reading, like Gayle's, would insist on a literature that "is a corrective— a means of helping black people out of the polluted mainstream of Americanism."[17] And it should perform all these tasks as an art form and not simple propaganda.

Most widespread, in theory and practice, is the belief that the Afro-American writer has an obligation to recreate his own American racial history. The bitter controversy following William Styron's *The Confessions of Nat Turner* was a flash point, illuminating the fact that many black intellectuals do not share a mainstream white reading of history and certainly not the heavily existential version issuing in Styron's work. The Marxist historian Herbert Aptheker prefaces his study of slave insurrections very aptly: "History's potency is mighty. The oppressed need it for identity and inspiration; oppressors for justification, rationalization and legitimacy."[18] This applies especially to history as it is dramatized in the history-binding structures of fiction, as the attacks on Styron demonstrate.

Basing his novel on the life of Nat Turner, leader of the most successful and bloodiest American slave uprising, Styron permitted himself the traditional right of the novelist to adapt materials to his own ends. Mainly, he imagined a pattern of motivation for Nat Turner, attributing his plotting to repressed homosexuality and religious fanaticism. His murderous insurrection is finally depicted as insane and anarchistic, however tight the bonds of slavery were. Black objections were numerous, focusing on the literary uses of history and the impact of Styron's vision of history during a racially troubled time. What sorts of attitudes and beliefs does Styron engender in shaping this putative black hero as a weak, aberrant, helplessly frustrated worshipper of white womanhood?

A year after *Nat Turner: Ten Black Writers Respond* appeared, the arguments continued.[19] Styron took a symposium on "The Uses of History in Fiction" as an opportunity for still another self-defense. Appearing with Ralph Ellison, Robert Penn Warren, and C. Vann Woodward, Styron stressed the novelist's license, "the free use and bold use of the liberating imagination which, dispensing with useless fact, will clear the cobwebs away and show how it really was." He began by invoking the judgments of Marxist Georg Lukács—surely *he* spins even yet in his grave—and fell back quickly on the primacy of the artist's freedom: "Facts *per se* are preposterous. They are like the fuzz that collects in the top of dirty closets. They don't really mean anything." Ralph Ellison took quick exception: "They *mean* something. That's why you're in trouble," and offered an excellent parallel example:

> If I were to write a fiction based upon a great hero, a military man whose name is Robert E. Lee, I'd damn well be very careful about what I fed my reader, in order for him to recreate in his imagination and through his sense of history what that gentleman was. Because Lee is no longer simply a historical figure. He is a figure who lives within us. He is a figure which shapes ideals of conduct and of forbearance and of skill, military and so on. This is *inside*, and not something that writers can merely be arbitrary about. The freedom of the fiction writer, the novelist, is one of the great freedoms possible for the individual to exercise. But it is not absolute. Thus, one, without hedging his bets, has to be aware that he does operate within a dense area of prior assumptions.[20]

Simultaneous with assaults on fictions like Styron's, on the deep structures, myths, images, characters, and psychologies that reinforce white stereotypes of black existence, Afro-American writers have begun the complementary affirmative process of creating new black visions of their pasts and futures. This is a battle for minds, evident immediately in the popularity of life stories and biographies—works by and about Malcolm X, Eldridge Cleaver, Gabriel Prosser, Sojourner Truth, W. E. B. DuBois, Richard Wright, George Jackson. The sensational impact of Alex Haley's *Roots* is obvious, but less apparent has been the wave of interest that ran through other ethnic subgroups in the United States. "What goes around comes around," an old blues riff tells us, and in this sense, much of the rekindling of interest by ethnic subgroups in the grain of their unique experiences derives from Haley's book and the subsequent television mini-series.[21] The pressure is seen in the special attention paid to repositories of a black heritage for children: children's novels by Carolyn Rodgers,[22] Julius

Lester's collections of slave narratives,[23] Toni Cade Bambara's *Tales and Stories for Black Folks*.[24]

Specific uses of history by the most talented younger Afro-Americans engaged in fiction have been equally diverse. Ishmael Reed's taste has been for satire and fantasy, for exotic strains of writing that take us away for a time but return us to this world slightly altered, with fresher eyes, ears, and minds. Reed's main interest is in language and literary structures as they control and dominate us, as he suggests in an introduction to his collection of Third World writing, *19 Necromancers From Now*:

> Sometimes I feel that the condition of the Afro-American writer in this country is so strange that one has to go to the supernatural for an analogy. Manipulation of the word has always been related in the mind to the manipulation of nature. One utters a few words and stones roll aside, the dead are raised and the river beds emptied of their content.
>
> The Afro-American artist is similar to the Necromancer (a word whose etymology is revealing in itself!). He is a conjuror who works Juju upon his oppressors; a witch doctor who frees his fellow victims from the psychic attack launched by demons of the outer and inner world.[25]

His recent work, *Mumbo Jumbo*, is a fantastic mythic history, pieced together for us by the metaphysical detective Papa La Bas, of the unfinished race between black and white Americans. Reed's recreation sees the origin of racial differences in crazy-quilt patterns of historical and cultural opposition between the early Eastern gods Osiris (black) and Aton (white).

Working stubbornly against the tide of black separatist thought in the late 1960s and early 1970s, Reed has arrived at a unique and valuable vision of multicultural America. *Shrovetide in Old New Orleans* defines his sense of America as a "cultural gumbo" and New Orleans voodoo as the perfect metaphor for multiculture. "Voodoo comes out of the fact that all these different tribes and cultures were brought from Africa to Haiti. All of their mythologies, knowledges and herbal medicines, their folklores jelled. It's an amalgamation like this country."[26]

Reed's work as writer, editor, and publisher has become extraordinarily important since his move to Berkeley, California, in 1967. His writing has always absorbed many other literary forms and traditions, and it now assimilates other nonwhite cultures: Asian-American, Chicano, Native American, even Eskimo. He has also sought to give his vision concrete form beyond his own writing. His journals *Yardbird* and *Y'Bird* have consistently introduced and retrieved Third World writers and artists, as have the publishing ventures of Reed, Cannon and Johnson, Inc. An active speaker and advocate for little magazines and grass-roots publishing, Reed's message has been consistent, defined well in *Shrovetide*, where he writes, "Anyone who tries to keep his cultural experience to himself is like a miser, moribund in a rooming house, uneaten beef stew lying on a table, and lonely except for the monotonous tick tock of a drugstore clock—all that gold stashed in the closet doing no one any good."[27]

William Melvin Kelley is a living example of the change in black consciousness. Educated at Fieldston School and Harvard, where he studied with Archibald MacLeish and John Hawkes, Kelley wrote in 1963: "The Negro was so completely cut loose from Africa that next to nothing is left. . . . American culture is the only culture he knows."[28] In a preface to *Dancers on the Shore*, he described himself as "an American writer who happens to have brown skin" and dismissed extraliterary approaches to his writing: "At this time, let me say for the record that I am not a socialist or a politician or a spokesman. Such people try to give answers. A writer, I think, should ask questions."[29] But by 1967, his attitude had undergone a remarkable development, and behind *Dem* and *Dunfords Travels Everywheres*, is the sense that a viable Pan-African culture flourishes in the New World. In the summer of 1967, Kelley left the United States to live in Paris, where he might be more in touch with African blacks and Third World peoples. Before leaving, Kelley described himself "formerly, as one of the most integrated people that the society has produced. And because I was one of the most integrated, I was one of the most messed up mentally, one of the most brainwashed." Further, he redefined his sense of the

93

importance of African culture to black Americans and stressed the need for new forms appropriate to their experience:

> Our literary tradition is essentially the African literary tradition, which is not written tradition. It is basically oral and I think black writers must begin to think in some of those terms, to use the fantastic oral language that has developed.
>
> If I find fault with the older black writers, with the exception of Richard Wright, it is that they have been working too much in the Western literary tradition and not enough in the African tradition. This is one of the things I want to do. I don't want to do anything in the psychological tradition. I think that the mythic and supernatural is much more the way we think. . . . To carry the weight of our ideas the novel has got to be changed. We are trying to tap some new things in a form which is not our form. So we must introduce some changes in the form.[30]

With *Dem* (1967), Kelley realizes at least part of his hopes and bids an incisive, satiric farewell to white America. But *Dunfords Travels Everywheres* (1970), his most ambitious work, takes him deepest into black mythic history by means of compressed folk forms. He describes the book as an experiment in language as sound, "a Joycean kind of prose . . . based on spoken language rather than written language."[31] It closes with a dialogue from the black unconscious: "'Mr Chigger, you vblunder, beeboy. You got aLearn whow you talkng n when tsay whit, man. What, man? No, man. Soaree! Yes sayd dIt t'me too thlow. Oilready I vbegin tshift mVoyace. But you llbob bub aGain. We cdntlet aHabbub dfifd on Fur ever, only fo waTerm aTime tpickcip dSpyrate by pinchng dSkein. In Side, out! Good-bye, man: Good-buy, man. Go odd-buy Man. Go Wood, buy Man. Gold buy Man. MAN! BE!-GOLD! BE!'"[32] His interest in black mythic history has been evident since *A Different Drummer* (1962), in which he projects a black exodus from several Southern states, working from black myths and folktales as his major sources: the black Jesus and the liberating African slave invested with superhuman powers. In *Dunfords*, he adapts slave-ship materials for his uses. Kelley recently described his fictions as "one big book" and promised a more explicitly historical dimension: "I'm trying to create a picture, to create or re-create a new picture of the experience of black people in the United States. Basically, in the last ten years, I've been dealing with the present—with the 1950's and 60's, my own lifetime. As I go on, I'm going to begin to move back in time. I'd like to write a novel about a slave on the plantation of the first President of the United States. I think I'll do that next time out."[33]

John A. Williams's recent fiction is of a very different order.[34] His second novel, *Night Song* (1961), is a powerful fictional rendering of the life and world of the jazz musician-folk hero Charlie "Bird" Parker. *The Man Who Cried I Am* (1967) is his most distinguished work, where Richard Wright is seen in the character Harry Ames; in the interplay between Max Reddick and Ames, "The King Alfred Plan" is discovered piecemeal, a chilling and convincing plan for mass black arrest and interment in "relocation centers." In *Captain Blackman*, Williams offers a remembered history of the black American soldier, mainly in the hallucinations and flashes streaming through Blackman's mind as he lies wounded in Viet Nam. Williams strongly senses that any black future must issue in an awareness of the Afro-American past, and his most dominant theme is the need for blacks to learn and remember, juxtaposed against the compulsion of whites to obliterate the past and seek escape. This is seen clearly in a rather staged scene between Captain Abraham Blackman and his white, career-Army adversary Ishmael Whittman: "'You're afraid of the past, Ish. You drop it in a hole and cover it over, like it was a stone, but it's a seed, sprouting a jungle.'"[35]

In this chapter I pay detailed attention to the prose works of Ernest J. Gaines, to his increasing use of black history and the forms that best sustain his vision.[36] The movement from his first work, *Catherine Carmier* (1964), to his most recent, *In My Father's House* (1978), is a movement from history rendered as a kind of bondage, an existential nightmare of dead ends from which a solitary black man finds no escape, toward history sensed as a natural cycle, wheeling slowly through the rebirth of a people and their inevitable liberation. As this vision takes shape, its modes of expression change. Gaines moves away from a personal version of the "white" existential novel and adapts folk forms like the sermon, slave narrative, and folktale, re-making the long fiction form to his unique ends. In so doing, he is an

95

instructive example of a novelist who reimagines a collective Afro-American past and culture that Richard Wright brought into being forty years earlier. They are politically and temperamentally very different, Wright and Gaines, but each in his own manner foresees an indigenous black American literature, a true proletarian art creating a human past from which a future grows naturally. Particularly, Gaines realizes *in his fiction*, what remained prescriptive for Wright, the strength of his own literary heritage:

> Negro folklore contains, in a measure that puts to shame more deliberate forms of expression, the collective sense of the Negroes' life in America. Let those who shy at the nationalist implications of Negro life look at this body of folklore, living and powerful, which rose out of a unified sense of a common life and a common fate. Here are those vital beginnings of that recognition of value in life as it is lived that marks the emergence of a new culture in the shell of the old. And at the moment that starts, at the moment a people begin to realize a meaning in their suffering, the civilization which engenders that suffering is doomed. Negro folklore remains the Negro writer's most powerful weapon, a weapon which he must sharpen for the hard battles looming ahead, battles which will test a people's faith in themselves.[37]

Ernest J. Gaines was born in 1933 during the heart of the depression, in Oscar, Louisiana, and worked his early years in the rural plantation fields that later wind through his fiction. He knew early the bittersweet life of the southern black family and community—broken and reset, pained and healing—and recalls himself working at age nine as a field hand chopping in hardscrabble for fifty cents a day. Like Jimmy Aaron in *The Autobiography of Miss Jane Pittman,* he came to his calling young, because Gaines was one of the few on the old place who had the gift of language. His halting words kept his people in tenuous contact with themselves and a larger world, and they kept him busy, interpreting official notices, writing letters, reading the Bible aloud, or dramatizing newspaper accounts of brighter lives, black and white, that brought hope: Jackie Robinson, Joe Louis, FDR, Huey Long. More important, he learned their stories firsthand, especially from the old people who came to his Aunt Augustine's home, an invaluable education of the heart that he carries with him and in his writing to this day. His fiction lives in the daily sorrow songs and gut-bucket blues of poor southern black folks, speaks of those hot doldrums, weary and long as the delta is flat, and the saving bursts of darkness that pull a life lovingly and violently together and apart. Raised by his remarkable aunt, for example, he recalls her being crippled from birth: "She crawled on the floor, as a seven or eight-month-old would crawl. She washed our clothes, cooked our food, kept our lives together. After her nap, she'd go outside to work her garden. She was the bravest, most courageous person I've ever known." One of the many black aunts in his work, her presence has been remembered well, particularly in his finest novel, in which she serves as "the moral basis for Miss Jane."[38]

When Gaines was fifteen, his family traced the path of many post-war southern blacks, chasing the dreams and jobs held out by a booming northern industrial economy. They drove north and west, to his stepfather's merchant marine position in Vallejo, California, settling there in 1948. Unlike Richard Wright, who also left his child-hood in the Deep South, he has never lost a sense of *place* in his work; all five of his published books, written over a period of fifteen years, are rooted in a richly imagined version of his native Pointe Coupee Parish and environs. Indeed, like many Americans, he has created a homeland by leaving it; in the thirty years since he left Louisiana, his sense of place and heritage has grown stronger each time he returns from a Mardi Gras visit "back home."

As a rough-hewn, bookish adolescent in California, he once again sensed the work before him. "When I came to Vallejo," he recalls, "I was reading books, *any* books that dealt with farm people, people who worked the earth—Steinbeck, Willa Cather, the Russians. But I didn't find *my* people in them, so I tried to write it. . . . When I first started writing in the summer of '49 or '50, I'd write for ten or twelve hours a day, but it wasn't until I left the Army and went to San Francisco State that I was really able to start."[39] Gaines graduated from San Francisco State University (then San Francisco State College) in 1957 and spent several years in Wallace Stegner's writing seminars at Stanford University. An adopted Son of the Golden West, he continues to live quietly in the Bay Area. While he has lived most of his life in California, the time spent there has not been worked easily into his fiction. "I've written four books out of my experience in California," he wryly admits. "But they're all dreadful." A sheepish smile crosses his face. "They're all stacked up in a foot locker at State, hidden where they belong. Maybe something'll be done with them after I'm dead. I doubt before."[40]

Gaines is a firmly rooted man, an uncommon meld of genuine humility and a fierce but quiet pride. He has eschewed political battles over the last decade, not because he lacks strong opinions or fears uttering them in difficult times but because he is convinced that the human story held in the craft of fiction is the writer's most eloquent voice. He refuses to be merchandized, makes few tours or national appearances (in contrast to some more recent and less talented black artists like Alex Haley and Toni Morrison, who are wed forever in the mind of television), and is an undistinguished performer; yet his work grows and draws attention because of its merits. His fiction has been praised by critics of diverse tastes—Addison Gayle, Jr., Jerry Bryant, Sherley Anne Williams, Hoyt Fuller—and his reputation has grown sufficiently outside the United States for Michel Fabre, the Richard Wright biographer and French critic of African and Afro-American literature, to speak of him as one of the three or four most significant novelists since Baldwin's generation.[41]

"Barren Summer," an unpublished novel, was completed in 1963, but Gaines's first published works were later collected in *Bloodline*—"Just Like a Tree" from *Sewanee Review* and "The Sky is Gray" from *Negro Digest*, both out also in 1963. *Catherine Carmier*, begun as a youth in Vallejo and completed as his first novel, came out in the following year and vanished quickly, but not before it attracted the attention and praise of Hoyt Fuller, then an editor at *Negro Digest*. In 1967 *Of Love and Dust*, a more substantial novel, followed. With *Bloodline* (1968), a thematically linked collection of five stories, Gaines attracted good reviews and hard-earned national praise, but only with *The Autobiography of Miss Jane Pittman* (1971) did he achieve the sales and serious critical attention that a fine writer seeks and deserves. The ensuing television film, adapted by Tracy Keenan Wynn, not only brought his fiction to a wider popular audience but also served as an example that prompted the adoption of Alex Haley's *Roots* for the national and international markets.

Gaines has held a Wallace Stegner Fellowship (1958), the Joseph Henry Jackson Award (1959), and a Guggenheim Award (1973–74); from these awards and modest royalties, he has been able to give his writing full-time attention. Throughout his career he has worked methodically and with a maddening patience; he is undaunted by the unpublished California books or by another unfinished work, "The House and the Field" (the first chapter appearing in the *Iowa Review* in 1972), a novel set aside to take up his most recent work, *In My Father's House* (1978).⁴² I sense a profound debt of gratitude and obligation behind his writing. The dialogue of his stronger characters, for example, is dotted with "must" constructions—a compulsion to honor the memories and people of his own black past. Such patience and desire are tested with each work. Early into *In My Father's House*, during a particularly bad stumbling block, he could write, "It's giving me a lot of hell, and it will take all of my strength and concentration to write it. I've tried to write this book several times before and failed each time. Maybe I will fail again, but I must give it my best."⁴³

Throughout the period 1963 to 1978, Gaines has allied himself with no coterie and has been promoted by no critical sponsor. He has maintained this aloofness in a time of heated debate about the role of black art and the proper stance of the black artist, a grueling and protracted argument around the "black aesthetic" during which the loudest voices and readiest formulas often seized attention. His work has rarely been inflammatory, did not urge the "killing of whitey" when it was a fashionable posture, and has seldom warned of the coming of a black apocalypse. Although he has refused to create black straw men and women as a response to white artistic and critical stereotyping, his heroines and heroes are most certainly alive; walking slowly and often painfully, they move nonetheless off the floor and step by step through an imagined South that was, until quite recently, everybody's national whipping boy.

Indeed, although Gaines would be slow to say it—he is a cautious and unrhetorical man—his interest in place and character and enduring human values suggests that he is a writer of "the old ways." Unlike many of his postmodern contemporaries, he delights in stories (often reinforced by plot) and in compelling characters. Some are noble, like Miss Jane and Aunt Fe and Joe Pittman; others, like Munford Bazille, Copper Laurent, the Cajun assassin Albert Cluveau, are tragic damaged cases. Many more are like Reverend Phillip Martin and his running buddy Chippo, neither gods nor devils, merely people trying to walk their time a little more upright. Gaines's skill and technique do not shout at you. His craft is more muted and does not seize the eye or draw attention to itself as often occurs in the work of his best Afro-American contemporaries: Ishmael Reed, Alice Walker, Toni Morrison, James Alan McPherson. It becomes apparent in consideration, emerges in retrospect, and consequently endures in effectiveness.

Like his grandest dame, the 110-year-old Miss Jane Pittman, he disavows "re-trick" (rhetoric) in his fiction, and his soaring moments of prophetic language are underscored by a balancing habit of understatement. Although Gaines regards the drift toward the cerebral or analytic as a taint in his work, he shows a painstaking concern for form and structure from *Catherine Carmier* through *In My Father's House*. "The artist must be like the heart surgeon," he suggests, "He must approach something with sympathy, but with a sort of coldness, and work and work until he finds some kind of perfection in his work. You can't have blood splashing all over the place."[44]

Above all, he senses his duty to speak of the modest and enduring lives of southern black folks, the true American peasantry. They are his bloodlines and nourish his work; in his best writing, as in *The Autobiography of Miss Jane Pittman*, their suffering and power are condensed into characters like Miss Jane, his narrator, who nears the end of a remarkable life. Composite lives become metaphors for great stretches of the pained ironic history of black and white together. History is not, in Gaines's work, the length of several long shadows; thus his central characters are not Nat Turner or Sojourner Truth or Martin Luther King but Jim Kelly, Jane Pittman, or Phillip Martin, the unsung folks always present in the buried life of a people. For all his interest in the past and the force of history, in the Louisiana breakdowns of races, classes, eras, and generations, he insists that "black writers must write about *people*." Lest we miss his emphasis, he continues: "*People. People. People.* And not just about problems."[45]

Although Gaines has cited Faulkner and Hemingway as formative influences, it is again a sense of the *folk*—timeless, at once ancient and modern—and the written sources giving it voice that inform his fiction. Most basically, his vision derives from the Bible, and a rich biblical stream of man's tragic and sustaining fate plays through his work. *In My Father's House* is a secular meditation on Christ's Passover words to his flock, passed down in the Book of John, a message of fathers and sons: "In my father's house there are many mansions. I am indeed going to prepare a place for you. I will not leave you orphaned. I will come back for you." Phillip Martin is a minister, and his painful confessions and discoveries enact an empty house and fatherhood, both of which must be renewed in suffering and death.

There is a literary debt, as well, to near and distant influences. Gaines admires the nineteenth-century Russians, particularly Tolstoy, and says of that connection, which spans more than a hundred years and twelve thousand miles, "The greatest writers of every country have dealt with their peasantry, and Tolstoy helped me see that the Southern black man and woman have been the deepest current of this country, the life, the peasant."[46] He mentions Turgenev's *Fathers and Sons* as an early model for his own first novel, *Catherine Carmier*, and its influence continues through his latest work. *In My Father's House* speaks again of the debts and treasures that are paid or passed on from father to son and son to father, black and white alike. But Gaines's peasants are far less romanticized than those of Faulkner, Tolstoy, or Turgenev, and he writes with a powerful sense of the Afro-American literary line that runs back from his work, beyond Wright, Baldwin, and Ellison, through Toomer's *Cane* and DuBois's *The Souls of Black Folk*, to the first black American tales found in the accounts of fugitive ex-slaves.

Ernest Gaines, Alice Walker, William Melvin Kelley, Ishmael Reed: they represent a rich new generation of Afro-American fiction writers. Although each claims a unique terrain, Kelley's assertion that "I'm really writing one big book" is apt for all.[47] Gaines's work, for example, is seeded in his native Pointe Coupee Parish, downriver along the Mississippi and the smaller Charles. The world composed in *Catherine Carmier, Of Love and Dust, Bloodline, The Autobiography of Miss Jane Pittman* and *In My Father's House* extends chronologically from 1865 to the late 1960s; geographically, Gaines's personal and fictional homelands—northwest of Baton Rouge on steamy bayous, tablelands, and marshy bottoms—are reconceived first as slave quarters and plantations, then as a series of crumbling buildings and backhouses, and finally as the modestly successful home of Reverend Phillip Martin. Upriver from Martin's Baton Rouge, beyond the corn and cotton and cane fields, lies the small town Gaines calls Bayonne, his main fictional stage. His characters are ordinary people, black, white, and "in-between." This latter group of mixed races and cultures is important, for his special interest is those who are caught in the middle: races or ethnic groups (poor blacks, Cajuns, Creoles, "'Mericans," Indians); traditions and institutions (slavery, religion, hoodoo, sharecropping, the web of folkways and unwritten laws that bind and separate all Southerners).

History Is a Wall: *Catherine Carmier*

So the struggle went on. The little incidents, the little indirect incidents, like slivers from a stick. But they continued to mount until they had formed a wall. Not a wall of slivers that could be blown down with the least wind. But a wall of bricks, of stones. A wall that had gotten so high by now that he had to stand on tiptoe to look over it.—*Catherine Carmier*

Jackson Bradley's plight in *Catherine Carmier* is familiar to readers of Afro-American fiction and is reminiscent of that of John in W. E. B. DuBois's story "The Coming of John" in *The Souls of Black Folk*.[48] At age twenty-two, gone ten years and recently finished college, Jackson returns to the Grover plantation and his Aunt Charlotte. He is not quite the impressionable Arkady of Turgenev's influential *Fathers and Sons*, nor is he as direly nihilistic as the foil Bazarov, but like them he is rootless and disillusioned. He can find no place in this old world and returns to say final goodbyes. For his Aunt Charlotte and the few blacks who remain, he is a last desperate hope, a way of reviving the dead era they sense being played out in themselves. The blacks are mostly old people, "enduring" like Faulkner's Dilsey, and though they sense their own demise, they resist it stubbornly, existing "like trees, like rocks, like the ocean" (171). Aunt Charlotte, the first in a gallery of old aunts peopling Gaines's fictions, implores Jackson to stay on: "You all us can count on. If you fail, that's all for us" (98).

The world of Grover is a southern wasteland: the plantation lacks even the full status of sharecropped land because many of the remaining older folks live in the "quarters," paying a token rental for the land. The bulk of the land has fallen from white to black to Cajun hands, and this latter group swarms like locusts in the novel, preying on the land and farming it mechanically and voraciously. Man does not live in organic relationship to his soil in *Catherine Carmier*; indeed, the only black to till the soil, Raoul Carmier, is an unhealthy influence, an anachronism. A light-skinned mulatto, Raoul is unable to work with whites and unwilling to live in a black world. He is landlocked, a blind end, and the backlands and bottoms to which he returns are more a tomb than a womb for him, a source to which he cannot return. Raoul is driven, "a magnet seems to be drawing him" (221), and he lives in recurrent references to mechanical devils. Although Jackson is unable to enter any future, Raoul cannot escape the past. There is no harmony and no order in his world, and the past is a recurring evil dream from which there is no awakening. This can be seen in his family. His wife Della is also a mulatto, taken as an early convenience and now scorned. She is less able to shut out the world and bears an illegitimate son by a black lover. Carmier fathers two daughters, Catherine and Lillian, the youngest taken away early to be raised by his relatives in New Orleans. Lillian and Jackson arrive separately on the same bus at the novel's opening, each returning to a ruined land. But it is her older sister, Catherine, jealously protected by Raoul, who is sought by Jackson.

Like many young southern blacks in the 1930s and 1940s, Jackson Bradley goes north for a better life. He finds no home there, only a series of smaller, more subtle dead ends, and manages only to kill off any viable past for himself: "The faults there did not strike you as directly and as quickly, so by the time you discovered them, you were so much against the other place that it was impossible even to return to it" (91). He does return to Grover but only to make a clean break of it. His rejection is protracted, complicated by his love for Aunt Charlotte, for whom he remains a twelve-year-old black boy. Severing his past has serious *human* consequences, but only in a series of conversations with his former teacher Madame Bayonne does he realize that there is no easy way out. Madame Bayonne is one of Gaines's "wise aunts"; she "knows people" and, though rumored to be a witch, she is simply and profoundly wise. Aware of Jackson's need to leave this past, she advises him of the human consequences, of the effect on his aunt: "It will be the worst moment of her life" (71).

Compelled by the words of one old woman to say words that will cause another to collapse, Jackson is damned by a third:

> A little old woman—somewhere between eighty and ninety— in a long gingham dress, carrying a walking cane, and smoking a corncob pipe that was so old it had nearly become the same color she was, changed his attitude completely. After threatening to beat Selina with her walking cane when Selina told her she could not see Charlotte because Charlotte was asleep, the old woman tore into the bedroom and remained beside the bed almost two hours. When she got ready to leave, she walked up to Jackson in the swing and told him if anything happened to Charlotte he would have no one but himself to blame. He tried to ignore the old woman just as he had the others, but she stood before him (she was so close that he could almost feel the pipe in his face) until he raised his head.
>
> "Yes," she said, "you. Yes, you." [171]

Liberation, then, is to cast this past aside, to be freed of the world laid out for him by his many "aunts" and "uncles." The prime difficulty for Jackson is that it is already dead for him, sterile. In the land he sees a projection of himself. Like the soil that drifts across his sight, he is desiccated, a mote of dust. He sees himself in images or organic sterility, confessing to Madame Bayonne, "I'm like a leaf that's broken away from the tree. Drifting" (79). Unable to join his aunt in the prayer she pleads for, unable to locate emotions to which he can respond, he sees himself in her garden, "half-green, half-yellow . . . dry, dead" (102). Even his childhood memories, idyllic and romanticized distortions of the past, hold little power for him.

After he systematically cuts old roots—family obligation, community ties, religion, past friendships—Bradley finds himself alone, purely alone, and it remains for him to find some means of existence, some way of breathing life back into himself. He attempts to move from sterility toward life, from the dying remnants of a community shaped by slavery toward a freer, more solitary, more existential present. Jackson's relationship with Catherine Carmier is the apparent means of achieving this ideal.

Catherine has been watched over by Raoul just as Jackson has been watched over by Charlotte. She is the only creature for whom Raoul shows love; she serves as an emotional mother-wife to him, and he shelters her jealously. The dark-skinned Jackson has been taught by all to stay away from the Carmier house, but he courts her resolutely. In their loving, he is again forced to face his past, to respond to it emotionally. Although he fears being "walled-in by fate" (126), Catherine feels obligated to Raoul, who has nothing else. As he tells her, "You're light. You're life," but a relationship with her does not guarantee a free and meaningful life (149). Through her, he hopes to rescue them both from their pasts and make for them a livable present.

Jackson's struggle to jettison the past is most apparent in structural terms, in recurrent scenes near the end of each of the novel's three parts. Each part closes with an image of Jackson in some relation to the church. At the close of chapter 22, he rejects his aunt's Christianity as a "bourgeois farce" (100) and refuses to pray with her, seeing in the dried-up world outside the window a projection of his own spiritual deadness. At the end of part 2, he returns to his former church-school building, rummaging memory for some living presence. He is momentarily poised between two modes of being, fruitful past and barren present: "How small was the yard. . . . What had happened? Had he grown so big or had the place actually shrunk in those ten years?" (192). But this scene also dies, surrenders its life, as he dwells on the barrenness of the old elms and pecans surrounding the yard. Near the end of *Catherine Carmier*, Jackson and Catherine attend a dance in a church near Bayonne. They make love in the churchyard, briefly revivifying the institution in a more personal, secular form. But the cycles of their experience are dominated by her sense of obligation to Raoul. Even after Jackson and Raoul fight, in a ritual scene of bloodletting, their relationship is ambiguous. Della advises that Raoul's beating will free them all, but the novel closes cryptically, with an image of Jackson isolated and behind more walls, as Catherine takes her father inside: "He watched her go into the house. He stood there, hoping that Catherine would come back outside. But she never did" (248).

Catherine Carmier is informed by a view of history as a prison, a tomb from which Jackson Bradley can never quite escape. There is little possibility anywhere in his world: South and North are equally unacceptable, and he is thrown back on his own scant devices, faced with the need to make a livable existential present from his isolation. But the single factor making this possible, at least for Jackson Bradley, is a bloodline, some possibility of human love or even human contact, and this is elusive. His inability to connect is partly a function of his own historical past. Bradley would be free, but finds himself a "freedman," a term taken idealistically in early Reconstruction but now galled with a bitter, ironic overtone. By design or not, Gaines suggests that his hero's need to vaunt the wall of his past is a form of racial self-loathing. His black past is a wall, shutting off the light, as it does in San Francisco when subtle racial slights "began to mount into something big, something black, something awful" (93). Catherine is "light and life" to him, depicted often at the window of the Carmier house in sunlight, able to see out. She is his bloodline, but they can live together only when each of them has made a separate peace with the past and their special obligations to it. In the world of the novel, they never do.

History Is My Face: *Of Love and Dust*

"No, it wasn't The Old Man. I had put my own self in this predicament. I had come to this plantation myself, when my woman left me for another man in New Orleans and when I was too shame-face to go back home. I had heard that Hebert needed a man who could handle tractors and I had come here for the job. . . . No, it wasn't The Old Man. The Old Man didn't have a thing in this world to do with it. It was me—it was my face."—*Of Love and Dust*

The sense of sparseness characterizing *Catherine Carmier* may well be a function of the vision informing the novel: that is, the emphasis on structural parallels and motifs might be seen as a literary means of miming the bleak helplessness pervading the lives of Gaines's characters. In my opinion, they rarely come to life and seem destined to scribe patterns, painfully and mechanically. The folk richness of later works—the play of black dialects and idioms, the vignettes and tales passed from memory to voice, the texture of manners and ways of postplantation life—are lacking. Gaines's stress on creating vibrant characters and his suspicion of "analytical" writing are recognitions of his own strongest suits, but not until *Of Love and Dust* are these skills realized.

Hoyt Fuller is very much correct in noting that Gaines's recurring themes "revolve around the conflict of eras. The new world of mobility and expanded possibilities impinges on the old world of land-love and solid, accepted social stratification. The old realities of the plantation culture gradually surrender to the demands of industrial pace and technology. The once-rigid poles which separated whites from cajun, and cajun from mulatto, and mulatto from black, have been bent out of shape."[49] But the collisions between races and eras are far off in the distances of *Catherine Carmier*. Jackson Bradley's dilemmas are more summarized than concretely rendered; they are most often recollected, handed indirectly to the reader by an omniscient third person narrator. Gaines admits to considerable difficulty in working with such a godlike role in the novel. In *Of Love and Dust*, he shifts to the first-person narrator-participant used in all his writing until *In My Father's House*. Jim Kelly's narration, particularly as he paraphrases what others about him have seen and told, allows Gaines to work more deeply in the grain of black oral narration, to flavor events with a natural richness of observation and response that is lacking in the first novel.

Although most of Jackson Bradley's trials are conducted offstage, the social disintegrations one can read in his state are also far too dim and sketchy to engage us. In *Of Love and Dust*, the locale and time are almost the same, but the conflicts and disorders are dramatized, and rendered as functions of the lives of fully developed characters. The world of Hebert plantation bears an air of active spirits, a world slowly eaten up by sharecropping Cajuns, with an "old side" worked by blacks and overseen by Cajun Sidney Bonbon and the entirety owned by a Creole, Marshall Hebert. The ways of an Afro-American past are also more densely realized in the individual lives of poor blacks living on the plantation. Gaines's interest in humans is properly placed in *Of Love and Dust*, for in the natural play between his characters—their races, eras, generations, values—the personal and historical dimensions enliven each other. Filtered through Kelly's mind and colored by his need for his people and their diversity, the world of Hebert is less skeletal and much more compelling.

The historical vision underlying this second novel is also more developed. *Of Love and Dust* grants that the historical legacy of racism or fate or a kind of social inertia may dominate, but it offers a partial reconciliation between a black man and his historical past (so binding in *Catherine Carmier*) and his psychic need for dignity and greater freedom. Jim Kelly is trusted by black and white alike, but he reads in "crazy nigger" Marcus's carrying-on a refusal to yield, however great the price. He comes to believe that he can act on principles, with dignity, without rejecting his entire racial history.

Hebert plantation before Marcus is a cosmos in the minds of those living there, a little world propelled and ordered by its own gravities, inertias, retrogressions. The rich front lands have fallen to Cajun sharecroppers. Hated by black and white, they have only recently worked up to the land from the bayous, and they hold on tenaciously. In the minds of landholding whites, Cajuns are racially inferior, though of greater status than blacks. Here, as in *Bloodline*, represented by men like Sidney Bonbon, they have a vested psychic and financial interest in white supremacy and serve to reinforce caste and color lines. The "old ways" become doubly important in their eyes; every time a black enters the formerly "unsoiled" Hebert family library or goes in the wrong door, he threatens an entire world and existence, and must be dealt with quickly.

The world of the blacks living at Hebert is at once utterly defined and unstable. "The Old Man," "The Master," we are told repeatedly, watches from his heavens, indifferent or exhausted. Marcus's stubborn violations are threatening, cosmically unnatural to Aunt Margaret and Ca'line and Bishop, as if God (himself) were powerless, asleep, or unconcerned. Gaines's old people are more numerous here and, though they do indeed live and think in "old ways," they are treated sympathetically in Jim Kelly's account. They have learned a simple lesson from the past—that all are punished for the transgressions of a few and that submission is necessary for basic survival.

Bonded out of jail by Marshall Hebert, Marcus can accept few of the laws governing the plantation. An unwilling killer, he is expected to work for five years in a kind of indentured servitude. Beyond the sentence of forced labor, he provides something more. His "breaking" by Bonbon and Hebert signals a warning to blacks and, representing as he does an urban, more contemporary existence, his submission is a sign that the past of white supremacy is alive and dominant. Marcus is unaware of his own significance, but his first experiences bring the message home. Jim recalls Marcus's arrival:

> He got in the middle and I got in beside him. It was blazing hot there with all three of us crammed together. Bonbon went down the quarter to turn around at the railroad tracks, then he shot back up the quarter just as fast as he had come down there. I knew what to expect when he came up to his house, so I braced myself. The boy didn't know what was coming, and when Bonbon slammed on the brakes, the boy struck his forehead against the dashboard.
> "Goddamn," he said.
> "All right, Geam," Bonbon said to me. He acted like he hadn't even heard the curse words. [5]

But Marcus does not break. He is tried by machines in the corn field, and by his fellow blacks—most of whom pray for his failure—in the fields, "house fairs," and stores of the plantation. Undaunted, he is the first of Gaines's rebellious black characters to resist the past, to assert his will. He is not romanticized, and his stubborn refusal to yield is not a function of any pattern of social or political considerations. Vain and foolish, he runs on appetites and intuitions, and whether his path is crossed by black or white, man or beast, he *takes*. Marcus's sexual exploits scandalize the gallery of black folks who watch him; to their horror, his first target is Pauline Guerin, Sidney Bonbon's black mistress. Pulling corn in the fields,

> He was thinking about Pauline. That evening he fell back again and he had to drag that sack on his shoulder again, and that black stallion was only about six inches behind him. But he didn't mind at all. He was thinking about Pauline . . . about the sweet words he was going to whisper in her ear. (He had told me what a great lover he was at dinner before we went back in the field. He had told me how once he got after a woman she couldn't do a thing but fall for him.) . . . So already he was thinking about him and Pauline in bed. He had already seen those long, pretty arms around his neck, and he had already heard the deep sighs from her throat. And after it was over, he was going to lay beside her and whisper words she had never heard before. He was going to tell her things Bonbon had never thought about. How could a white man—no, not even a solid white man, but a bayou, catfish-eating Cajun—compete with him when it came down to loving. So he was glad Bonbon was there on the horse. He was glad the horse was so close he could feel his hot breath on the back of his neck. He was glad he could hear the *sagg-sagg-sagg* of the saddle every time the horse moved up. And even that hot, salty sweat running into his eyes couldn't make him hate Bonbon. [57]

Pauline rejects Marcus, and only then does he turn to Louise Bonbon, Sidney's wispy, ghostlike wife—a lifeless, pathetic figure—who has been on her gallery watching, watching since he arrived. Grown out of a mutual desire to hurt Bonbon, their affair develops quickly into a kind of love, impossible and grotesque, and the scenes depicting their rompings have a frenzied, surreal character not unlike those of Joanna Burden and Joe Christmas in Faulkner's *Light in August*. These scenes are some of Gaines's best. He has developed his characters and their world, and this alliance is as unreal and removed of this earth as that of two children in a playhouse: "'Let me kiss you,' he said. 'Oooooo, you sweet. Good Lord—Lord, have mercy. He know

you this sweet? Let me kiss this little pear here . . . now this one. Two
of the sweetest little pears I ever tasted. 'Specially this one here. . . . Go
on touch it. That's right, touch it. Won't hurt you. See? See?' " (160).

If his courting of Pauline upset the quarters, this affair with Louise
foreshadows disaster for everyone. Jim Kelly's first response is violent
and profane, but he gradually takes on the stoicism and resignation
expressed by Aunt Margaret: " 'Y'all ain't going nowhere . . . y'all
go'n die right here. 'Specially him there. . . . There ain't nothing but
death—a tree for him' " (207). Marcus and Louise conspire to escape
"to the North," taking Bonbon's daughter Tite with them. It is a grisly
satirical twist of slave narratives of escape, as Louise and Tite lamp-
black their skin, intending to travel only by night. Marcus goes to
Hebert for help, offers to kill Bonbon in return, and the owner sets
them up. The inevitable disaster occurs before they can leave the
house as Bonbon intercepts them. Gaines enriches the dimensions of
Kelly's narrative by having him paraphrase firsthand accounts of
others. Here, Sun Brown was the unwilling witness.

> The car stopped and Bonbon got out. . . . Sun could tell that
> Bonbon didn't know what was going on, either. . . . Sun could tell
> by the slow, careful, thinking way he went before the house.
> Then as he came in the small yard, Marcus threw the package to
> the side and jumped on the ground to fight him. . . . Bonbon
> moved toward the house quickly now. When he came to the end
> of the gallery, he stooped over and picked up something by the
> steps. Sun could tell it was a scythe-blade, and not a hoe or a
> shovel, by the way Bonbon swung it at Marcus. Marcus ran to the
> fence and jerked loose a picket. . . . Marcus was blocking the
> scythe-blade more than he was trying to hit with the picket. Sun
> could hear the noise that steel made against wood and that wood
> made against wood. . . . Then, for a second, everything was too
> quiet. Then he heard a scream, and he jerked his head to the left.
> He saw that Marcus had lost the picket and he saw Bonbon
> raising the blade. He had time to shut his eyes, and even though
> he couldn't see, he saw Bonbon standing there with the blade in
> his hand. Bonbon swung the blade far across the yard and went

up on the gallery to get his little girl. He sat down on the steps with the little girl in his arms. [276]

In the days following, Louise is taken to the insane asylum at Jackson, Bonbon is acquitted of murder, and Hebert orders Jim Kelly to leave the plantation, ostensibly because the "Cajuns might start some mess" (280).

But the import of the tale is the effect it has on Jim Kelly, on his development to a point where he believes once more in his ability to act and shape his own dignity and life and in the need for black people to shape their histories rather than be enslaved by them. The real reason for Kelly's leaving, as he and Hebert know, is that he knows "the truth about what had happened. He was afraid I might start blackmailing now and he would have to get somebody to kill me" (278). Kelly's danger is that he is able to comprehend the past and act upon it, to see through the imperatives of history the possibility and necessity for a black man's action.

When *Of Love and Dust* opens, it is clear that Jim Kelly is trusted by white, Cajun, and black. As Hebert's machine operator, he is a trusted employee, and as overseer Bonbon's "man," he serves as both a liaison with blacks in the quarters and occasionally as Bonbon's sole confidant. Kelly is an honest and decent man with a sense of racial and generational boundaries, trusted by Gaines's flinty "aunts" and by the younger black men and women on Hebert. But Marcus's earliest response to him is based on Kelly's role at Hebert, and he calls him "whitemouth." Thereafter the relationship between Marcus and Jim is at the heart of the novel.

Like Bishop, Aunt Margaret and Ca'line, Jim is initially put off by Marcus, fearful that his antics will trip the tenuous balance of black plantation life. Unlike Marcus, he has been dominated by his own recent past. At several points early in the novel he daydreams about women, especially a former New Orleans lover, Billie Jean. Two poignant passages stand out, and Gaines gives us a view of Jim as a man whose most passionate living moments are the two years in the past with Billie Jean. Content to ride behind Red Hannah as she traces and retraces furrows in the corn field, he walks also in more human furrows: "I went around the other side and had myself a couple of beers. You could buy soft drinks in the store or if you were a white man you could drink a beer in there, but if you were colored you had to go to the little side room—'the nigger room.' I kept telling myself, 'one of these days I'm going to stop this, I'm going to stop this; I'm a man like any other man and one of these days I'm going to stop this.' But I never did" (43).

Jim is in essential agreement with the old folks who accept and submit, who mark their fates off as determined by the will of "The Old Man." But gradually, Marcus's actions stir him up, force him back on himself. He rediscovers in his sentimentalized past a basic truth, that "man has to do it for himself now. No, he's not going to win, he can't ever win; but if he struggle hard and long enough he can ease his pains a little" (52). In response to Marcus's stubborn refusal to give in, Jim grows more self-reliant, realizing finally—as our headnote quotation expands—that "it wasn't The Old Man. . . . it was me—it was my face" (148). And although he cannot absolve Marcus of the killing that brought him to Hebert, he grows to respect him, to see in his seemingly futile affair with Louise the roots of human liberation. Shortly before Marcus's death, he admits: "I admired Marcus. I admired his great courage. And that's why I wanted to hurry up and get to the front. That's why my heart had jumped in my throat when the tractor went dead on me—I was afraid I wouldn't be able to tell him how much I admired what he was doing. I wanted to tell him how brave I thought he was. . . . And I wanted to tell Louise how I admired her bravery. I wanted to tell them that they were starting something— yes, that's what I would tell them; they were starting something that others would hear about, and understand, and would follow" (270).

Jim's movement toward an awareness of the need for a black man to chart his own way is not purely existential or individual. He does begin to recognize social realities in large terms, for instance, that "they" manipulate "the little people." And he agrees with the Bonbon that "we is nothing but little people," adding that "Marcus was just the tool. Like Hotwater was the tool—put there for Marcus to kill. Like Bonbon was the tool—put there to work Marcus. Like Pauline was a tool, like Louise was a tool" (269–70). But through Marcus, Jim Kelly sees a willingness to walk out of the furrows, glimpses a black past and the basis for a black future. Marcus was a solitary bloodline, one who sensed in every breath the course demanded by his own eulogy: "Man is here for a little while, then gone" (270).

Marcus's recent history revives Jim's own more distant past, and the past eventually reveals the possibility of individual existential choice and action. Cycles and ritual patterns are again significant in this second novel. There is a three-part structure again, and though Gaines carefully constructs the repetition of key scenes (Jim talks with his "aunts" near the opening of each part), he emphasizes character evolution. The opening scenes of parts 1, 2, and 3 depict Marcus's growing freedom (1: Marcus riding in Bonbon's car; 2: Marcus riding with Jim on Red Hannah; 3: Marcus walking willingly into the Bonbon and Hebert houses). Each part closes with Marcus involved in a fight or struggle. As part 1 closes, he is lying down unconscious, defeated in a fight, but in part 3, he is lying down, he is dead, as near victory as a black man can be in the world of Hebert. The tale runs full cycle, opening with Marcus's bonding-out for murder and closing with his own liberation in death. Marcus exists, however, to throw light on Kelly. Through Marcus he can see his own face more clearly, that of a black individual whose features have been forgotten for a time but which can be reimagined in his struggle to shape a life with human dignity.

History Is the Wind on the Water: *Bloodline*

"She's not the only one that's go'n die from this boy's work. Many mo' of 'em go'n die 'fore it's over with. The whole place—everything. A big wind rising, and when a big wind rise, the sea stirs, and the drop o' water you seeing laying on top the sea this day won't be there tomorrow. 'Cause that's what the wind do, and that's what life is. She ain't nothing but one little drop o' water laying on top the sea, and what this boy's doing is called the wind. . . . Go out and blame the wind. No, don't blame him, 'cause tomorrow, what he's doing today, somebody go'n say he ain't done a thing. 'Cause tomorrow will be his time to be turned over just like it's hers today. And after that, be somebody else time to turn over. And it keep going like that till it ain't nothing left to turn—and nobody left to turn it."—"Just Like a Tree," *Bloodline*

With *Bloodline*, Ernest Gaines sounds a very different historical emphasis. The vision of history as fate, as a cycle from which one cannot escape and during which the slayer must be slain (Marcus), is expanded. As the title *Bloodline* suggests, the book is concerned with the living and organic. Gaines writes with a vision of the natural history of a people. It is not simply a collection of stories but a gathering of linked tales in the tradition of Faulkner's *Go Down, Moses* and Richard Wright's *Uncle Tom's Children*. The dominant concern through these five stories is with natural patterns of growth and decay, the evolution from childhood to maturity to old age as seen in the lives of people, races, generations, and eras. In the shapes of these stories and in their recurrent images and metaphors, the past, present, and future are all of a piece; history is part of a natural process and humans who live within it find their lives infused with significance.

These stories focus on individual growth. Only rarely do we encounter intruders like Jackson Bradley and Marcus, men who can never really fit in Gaines's worlds. Instead, as suggested in the organic metaphors, the characters are alive and seem to evolve naturally. They go through their cycles and changes almost unconsciously, like Aunt Fe's beloved giant oaks in "Just Like a Tree." The five stories are ordered from childhood experiences to those of old age. The first, "A Long Day in November," is filtered through six-year-old Sonny's mind, as it deals with the breakup and reconcilation of his parents' marriage throughout the course of a single day. The emphasis is on the simultaneous growth of several people toward maturity and secondarily on the growth of a race toward true autonomy. Amy, the mother, leaves Eddie because he is infatuated with a new car and ignores his family for the all-night experience that his toy opens for him. Faced with her decision, Eddie begs his wife to reconsider; he is systematically stripped of respect by the females he copes with in trying to win her back—by his wife, her mother, the seer Madame

Toussaint. Scorned, shot at, Eddie agrees to burn his car, a public admission of his inadequacy. He is a portrait of inadequacy, a man who *must* grow toward some sense of pride, a fact suggested at the story's end. At the close of the day, back in their home, Amy insists that Eddie beat her. Sex roles are well-defined in this world, and to be a man is to dominate. He realizes only gradually that his wife is almost forcing him through an evolution, as she says, "I don't want you to be the laughingstock of the plantation. . . . Now they don't have nothing to laugh about" (76).

Similarly, Sonny matures in the story. He is a naive narrator, unaware of the significance of much of what he relates. As he does become more self-conscious, he grows faintly aware that he must stop wetting the bed and his pants and must stop allowing schoolmates to abuse him. By the end of his day—once more back in the womb of his bed as he was when the story opened—he has formed these "resolutions" in his mind. Ironically, Sonny challenges his father for the first time when he beats his mother: "'Leave my momma alone, you old yellow dog,' I say. 'You leave my momma alone.' I throw the pot at him but I miss him, and the pot go bouncing 'cross the floor" (74). But sex is still a mystery to him; inside his bed, he remembers that "mama say she didn't do her and Daddy thing with Mr. Freddie Jackson" (79) and drifts to sleep to the muted creakings of bed springs. A secondary emphasis is also apparent in Gaines's underscoring of the need for strong black men in this world of Bayonne. Gaines's fictive world is very much one of young men and old women; his focus on the development of proud black men who can grow and survive looms near the surface of "A Long Day in November."

This is a basic theme in the second story, "The Sky Is Gray." At age eight, James recounts the experiences of another important day. He and his mother take a bus to Bayonne, where he will be treated for an abscessed tooth. The underlying pattern of James's experience is also growth toward manhood: his father has left the family, and at age eight he is already very aware of the need in his culture for strong men "who can make it." His trip immerses him in every color of experience: pain, death, lust, racial and generational hatred—every hue of which is observed and marked off by a strong sense of ritual. James is very much aware that this painful and chilling trip is one of a continuing series of lessons. Aboard the bus he recalls his first, one of male obligation and the power of death. He remembers having to trap small birds for food, his mother ordering him to snap their necks with a fork. Bewildered then, James now realizes that this was his earliest lesson in masculine survival, obligatory personally and racially: "I know now; I know why I had to do it. . . . Suppose she had to go away? That's why I had to do it. Suppose she had to go away like Daddy had to go away? Then who was go'n look after us? They had to be somebody left to carry on" (90).

A subsidiary theme, the conflict between generations, is also developed in "The Sky Is Gray." Change may well be inevitable, but it need not be welcomed, and it is not in the dentist's office at Bayonne. James moves in a segregated world where white contempt is accepted and expected. Submission is a mode of survival here; it may be seen as the blacks discuss the whys of pain and suffering, howls of which come from the next room. "I wonder why the Lord let a child like that suffer," a woman asks rhetorically, and she is quickly offered an answer by a black preacher: "Not us to question. . . . He works in mysterious ways—wonders to perform" (94–95).

James watches a younger man enter the conversation, asserting "that's the trouble with the black people in this country today" (95). He has no faith in traditional structures of any sort. He and the preacher, representing two generations and two eras with very different notions of black conduct, lock horns:

> "Show me one reason to believe in the existence of a God," the boy says.
> "My heart tells me," the preacher says.
> "'My heart tells me,'" the boy says. "'My heart tells me.' Sure, 'My heart tells me.' And as long as you listen to what your heart tells you, you will have only what the white man gives you and nothing more. Me, I don't listen to my heart. The purpose of the heart is to pump blood throughout the body, and nothing else."
> [96]

The preacher is enraged and slaps the boy, leaving the office. But the conversation continues with the black ladies who do accept the elder's counsels of submission. The young man is a familiar face in Gaines's gallery, very like Jackson Bradley of *Catherine Carmier*:

> "Let's hope that not all your generation feel the same way you do," she says.
>
> "Think what you please, it doesn't matter," the boy says. "But it will be men who listen to their heads and not their hearts who will see that your children have a better chance than you had."
>
> "Let's hope they ain't all like you, though," the old lady says. "Done forgot the heart absolutely."
>
> "Yes ma'm, I hope they all aren't like me," the boy says. "Unfortunately, I was born too late to believe in your God. Let's hope that the ones who come after will have your faith—if not in your God, then in something else, something definitely that they can lean on. I haven't anything." [102]

We should note that both the boy and the preacher represent imbalances. Gaines undercuts each with reserved irony, implying the necessity of a natural resolution between head and heart.

The heart of the story is again a boy's gathering awareness of his own need for resilience and dignity. These notes sound repeatedly in Gaines's work, and here James is taught a fierce and complex lesson by his mother. He has begun to mature early; aware of his family's poverty, he works to ease the burden. One would judge that his mother's most insistent command will not be wasted: "'You not a bum,' she says. 'You a man'" (117).

Of Gaines's five books, *Bloodline* and *In My Father's House* are the most persistent in examining the obligations of black manhood, particularly as it is thwarted and destroyed in the South. This is a universal torture, though, reserved by all oppressors for the oppressed and not limited to this time or that place. "Three Men" is an examination of the growth of a bloodline, an imagined instance of development from personal self-esteem toward more public, more political forms of resistance to oppression. Gaines uses the same premise in *Of Love and Dust*, that the bonding-out of an arrested black is a means of breaking him, splitting his will between false choices: prison or plantation. But we see Marcus only after he has been bonded out; here, narrator Procter Lewis gives himself up after killing another black in a nightclub fight over a woman. He is led through a catechism of self-abnegation by two white deputies—a scene in which the tissue of black and white racist folkways is masterfully evoked—and placed in a cell with two other men. Hattie is a homosexual, jailed on a morals charge. "They caught him playing this man dick," the third man advises Lewis, "At this old flea-bitten show back of town there. Up front—front row—there he is playing with this man dick. Bitch" (127). Hattie is tender and concerned, but his sympathies are misplaced and harmful. He is like John and Freddie, the black "punks" who pull corn furiously, trying to humiliate Marcus in *Of Love and Dust*. Because he is more feminine, he is ultimately unnatural, another means by which white oppressors can defeat black men.

Gaines depicts the third man, Munford Bazille, with the distanced irony reserved for his black rebels. Like Marcus and like "Copper" in "Bloodline," Bazille is in no way romanticized. He is more than a little crazy but, for all posturings and excesses, he conveys truth and can move black men. Bazille is a habitual offender, bonded out repeatedly by plantation owner Roger Medlow. In the nineteen-year-old Lewis, he sees himself some years earlier; he therefore views him with a peculiar blend of disgust and affection, urging him to refuse bond and go to prison. "He felt sorry for me," Lewis observes, "and at the same time he wanted to hit me with his fist" (141). A local phenomenon, Munford Bazille is, like Hattie, a psychological distortion encouraged by whites, still another misshapen version of black manhood. But though he has little control over his will to violence against other blacks, he is aware of what he is doing and why it is encouraged. In one of his lucid moments, he speaks thoughts very much like Bigger Thomas in *Native Son*:

> Been going in and out of these jails here, I don't know how long . . . forty, fifty years. Started out just like you—kilt a boy just like you did last night. Kilt him and got off—got off scot-free. My pappy worked for a white man who got me off. At first I didn't know why he done it—I didn't think; all I knowed was I was free, and free is how I wanted to be. Then I got in trouble again, and again they got me off. Didn't wake up till I got to be nearly as old as I'm is now. Then I realized they kept getting me off because

they needed a Munford Bazille. They need me to prove they
human—just like they need that thing over there. They need us.
Because without us, they don't know what they is. With us
around, they can see us and they know what they ain't. They ain't
us. Do you see? Do you see how they think? . . . But I got news
for them—cut them open; go 'head and cut one open—you see
if you don't find Munford Bazille or Hattie Brown. Not a man
one of them. 'Cause face don't make a man—black or white.
Face don't make him and fucking don't make him and fighting don't make him—neither killing. None of this proves you
a man. 'Cause animals can fuck, can kill, can fight—you know
that? [137–38]

Munford is bonded out again, but his advice is not wasted. A third
man joins Lewis and Hattie, a boy of fourteen or fifteen arrested for
stealing cakes. By this point well advanced in the story, Gaines has had
Lewis recollect the fight and killing; as Lewis proceeds, he can gradually read his future in Munford Bazille's grizzled face. He accepts
Bazille as a truthful man. Lewis then decides to refuse bonding-out
and assumes Bazille's role in dealing harshly with the new boy. Again,
Gaines invests the end of Procter Lewis's night with a strong sense of
ritual, because his actions bear much more than individual significance. Lewis seems to become a better Munford Bazille. "Deep in my
heart I felt some kind of love for this little boy," he admits and rudely
awakens the crying boy to some semblance of self-respect. The boy is
frightened, because Lewis is at first violent, bullying him into accepting responsibility for his crimes. Then, puzzled, as Lewis orders him
to pray: "I don't believe in God. But I want you to believe He can hear
you. That's the only way I'll be able to take those beatings—with you
praying" (153). Like Bazille, he is a bloodline, a living graph of past
and future, and his disgust gives way to affection that is dramatized in
the small intimate ceremony of tending the boy's wound: "I wet my
handkerchief and dabbed at the bruises. Everytime I touched his
back, he flinched. But I didn't let that stop me. I washed his back good
and clean. When I got through, I told him to go back to his bunk and
lay down. Then I rinched out his shirt and spread it out on the foot

of my bunk. I took off my own shirt and rinched it out because it was filthy" (154–55).

Although "Bloodlines" is a very resonant metaphor and the title story, it is the least successful in the collection. Races and generations with very different visions clash in the story, whose main action is the return of Copper Laurent (mulatto son of the former owner of Laurent plantation) to reclaim his "birthright." In owner Frank Laurent, Gaines condenses the plight of liberal white slavers who lacked the requisite callousness to work slaves "properly" and paid dearly for their limited compassion. Frank has inherited a legacy of racial devastation: though he realizes the cruel history of the institutions around him, he professes himself powerless to undo the past. He is matched with Copper, slightly insane and certainly Gaines's most militant black figure. Copper exists mainly to give eloquent voice to the millions of lives wasted by slavery and its remnants and delivers several compelling speeches on the historical retributions due the sufferers. But his monologues are too long and strained, as are Frank Laurent's, and the actions of the story do not effectively absorb the burdens of history and rhetoric that Gaines packs in. "Bloodline" is too poised, static, one-dimensional. What it lacks, perhaps, is the dimension of a narrator-participant who can weigh the impact of the experience he reports and grow and change in response to it. Here he is a functionary, a literary device. The final effect of the story resembles an attempt to read the storms and blights of the past in the rings of a sectioned oak instead of witnessing the naturalness and power of the tree in full growth.

"Just Like a Tree" is a fitting end piece for *Bloodline*. It is Gaines's first published work, one of his most assured and moving stories that makes full use of Afro-American oral and rhetorical folk materials. The title is taken from an old black spiritual, a hymn of determination and endurance. It closes:

> *I made my home in glory:*
> *I shall not be moved.*
> *Made my home in glory;*
> *I shall not be moved.*

Just like a tree that's
planted 'side the water.
Oh, I shall not be moved. [221]

The story is made of ten overlapping first-person accounts—by black and white, young and old, sympathetic and cynical—spanning the events of a family farewell supper for the most stately of Gaines's matriarchs, Aunt Fe. While she does not speak directly, her being is refracted powerfully through the accounts and she serves as a common center. The story line is easily reconstructed: a civil rights movement flourishes in a rural Louisiana county, and local whites bomb a house as a warning. Fearful that she will be injured, the family decides that Aunt Fe must indeed be moved north to live with her daughter. They gather on this stormy evening for one last family celebration.

As in other *Bloodline* stories, there are clear conflicts in "Just Like a Tree." The most blatant is a racial struggle between blacks led in civil disobedience by Emmanuel and poor whites outraged at their wish for liberation. But the conflict between black generations is more pervasive, as Emmanuel finds himself bitterly chastised during the evening, blamed for causing the trouble that forces Fe north. Emmanuel's defense is delivered through Etienne's commentary; it is clear that his leadership is motivated by love and by a strong sense of historical obligation:

> "I love you Aunt Fe, much as I do my own parents. . . . I'm going to miss you, but I'm not going to stop what I've started. You told me a story once, Aunt Fe, about my great-grandpa. Remember? Remember how he died? . . . Remember how they lynched him—chopped him into pieces? . . . Just the two of us were sitting here beside the fire when you told me that. I was so angry I felt like killing. But it was you who told me to get killing out of my mind . . . told me that I would only bring harm to myself and sadness to others if I killed. Do you remember that, Aunt Fe? . . . You were right. We cannot raise our arms. Because it would mean death for ourselves, as well as for the others. But we'll do something else—and that's what we will do." [246–47]

This first of Ernest Gaines's writings is, significantly, a paean to one of his enduring "aunts," but her importance is greater here than in any other work. Fe is described in organic terms; and like the tree in the spiritual, she will indeed be moved when her time arrives. It seems cruel to the family that she must migrate, and though she is stoic during the evening, she gives way to her fears later. She is making the same trip slaves made a hundred years earlier, but now it seems wrong and appears in local minds as a violation of natural order. Aunt Clo, one of her nearest friends, summarizes the nature of this violation. Her section is masterfully written; the tang of her figures and language evokes a black oral past, suggesting other times when truths have been told at a drafty cabin fireside:

> Be just like wrapping a chain round a tree and jecking and jecking. . . . Jeck, jeck, jeck. Then you hear the roots crying, and then you keep on jecking, and then it give, and you jeck some mo', and then it falls. And not till then do you see what you done done. Not till then you see the big hole in the ground and piece of the taproot still way down in it—and piece you won't never get out no matter if you dig till doomsday. . . . You never get the taproot. But, sir, I tell you what you do get. You get a big hole in the ground, sir; and you get another big hole in the air where the lovely branches been all these years. Yes sir, that's what you get. The holes, sir, the holes. Two holes, sir, you can't never fill no matter how hard you try. [235–36]

Aunt Clo's monologue later stresses the brutality of Fe's being uprooted, a distinctly unnatural development, for she cannot relate the North to any sort of organic existence. Dragged there, Fe will perish. But the extended image she draws of this old woman—as a living creature, a taproot whose presence can never be undone—is striking and appropriate. And the "two holes," in the ground and in the air, are not merely absences, emptinesses. They are active; they seem to suggest that Fe's being does not perish but instead is retained as a powerful memory, an immediate and felt history, a bloodline to nourish later Emmanuels.

The emphasis in "Just Like a Tree" is not on conflict but on reconciliation. Gaines's final comment on Aunt Fe's importance is an expression of his most sweeping historical vision. The language and rhythms of Etienne's testimony grow from the Bible and the folk sermon; it is a cosmic vision, simply and dramatically built, and in it all of the apparent conflicts and contradictions between people and races and eras are resolved:

No, I say; don't blame the boy 'cause she must go. 'Cause when she's dead, and that won't be long after they get her up there, this boy's work will still be going on. She's not the only one that's go'n die from this boy's work. Many mo' of 'em go'n die 'fore it's over with. The whole place—everything. A big wind is rising, and when a big wind rise, the sea stirs, and the drop o' water you see laying on top the sea this day won't be there tomorrow. 'Cause that's what wind do, and that's what life is. She ain't nothing but one little drop o' water laying on top the sea, and what this boy's doing is called the wind . . . and she must be moved. No, don't blame the boy. Go out and blame the wind. No, don't blame him, 'cause tomorrow, what he's doing today, somebody go'n say he ain't done a thing. 'Cause tomorrow will be his time to be turned over just like it's hers today. And after that, be somebody else time to turn over. And it keep going like that till it ain't nothing left to turn—and nobody left to turn it. [245]

History Is Your People's Bones:
The Autobiography of Miss Jane Pittman

"This earth is yours and don't let that man out there take it from you," he said. "It's yours because your people's bones lays in it; it's yours because their sweat and their blood done drenched this earth. The white man will use every trick in the trade to take it from you. He will use every way he know how to get you wool-gathered. He'll turn you 'gainst each other. But remember this," he said. "Your people's bones and their dust make this place yours more than anything else. . . . Your people plowed this earth, your people chopped down the trees, your people built the roads and built the levees. These same people is now buried in this earth, and their bones's fertilizing this earth."—*The Autobiography of Miss Jane Pittman*

The dust that drifts through *Catherine Carmier* is what remains of a dead past, stifling Jackson Bradley. But for Miss Jane Pittman the dust is alive, a vivid reminder of the price paid by her black ancestors for her own meager freedom and by those younger than she, such as her adopted son Ned Douglass, shot down by a hired white murderer. The epigraph for this section is taken from Douglass's last sermon on the St. Charles River and, lest we overlook his message, Jane drives it home at his graveside: "I remember my old mistress, when she saw the young Secesh soldiers, saying: 'This precious blood of the South, the precious blood of the South.' Well, there on the riverbank is the precious dust of this South. And he is there for all to see" (113).

The Autobiography of Miss Jane Pittman is a fiction masquerading as an autobiography, but mostly it is a folk history of Afro-American life from the Civil War to the mid-1960s. If such comparisons are helpful, it is less a novel than a racial repository, sui generis like W. E. B. DuBois's *The Souls of Black Folk* and Jean Toomer's *Cane*. Jane Pittman's life is a framing metaphor, complex and vibrant, like Toomer's sugar cane. Both her life and his field are poetically imagined, specific and concrete; people go in and out of them—they can be sweet and raw, can harbor love and lust, spawn tragedy and hatred. And like DuBois and Toomer, Ernest Gaines taps the languages and forms and powers of black folk-rooted art forms. The bones of his book are oral and rhetorical: spirituals, black folk sermons, slave narratives, biblical parables, folk tales, and primitive myths. These are spoken, declaimed forms issuing in a human voice. As the putative "editor" tells us in his "Introduction," it is built on a series of interviews with Miss Jane Pittman, a 110-year-old former slave, and many of her friends. What results is "the essence of everything that was said" (ix). He preserves the figures, dialects, and rhythms of their speech, as well as the content. Although there are natural shapes to this work, it is inevitable that in so rich a book—as Miss Jane warns us through our editor—"all the ends do not tie together in one neat direction. Miss Jane's story is all of their stories, and their stories are Miss Jane's" (x).

Gaines speaks of the growth and development of the novel in a recent discussion:

> *Miss Jane* came out of the stories I heard at Auntie's house back home. Since she was crippled and couldn't go out, people'd come over in the evening, make a fire—out of wood and corn shuck— and sit on the ditch bank and tell stories for hours at a time. I first thought of the book about twenty years ago in San Francisco. When I finally decided to start *Miss Jane* in 1968 or so, I began it as *A Short Biography of Miss Jane Pittman*. I did it conversationally, that is, after Miss Jane died, a lot of her friends gathered on the porch to talk about her. I started with three friends—one white and two black—and the idea was to use something like the structure of "Just Like a Tree." I worked and worked, but couldn't get the language right, so I tore up a year's work and started over. The key was getting Miss Jane's voice. Once I had that, the point-of-view worked properly. What I wanted was a kind of folk autobiography, and once I had her voice, I was permitted to work in a lot of the reading I had begun to do.[50]

There are four sections to *Miss Jane Pittman*: "The War Years," covering the years 1865–66 and the child Ticey's (Jane's slave name) wanderings as a newly freed slave from plantation to plantation; "Reconstruction," extending from 1876 to about 1912, in which Reconstruction fails, Jane is married and loses her husband (one of the early black cowboys) and her adopted son; "The Plantation," moving from 1912 to the 1930s, during which she comes to Samson plantation and experiences the very different declines of poor blacks and ruling whites; and "The Quarters," an unbroken memoir running from the 1930s to the book's present, drawing together events of those years about the life of Jimmy Aaron, "The One." Summary serves few fictions well and in this it is particularly inappropriate. The power of the book lies precisely in the ways Gaines concretely dramatizes a vision of human history; so thoroughly does he absorb his materials and their modes of expression that the result is a truly unique creation. But there are deep structures and patterns of experience that we might examine with minimal reduction.

The informing vision behind the events of Jane's life is a cosmic resolution of a different sort than that expressed by Etienne in "Just Like a Tree"; mainly, it offers greater hope for man in the here-and-now and reconciles black generations through a common course of social action. It is summarized best in Ned Douglass's riverbank sermon. Rescued by Jane at age four, he watches enraged "patrollers" beat and dismember a band of wandering ex-slaves, including his mother. Ned goes on and, along with Jimmy Aaron in a later section, serves as "The One" for his own time and people. He is born to lead and, true to his surname, is a black renaissance man of sorts: teacher, preacher, architect, martyr. On this cool Sunday morning, he preaches at the St. Charles River near Bayonne, while his killers sit quietly in a rowboat offshore, straining for proof to effect his murder. As the epigraph suggests, Douglass's text is about redeeming a black birthright. He urges blacks not to migrate to Canada or Africa or South America and asserts that this country has been built of their bodies and souls. "I'm as much American as any man; I'm more than most," he argues, but insists that one's birthright must be claimed in dignity. There are shades of darkness and degrees of manhood, but the latter has little to do with race:

> "Be Americans. But first be men. Look inside yourself. Say, 'What am I? What else beside this black skin that the white man call nigger?' Do you know what a nigger is? . . . First, a nigger feels below anybody else on earth. He's been beaten so much by the white man, he don't care for himself, for nobody else, and for nothing else. He talks a lot, but his words don't mean nothing. He'll never be an American, and he'll never be a citizen of any other nation. But there's a big difference between a nigger and a black American. A black American cares, and will always struggle. Every day that he gets up he hopes that this day will be better. The nigger knows it won't. . . . I want my children to fight. Fight for all, not just a corner. The black man or white man who tell you to stay in a corner want to keep your mind in a corner too." [110]

Ned's counsel at the river is a key to understanding the ways of three heroic black men that stand out in *Miss Jane Pittman*. The first is Ned Douglass himself. "People's always looking for somebody to come lead them. . . . Anytime a child is born, the old people look in his face and ask him if he's The One" (197). Jane's remarks open "The Quarters" but apply to Ned some thirty-five years earlier. An unlikely "One," he sensed his duty as a black man at a young age. As we read through each incident, he is fully conscious, performing what seem to be fated obligations. In retrospect, he may be seen as a basic element in Gaines's vision of Afro-American history. Jane pleads with him to stay home; but he senses that a slave can have no true homeland and he thus moves actively toward an unknown future. Working first with whites to resettle former slaves and later with his own southern black people, he is pursued constantly and realizes that he cannot live very long.

Like DuBois, Ned envisions a pluralistic America. He is properly suspicious of white people, warning that "he will use every trick in the trade to take it from you." But he also remembers an old white man who led two children out of the swamp briars to his hearth. Met with suspicion, he widened their minds with his words. His kindnesses were unasked and substantial, but he is a kind of sphinx, the unknowable element in human affairs that returns attention to the specific, humane gesture: " 'I might be a Secesh. . . . Then I might be a friend of your race. Or maybe an old man who is very wise. Maybe an old man who cries at night. Or an old man who might kill himself tomorrow. Maybe an old man who must go on living, just to give more children a pan of meatless greens and cornbread. Maybe an old man who must warm another man at his fire, be he black or white. I can be anything, now, can't I?' " (51).

But Ned's suspicions of whites are usually appropriate. In one of the most remarkable sections of the novel, we read of Ned's achievements and his killing in "Reconstruction." Through his murderer Albert Cluveau—a sort of savant obsessed with the many killings he performs but who fails to comprehend his own unhumanity—Gaines invests much of his sense of ambivalence and retribution. As Jane recalls him: "Sometimes I got him off talking about killing. I would make him talk about fishing and raising crop. He could talk about anything. . . . But in the end killing always came back to Albert Cluveau's mind. He wasn't bragging about it, and he wasn't sorry either. It was just conversation. Like if you worked in the sawmill you talked about lumber more than you talked about cane. . . . Albert Cluveau had killed so many people he couldn't talk about nothing else" (103). Cluveau is an unsettling creation. When he tells Jane he *must* kill Ned if he is ordered, he cannot understand her anger or shock. He is literally an instrument and in him we see a prevalent emphasis on "them"—those with power and wealth, most often white, who kill to preserve their status. "They" are responsible not only for Ned's death, but for Jimmy Aaron's too, and Huey Long's as well. Of Long's death, Jane notes tersely: "Look like every man that pick up the cross for the poor must end that way" (150). Cluveau, like many other whites in this book, is a cleaver, a mechanical man. It is the function of such whites to blight and cut the natural, which is symbolized here by the growth of black manhood. In Jane's mind, blacks and Indians have natural totems, sacred phenomena with which they can commune. For the earliest Americans, it was the river; for the blacks following them, the oak tree. But the white man—first seen with the arrival of the French—is fated to be the levee, the human version of the concrete spillways that possess the rivers and cut man off from the sources of life. Later on, one of the more decent whites, Jules Raynard, assesses his godson's suicide after an impossible love for a black woman. However kind, Raynard is bound in by his history, a sort of levee: "Way, way back, men like Robert could love women like Mary Agnes. But somewhere along the way somebody wrote a new set of rules condemning all that. I had to live by them, Robert at that house had to live by them, and Clarence Caya had to live by them. Clarence Caya told Jimmy to live by them, and Jimmy obeyed. But Tee Bob couldn't obey. That's why we got rid of him. All us. Me, you, the girl—all us" (191).

Later in the novel, Jimmy Aaron is another strong young black leader. It is his function to lead toward an unknown future, and his leadership is not what the church elders wish from "The One." He is a political figure who organizes a demonstration in New Orleans and is shot to death for his efforts. In the actions of Aaron and Douglass, Gaines suggests that political activity is natural and necessary, a move historically dependent on the past. At the opening of the novel, Unc Isom urges all newly freed slaves to stay at the plantation, not to separate the tribe. Led by Ticey and Ned, the young walk ignorantly into a mysterious and dangerous world. Near the end, the elders again advise staying at home, rebuffing Aaron and his plea for support. But Jane, like Unc Isom, urges that young and old not part. However, she follows Jimmy Aaron's spirit into New Orleans; in so doing, past and present can harmonize again and blend into a future.

Jane's husband, Joe Pittman, is the third strong black figure in her life. After they settle in Texas, Jane fears for his life, and goes to Madame Eloise Gautier, a hoodoo. Madame Gautier is a seer, and she confirms Jane's fear that Joe will die. She also explains the obligation of black manhood in another sense. Not only are black men historical and political instruments, they are existential and supremely individual as well. She defines the masculine principle in this world: "'That's man's way. To prove something. Day in, day out he must prove he is a man. . . . If not the horse, then the lion, if not the lion, then the woman, if not the woman, then the war, then the politic, then the whiskey. Man must always search somewhere to prove himself. He don't know everything is already inside him'" (93–94).

Madame Gautier also defines the feminine principle in this world. If man must go forward, risking himself and living for a shorter, brighter time, the woman must endure and sustain her people. Man dies in opening the future; and although woman seems to sense intuitively that he will be destroyed, she is powerless to stop him. It falls to her lot to watch and *remember*, at all costs to *remember*—as Jane does so well—and walk through the doors opened for her.

As I suggested earlier, the power of *The Autobiography of Miss Jane Pittman* does not lie in the patterns and motifs of recurring characters, actions, and themes. There are familiar patterns, to be sure: black leaders are consistently thrust up, only to be slain and to dash the hopes they inspired; again and again, Jane and her people take to the road on still another exodus, in search of another homeland. But Gaines shows much less concern with shoring up the structure of the novel than with allowing his material its own natural course; indeed, the richness of the fiction lies in the momentary eddies and pools into which the narrative stream is deflected. When Gaines speaks of Richard Wright's decline, he attributes it to an inability to continue writing from black "American soil [instead of from] a European library."[51] This is true of his own writing; there is a strong suspicion that the traditional techniques of the novel are too analytical and schematic to properly define his materials or express his vision of the natural history of black people. Gaines seems to agree with William Melvin Kelley's assessment that "to carry the weight of our ideas, the novel has got to be changed. We are trying to tap some new things in a form which is not our form."[52]

The power lies in Gaines's careful assimilation of Afro-American folk materials, particularly those of the South, in which his historical vision is absorbed and vivified. His debt is to the rich fund of customs and folkways of the black American past, to the unique forms grown out of them: to the spirituals, determination songs, and church music like Jane's "Done Got Over," which urge a rocklike perseverance even as "they tell . . . of death and suffering and unvoiced longing toward a truer world, of misty wanderings and hidden ways."[53] From the church he also draws on folk sermons and church talks, adapting them to his own more secular uses; to these he owes the compelling rhetorical power running through the speeches of Ned Douglass and Jimmy Aaron and the broad historical apology for pain and suffering. He is likewise indebted to slave narratives, like that of Frederick Douglass, which testify to the moral diseases incipient in human bondage and to the psychic devastations resulting in both black (Black Harriet) and white (Cluveau and Tee Bob). A more regional Louisiana folk heritage is spun out in the presence of hoodoo Madame Eloise Gautier and in the many webs of prophecies bound in dreams, visions, or superstitions. These superstitious presences suggest a world more alive and mysterious beyond our own and are characteristic of the folk tale, as in the remarkable account of Albert Cluveau's suffering and death, "The Chariot of Hell." Many of Gaines's figures are familiar to black myth: Singalee Black Harriet and her return to the shelter of her homeland via insanity; the hunter in search of his mother, pausing in the swamps to trap food for Ticey and Ned. To this rich stream, played through Gaines's shaping contemporary imagination, we owe the spectrum of Afro-American life and language set loose in *Miss Jane Pittman*.

His direct concern with history and those who record it is apparent from the start. The putative "editor" is a teacher of history; he explains to Jane and her friends that her life will help students to better learn their lessons. "What's wrong with them books you already got?" her friend asks. "Miss Jane is not in them," is his reply. Teachers are important throughout Jane's story. Good ones such as Ned Douglass and Mary LeFabre are treasures; the poor ones, like Miss Lilly and Joe Hardy, are quietly indicted, damned simply as being "among the worst human beings I've ever met" (154).

But teaching is not easy: we are often reminded of the difficulty of knowing a truth, of daring a vision of history. Jane is first made aware of this painful fact by the riddling old man in whom a world of mystery is refracted. Discouraging her trek to Ohio in search of a kind "Yankee soldier name Brown," he images a detailed account of her fruitless travels: " 'And the only white Brown people can remember that ever went to Luzana to fight in the war died of whiskey ten years ago. They don't think he was the same person you was looking for because this Brown wasn't kind to nobody. He was coarse and vulgar; he cussed man, God, and nature every day of his life' " (54). Thus, as long as man can speak it and shape it, history can deceive, can be a weapon against one's foes. Remembering Herbert Aptheker's adage that "history is mighty," especially for the oppressor, we listen to Jules Raynard's account of Robert Samson's suicide. His reading of the past is historically myopic and consciously blurs the pattern of cause and effect. In his account of slavery, for example, the lion and the lamb lie down together, and each is equally guilty and helpless before the fated retribution for the sins of a common past. Raynard drives Jane home from the plantation to the old slave quarters, and she listens quietly from a back seat, suspicious of his version of "the gospel truth." For all his decency, Raynard is still another white man whose dream of the past makes those in the present impotent; history is a wall for him, before which master and serf can do little but surrender.

For Ernest J. Gaines, like his creation Jimmy Aaron, there is immense power in language, and its use is a sacred trust. Like Aaron, he assumes his obligations cautiously and naturally. Aaron's simple skills of reading and writing family letters and papers and his later rhetorical talents; Gaines's powers to create fiction: each is a way to preserve a people, to pass on a heritage. Ned Douglass's last text is a popular folk sermon, adapted from the "Vision of Dry Bones" in

Ezekiel, in which it is taught that words can bring a past to life, put flesh on bones and a seed in the soil. "Son of man, these bones are the whole house of Israel: behold, they say. Our bones are dried up, and our hope is lost; we are clean cut off" (Ezekiel 37:11). Ernest Gaines writes from this lament, and *The Autobiography of Miss Jane Pittman* is his mighty attempt to open the graves and make these bones live.

History Is a Gap

"Yes. All the time. Every day. About a month ago I was talking to a newspaperman—a man who's covered executions all over the South. Not just here in Louisiana—Texas, Mississippi, Georgia—all over. He's seen fifty, sixty of them. Most of them, black men. Said he never heard one called daddy's name at that last hour. Heard momma called, heard gran'mon called, nanane, Jesus, God. Not one time he heard daddy called. . . . There's a gap between us and our sons, Peters, that even He," Phillip said, nodding toward the Bible, "even He can't seem to close."—*In My Father's House*

"It's more subdued in my earlier books, but it's there," Ernest Gaines says of the central theme of *In My Father's House*. "The new novel is about a young man's search for his lost father (and the other way around). The black father and son were sold apart up on the auction block, and have searched for each other—often blindly and violently —ever since."[54]

If *The Autobiography of Miss Jane Pittman* is a fictive study of the black matriarch, Gaines's most recent work searches the tragic destructions of black fathers, specifically the separation of patriarchs and children from the ancestral homeland and the auction block to the present day, and the many ensuing attempts to heal that breach. His title is borrowed from the Gospel of John (part 3: "The Book of Glory"), and the novel itself is a secular meditation on Christ's last discourse at the feast of the Passover, a message from the supreme Father to his children:

In my Father's House there are many dwelling places;
Otherwise, how could I have told you
That I was going to prepare a place for you?

I am indeed to prepare a place for you,
And then I shall come back to take you with me,
That where I am you also may be.
. . . .
I will not leave you orphaned,
I will come back to you. [John 14:2–3; 18]

Gaines's modest Christ is Reverend Phillip Martin, at sixty a respected Louisiana family man, pastor of the local Solid Rock Baptist Church, area civil rights leader. *In My Father's House* is set in the black suburbs of St. Adrienne, across the Mississippi and a lifetime away from urban Baton Rouge. It is the author's most contemporary work. The action unfolds in the rainy winter of 1969, in the chilly abyss of the spirit after Martin Luther King's death. Once again, Gaines's history is not the length of one or two long human shadows; thus this novel centers on one of many thousands of King's successors who carried on the work in the bitter depths after his assassination.

King is in many ways a model for the fictive Martin. King radiated power, and Martin is also a bull of a man. Like King at his height, Reverend Martin's regional successes and leadership mark him clearly as future congressional material. Faint whispers of prowess with women are heard in the lives of the historic man and the fictive character, but in the case of Phillip Martin, rumor is borne out when he is disgraced and rejected—by friends, wife, congregation—in trying to secretly retrieve a lost bastard son.

Reverend Phillip Martin is early depicted as a decent man, well regarded not only in the pious houses of church and black family but, more grudgingly, in bars, pool shacks, and concrete block gambling houses. Reverend Martin has shaped the town's character by fifteen years of countless small actions and daily attentions. Community spirit is at low ebb as a gray rain falls on the pecans and live oaks and cypress sheltering this levee community, and Martin's leadership proceeds against a chorus of cynical teachers drinking dead evenings through at the Cotton Club. Although they harbor a guarded respect for Martin, they agree with Chuck, as he insists: "That shit's over with, kiddo. Them honkies gave up some, because of conscience, because of God. But they ain't giving up no more. Nigger's already got just about everything he's getting out of this little town" (21).

Against the welter of their disbelief, Martin's life strikes a bright figure, particularly on the eve of his planned march and boycott against Chenal, a racist department store owner. But respected as he is, his own house is cold and more than a little empty, for out of the cold rain walks a mysterious and pitiful young man, Robert X, who announces that he has a "meeting" in St. Adrienne. He is not a Black Muslim; the X suggests his cipherhood, his ghostliness. Robert X arrives on the bus, takes a rented room, and lingers like a painted wraith in the early chapters of the novel, a true dead soul; he is finally shown to be Martin's abandoned son, one of three hidden illegitimate children. He has returned with a gun, perhaps to murder his father, most certainly to confront him and force this servant of the Lord to place his own house in order.

His fifteen years of responsible life having come to naught, Martin undertakes a nighttime trip across the Mississippi, back into his roistering past and through the squalid ghetto of Baton Rouge in search of his old running buddy, Chippo Simon. Gaines's touch is masterful in these scenes, for he creates a nocturnal past that is in every way an inverted mirror to the mundane respectability of St. Adrienne. Unlike Miss Jane, who never does make it, Phil Martin crosses the mythical one more river, that literal American Jordan, and goes back twenty years.

In My Father's House is perhaps the author's most painstakingly structured book. At its core is an understated pattern of contrasts between the daytime world of the present in St. Adrienne and the hellish nocturnal past of Baton Rouge. Martin's long evening brings him across his forgotten god-family, a fellow pastor, old lovers, some shiftless brothers to the calloused teachers who drink promise away across the river—all here in Hebert, Domico, the Red Top Saloon. In Billy, scarred by Viet Nam battle and racism at home, he finds an active, enraged image of his own mist-shrouded Etienne (Robert X). His conversation with Billy, who advocates a fiery apocalypse against racist America, directs our attention to the gap discussed in the epigraph preceding this section. Martin and his surrogate son speak of fathers and sons, and Martin finally asks, "How do we close the gap between you and your daddy, between me and my boy?" (166). The young veteran's response is embittered—he depicts his ailing father as "forty-five, a massive heart attack" and Martin's protecting church as "nothing but more separation" (166). Billy is a saner "Copper" Laurent ("Bloodline") but no less obsessed with violence; he stands for healing by cauterizing fire, an attitude with which Martin can commiserate but never accept.

Phillip Martin moves beyond Billy and, with his boyhood friend Chippo's help, reconstructs his own lost past. Chippo is a ruined derelict vision of what Martin might easily have been. From his story, Martin puts together the fruits of desperate escape some twenty years earlier: his lover Johanna Rey, abandoned in 1949, is now wasted and forlorn in a West Coast slum, with three ruined bastard children shucked off with her. The lives of Antoine, Justine, and Etienne have been ravaged by poverty and violence, but most of all by the consequences of having been deprived of a loving father.

The Reverend Phillip Martin is devastated by his experience in *In My Father's House,* as he is brought face to face with his hidden sins. Although his stature has been diminished, he is finally neither a Christ nor a Satan, just a man trying to walk a little more upright. He is many times a father here: to his three bastards, to his legitimate family in St. Adrienne, to his pastoral flock at home, but at the novel's close he is as weak as a child. He is about to piece himself together with the scraps of his past, almost ready to "bind the gap between father and son," the first step of which is to heal himself and to bring decent order into his own house. Though a teacher, he must be taught by his former students. Beverly, who teaches his son Patrick, advises that his life and work have not been in vain, that "we work toward the future. To keep Patrick from going to that trestle. One day I'll have a son, and what we do tomorrow might keep him from going to that trestle" (213).

Like Miss Jane Pittman, who opens her fictive life afoot and ends the novel walking on the same long journey, Phillip Martin gets up from the floor an aging man. He is weakened but less paralyzed; supported by his wife and Alma, who sets her own humiliations aside, he agrees unsteadily when she instructs "We just go'n have to start again" (214).

In My Father's House, Ernest Gaines's fifth fictional work, once again depicts the author's concern with history and its unique uses in the contemporary black American novel. And once again we realize that history—in this case, the tragedy of the failure of the black father and his relationship to his son—is alive, vital, and not to be denied or escaped. "I was telling my boy today what keep us apart is a paralysis we inherited from slavery," Martin sadly advises Chippo Simon (202). What he learns painfully is that this "paralysis" is not so easily healed, but if it is to be so, the starting point is recognition of the black father's historical plight. Furthermore, one must acknowledge that the sins of the fathers are indeed visited on the sons and that those sons are very quickly fathers of another generation of sons. As expressed in the closing verses chosen by Gaines, "I am in my Father,/ And you in me, and I in you" (John 14:20).

We have thus come full circle from *Catherine Carmier,* in which the emphasis is on the son Jackson Bradley's coming back to prune a dead past. *In My Father's House* dramatizes the impact of the son's return. If a man and his son are indeed separated by a gap, Phillip Martin learns, the healing of that divide starts in a kind of psychic regeneration, a conscious moral and political attention to "the paralysis we inherited from slavery" (202). Liberation is both personal and political, and it lies in accepting the mighty river of the past, particularly as it trickles down into one man's life. Martin learns two lessons: history paralyzes us only if we deny it, and we can and must act on the personal consequences of ancient outrage, if only to assure that it is not repeated. *In My Father's House* finally shares the ancient wheeling vision found in the Bible and the blues—history is alive in each of us, but it lives with a particular vibrance in Afro-American experience. Or, in the proper languages, that of the blues phrase "what goes around comes around," and the biblical "I am in my Father,/ And you in me, and I in you." Roll on, Jordan.

Four

Fiction from the Counterculture:
Marge Piercy, Richard Brautigan, Ken Kesey

A third very visible result of American cultural fragmentation over the last several decades has been the body of "countercultural" writing that has accumulated since the mid-1960s. The term "counterculture" has, like all American catch phrases, been long since exhausted of meaning by the marketplace. Originally, it implied the presence or possible presence of alternate life-styles, genuine alternatives to "straight" middle-class American life. It very quickly became a vast umbrella under which every sort of thinker, artist, or performer—sage and charlatan and every shade between—could be placed. Very generally, the writers I place in this category share an active concern about the psychic, sexual, social, and political configurations in quotidian American life, but choose fiction as their means of projecting or evoking alternative semiutopian worlds. This is not to say, by any means, that fiction was a dominant mode of expression for the young experience of the period. Tom Wolfe is essentially correct in asserting that the period will be remembered as "the decade when manners and morals, styles of living, attitudes toward the world changed the country more crucially than any political events . . . all the changes that were labeled, however clumsily, with such tags as 'the generation gap,' 'the counter culture,' 'black consciousness,' 'sexual permissiveness.' . . . This whole side of American life that gushed forth when postwar American affluence finally blew the lid off."[1] And he is certainly correct in observing the relative paucity of fiction written from this heady and turbulent experience.

Perhaps the period 1965 to 1972 was simply a time in which other media, mainly the technologically appealing film and popular music, somehow proved more appropriate to our experiences. Perhaps the psychic changes were too intense and too prolonged to ponder very quickly, to run through the fine mills of fiction. Mainly, I suspect that living through that ecstatic time—when many of the young felt themselves living outside of history, when prophets like R. D. Laing, Norman O. Brown, and Timothy Leary offered regular glimpses of the New Jerusalem, when each evening failed to deliver that apocalypse, that new Eden, NOW!—at the peaks and valleys of one's nervous system drained energies so thoroughly that the hours of concentration at the writer's desk were an impossible demand. As the young withdrew into a tight circle of interest, from mass demonstration to communal life to "getting your head together," the appeal to another implicit in the act of writing seemed even more improbable. Whatever reasons one offers, countercultural fiction was and is scarce in kind and in fine quality. As Tom Wolfe comically concludes:

> I wrote the The Electric Kool-Aid Acid Test and then waited for the novels that I was sure would come pouring forth out of the psychedelic experience . . . but they never came forth, either. I learned later that publishers had been waiting, too. They had been practically crying for novels by the new writers who must be out there somewhere, the new writers who could do the big novels of the hippie life or campus life or radical movements or the war in Vietnam or dope or sex or black militancy or encounter groups or the whole whirlpool all at once. They waited and all they got was the Prince of Alienation . . . sailing off to Lonesome Island on his Tarot boat with his back turned and his Timeless cape on, reeking of camphor balls.[2]

Thus few young writers associated with the "counterculture" accumulated a body of work during the 1960s. For this reason, I deal with single works of fiction by three young American authors, dwelling on the particular attitudes that shape and inform their works:

Marge Piercy's *Dance the Eagle to Sleep*, a fictive exploration of a future political revolution in the United States; Richard Brautigan's *Revenge of the Lawn*, a sustained series of instances of creatively imagining oneself out of a hostile environment; and Ken Kesey's *One Flew Over the Cuckoo's Nest*, a dream about the necessary evolution of heightened states of human consciousness.

The effects of the political and cultural rifts so evident in America during the 1960s and early 1970s were nowhere more evident than in the literary counterculture, spawned in tabloid free presses and underground newspapers, street theater, and political demonstrations; out of it a style of life and a series of exemplars and their works continue to grow. The movement has most obviously included journalists and poets, but it has also taken in fiction writers and cult figures such as Richard Brautigan, Ken Kesey, Kurt Vonnegut, and Leonard Cohen. Very slowly over the last decade, a small body of fiction has grown out of the concern for alternate life-styles in the late 1960s and early 1970s. Ishmael Reed, cofounder of the *East Village Other*, one of the early underground newspapers, continues to build a reputation as a bright novelist. Rudolph Wurlitzer, advocating a "politics of displacement," writes both films ("Two Lane Blacktop") and novels—hallucinatory, disordering works depicting the often self-induced pressures on young selves during the period. *Nog, Quake,* and *Flats* have developed a following among young aficionados of "head cultures."[3] More popularly, Tom Robbins and Robert Pirsig present real, if unformed, narrative talents in *Another Roadside Attraction* and *Even Cowgirls Get the Blues* and in *Zen and the Art of Motorcycle Maintenance*.[4] Robbins has a flair for the richness of language and wild invention characterizing his sensuous fictions and Pirsig for an ingenious, if long-winded, grafting of popular Western and Eastern philosophy to a stock of American psychic breakdown.

But the most effective literary outgrowth of counterculture impulses is neither fiction nor poetry, but nonfiction. Older writers like Norman Mailer, I. F. Stone, and Paul Goodman, who worked from a more traditional left perspective, wrote directly about the shame and power of U.S. incursions in Viet Nam. Younger writers, however, chronicled wars at home, the many domestic southeast Asias that utopian communal schemes hoped to remedy. Four of the most significant works are Elia Katz's *Armed Love*, Michael Rossman's *The Wedding Within the War*, Raymond Mungo's *Total Loss Farm*, and Ernst Callenbach's visionary *Ecotopia*.[5] Journalists were particularly fascinated with altered states of consciousness, and Carlos Castaneda's five golden notebooks have finally tapered in appeal after enormous popularity.[6] From *The Teachings of Don Juan* to *The Second Ring of Power*, Castaneda enthralled college audiences with Carlos in the Yaqui underworld, a perfect fantasy for the American college youth's daydream of unsuspected darker powers. "Gonzo journalism" has also been very popular, particularly works like Hunter S. Thompson's *Fear and Loathing in Las Vegas*, *Fear and Loathing on the Campaign Trail*, and *The Great White Shark*.[7] Thompson's raucous, drug-crazed adventures encountered in attempts to cover stories in Vegas, on the campaign trail, or at the Superbowl, have made him a culture hero to many young extremists. There have been more serious non-fictions as well; among the books by younger writers, *Dispatches*, Michael Herr's collection of startling essays, is outstanding.[8] Herr's first book, much of which was written as a war correspondent for *Esquire*, conveys the absolute surrealism of grunt life in Viet Nam—as if the drugs and music and life-styles of American freaks were transported wholesale to Hue, Saigon, and Khe Sanh, along with recoilless rifles, B-52s, napalm, and M-16s. It conjures up Janis and Jimi Hendrix in a free fire zone.

As the 1980s seize us in their grasp, countercultural macropolitics have become more decentralized and populist. Mass demonstrations and movements by an inchoate left have wisely dissolved into nodes of special-interest activist groups concerned with locales like the southwestern deserts or the redwood forests of the Pacific Northwest and with issues such as our national addiction to fossil fuels and our seeming lack of concern for vanishing species. The development is still too young for a full body of writing to emerge, but controversial and popular work by Edward Abbey, a writer who now bids to replace Hunter Thompson as a favorite with college readers, may give us a glimpse of the near future. In luddite romances like *The Monkey Wrench Gang* and backcountry jeremiads like those collected in *Desert Solitaire* and *Abbey's Road*, Abbey turns our moral imaginations back toward our natural homes outside, toward a national illusion that our land and people are infinitely renewable.[9]

Writing in 1970, Todd Gitlin, one of the more astute commentators on the left in recent years, is correct in lamenting the paucity of politically committed fiction: "The direct insight of fiction has been sorely missing at a time when the radical movement's own journalistic accounts of itself have grown stale, glib, shrill and blindly celebratory, and the future has faded into one-dimensional images of guerrilla warfare on the one hand and 'the greening of America' on the other."[10] But as Gitlin goes on to observe, a small but active band of writers sharing an essentially radical left perspective has labored to reintroduce American political experience to the novel. The most impressive of such fictions is Sol Yurick's *The Bag*, a mammoth novel imagining a future revolution starting in New York, an orchestration of unleashed oppression by every sort of desperate special-interest group.[11] Yurick's method of operation is to organize characters around a matrix of psychological responses to social repression; he does not question *whether revolution can occur*, but *why it is humanly and culturally inevitable*. Befitting the introspection of the time, Yurick suggests that the "Revolution" must begin inside, at the root of human consciousness; thus his hero, white social worker and writer Sam Miller, is gradually so overwhelmed by his case work that he is absorbed into the surrogate identity of Mr. Alpha, his own fictional black ghetto victim. Alpha is, in turn, absorbed into the energies of the angry mob that sweeps through the final sixty pages of *The Bag*.

Several other writers work with similar material. Norman Fruchter and E. L. Doctorow write strains of social realism from a left perspective. Doctorow, in particular, writes with a sense of the chilly political atmosphere in the American 1950s in *The Book of Daniel*, a far more accomplished novel than his more recent flashy novel, *Ragtime*.[12] M. F. Beal writes from a feminist, Marxist perspective in a guerrilla underground work, *Amazon One*.[13] At least one serious novel by a major young talent did come out of the cauldron of the late 1960s—*Rabbit Boss*, by Thomas Sanchez. Although his politics are less doctrinaire than Yurick's or Marge Piercy's, his sense of outrage at our historical racism and imperialism is no less intense. *Rabbit Boss* is a carefully wrought and researched book about four generations of Washo Indians; it traces their tragic and inevitable decline as white, gold-seeking, railroad-building Americans westered through their sacred lands.[14]

But the largest and most distinguished body of fiction by a politically committed writer during this period is by Marge Piercy, and I thus examine her visionary novel, *Dance the Eagle to Sleep*, in greater detail.

The Saying Is Not the Magic:
Dance the Eagle to Sleep

Every soul must become a magician; the magician is in touch.
The magician connects: the magician helps each thing
to open into what it truly wants to utter.
The saying is not the magic: we have drunk words and eaten
manifestoes and grown bloated on resolutions
and farted winds of sour words that left us weak.
It is in the acting with the strength we cannot
really have till we have won.—Marge Piercy

Marge Piercy has published extensively in the twelve years since her first book, *Breaking Camp* (poems) in 1968. Five more collections of poems have followed. An excerpt from "Maude Awake" (an unpublished novel) appeared in a feminist anthology in 1966, her first published fiction.[15] Since then, she has published six novels, from *Going Down Fast* (1969)—a very solid first work—to *The High Cost of Living* (1978) and *Vida* (1979). Her most balanced and impressive work to date is *Woman on the Edge of Time* (1976), in which she successfully blends techniques of social realism and prophetic science fiction.[16] I focus on her second prose work, the "cautionary tale" *Dance the Eagle to Sleep*.[17]

Because of her involvement in Students for a Democratic Society during the early 1960s, Piercy has defined herself as "a committed radical artist."[18] Her work has grown increasingly sympathetic to the plights of women in a capitalist, sexist culture, but her earlier comments on *Dance the Eagle to Sleep* still serve as a personal, artistic, and political credo:

> I wanted to examine alternatives and choices and daydreams and
> accepted mythologies and tendencies of behavior in the New

Left. I am a revolutionary, my work is all committed and engaged writing. I make poems for people as people bake bread for people and people grow corn for people and people make furniture for people. This novel, like my poems and other writing, is intended to be useful: I live in a situation of feedback. I articulate what I perceive needs to be articulated out of me, out of those around me, out of those I work with, out of those who push on me, out of those who are trying to kill me. . . . I am involved in showing people changing through struggle, becoming, always in process. I am concerned with drawing characters who are full and able to be identified with, but not heroes or heroines of impeccable revolutionary virtue.

I get a lot of flak for that. But the people I love and thus the characters I can make out of my life and those around me are mixtures, products of a society that socializes through guilt and competition and fear and repression.[19]

I work with Piercy's cautionary tale for several reasons. First, it was written in the midst of radical dissent in the late 1960s, examining, as she explains, "alternatives and choices and daydreams and accepted mythologies and tendencies of behavior in the New Left."[20] Second, I wish to examine flaws in the work. Its considerable narrative powers are diluted by long stretches of a "saying" and by a wide streak of rhetorical preaching and posing of the sort criticized by Piercy herself in the epigraph (page 143), "The Aim." I believe the fiction's weaknesses, perhaps even more than its virtues, are instructive and exemplary.

Dance the Eagle to Sleep is set in an indefinite future, a time when a small army of alienated and oppressed youths band together to create an alternate culture. As Piercy explains, "the emphasis is on significant episodes of a collective action. There are five major characters, four of them viewpoint characters and one seen only from the other's eyes."[21] Her major characters are familiar "youth culture" types: Corey is half-Indian, an outlaw, a strongly mystical figure given to fasting and seeking visions in which America is redeemed by her tribal children:

They could turn away from the ways of metal to the ways of the flesh. They could learn the good ways of being in harmony, of cooperating, of sane bravery in defense of each other, to be one with their bodies and their tribe and each other and the land. The children would turn away from being white. For the whites were crazy. The whites were colonizers and dominators and enslavers. They came to rob and steal and develop and conquer. Already the children wore beads and headbands and smoked ritually. They were awaiting the coming of the real tribes. [36]

Closest to Corey is Shawn, cooler and more aristocratic, the leader of a rock band and a youth culture hero. Through Shawn's summarized experiences, Piercy relates her unsettling vision of "The Nineteenth Year of Servitude," brainchild of a "Task Force on Youth Problems." Implemented by a liberal president, The Nineteenth Year seems to be the ultimate in social programming:

> Most guys still ended up in the Army, and a great many went into street patrols and the city militia. But a number were channeled into overseas aid and pacification corps, the rebuilding programs in the bombed-out ghettoes, and pollution clean-up corps. Girls who weren't rushed into the nursing corps worked in the preschool socialization programs in the ghettoes, or as teachers' aides or low-level programmers for the array of teaching machines. Of course, students in medicine, engineering and the sciences just kept trotting through school.
> School records, grades, and counselors determined some of the channeling, but the prime tools were the mass exams everyone took, separating out levels of skill and verbal intelligence, and locating potential troublemakers. . . . For two years now, The Nineteenth Year had bottled up the so-called Youth Revolution. [10-11]

Shawn's involvement with the rebels is much more uncertain than Corey's. He drifts through life, and his only strong interests are his music and the passion it compels. Channeled as a musician for The Nineteenth Year, he finds his talents being used to manipulate his peers; he rebels, is arrested and court-martialed. Befriended by Corey, Shawn joins the commune and lends his music to serve the ends of the Revolution.

Bill Batson is a third major figure. Named for the human weakling in which comic book superhero Captain Marvel hid, Billy is a scientific genius, cynical and dispossessed. He joins The Indians when they occupy his high school—their first act of secession. Billy's mind and skills are quickly assimilated; even more than Corey, he comes to argue for militant, violent face-offs with the government. Piercy's rhetorical excesses are especially blatant in her descriptions of Billy:

> Born twisted, born warped, born in the center of the empire, he could only pride himself that they had not succeeded in using him. They had come close. But he had escaped them and turned. For the society, the system was mad: it caused the people in it to go slowly mad. They could not care for each other. They could only hate and fear and compete and fantasize; they could only rub against each other and try to use each other and suck on their own anxieties.
>
> He would never live to be human. Nobody like him or these people could imagine what it might be like to be human, in a society people ran for the common good instead of the plunder of the few. . . . Tenderness swept his body. He could almost imagine. Someday there would be people. But that coming would not be gentle. It would sprout from struggle and death. Someday there would be human people. [104–5]

Joanna is the major female character. Like the other four, she is virtually a sociological type: an army child, an inveterate runaway, she finally attaches herself to The Indians at their lower East Side commune. Sleeping her way through the tribe, she finally settles as Corey's woman. Joanna is the most static of the cast, revealed to us in skeletal form; indeed, her "brainwashed" character remains unconvincing throughout the novel. She too serves as a handy mouthpiece for the preachiest of political lectures:

> It depressed her that she could only define herself in negatives. She was not like her mother. She was not like her father. The conventional masculine and the conventional feminine roles were for shit. The primary business of base ladies was to talk about each other. What her mother knew could be contained in a

greeting card and consisted of You're Supposed To's and Don't You Dare's. It could be summed up as, "Don't sit with your knees apart, Jill, you're a big girl now."

She did not want to be somebody's wife or somebody else's mother. Or somebody else's servant or somebody else's secretary. Or somebody else's sex kitten or somebody else's keeper. She saw no women around who seemed to be anybody in themselves. They all wore some man's uniform. She wanted to be free, and free meant not confined, not forced to lie, not forced to pretend, not warped, not punished, not tortured. [54]

After the initial rounds of this sort of crude exposition, *Dance the Eagle to Sleep* picks up markedly. Her characters swing into action: after occupying a school, forming a sizeable youth commune in New York, directing the formation of the Warriors (their guerrilla wing under Billy's leadership), and setting similar movements off throughout the country, The Indians move to a rural New Jersey commune, where they hope to build a serious land base.

Although her central characters share a marionettelike quality early in the novel, they become less wooden and more convincing in action. Drawing directly on her own movement experiences, Piercy does indeed "examine alternatives and choices and daydreams and accepted mythologies and tendencies of behavior in the New Left."[22] As The Indians work hard to establish a revolutionary base, take "bread" (a kind of psychedelic sacrament), and dance out their visions in tribal gatherings, personal and political relationships become strained and factions develop. Corey and his "water people" argue for continuing the commune farms and tribal families: "Creating something better is struggling, too. We need to keep it up on both fronts: making real, visible alternatives, and confronting the system. . . . Here they're all the way out of the system. That's the biggest trouble we can make. . . . But we have to gather all the tribes. Everybody can't make it on the streets. We have to grow or we perish. The tribe is the core. The whole tribe" (94–95).

His brother-antagonist Billy Batson is more urban directed, insisting on militant, confrontation-provoking tactics. Modeled closely after several of the Weathermen, most violent of the New Left factions in the late 1960s, Billy scorns tribes and farm communes: "If you had bothered with nineteenth-century history, you'd know that this whole farm business is a throwback, Brook Farm-utopian cranks off in the woods to start the good society, and at each other's throats in six months. . . . So we set up a summer camp in the Jersey hills for wayward adolescents. The man can let us get away with that. What would it matter to General Motors if we set up twenty?" (93–94). Factions flourish: faced with revolutionary paradoxes—the need to murder and to create, for example—The Indians drain their energies by squabbling. The liberal American government is replaced by a harder line, and "The System" methodically and harshly eliminates their numbers. Billy's warriors use bombings and terrorism to force a showdown and are quickly crushed. The authorities move into the farm commune; after a time lapse at the end of the tenth chapter, we see what is left: Billy is dead, Joanna captured, Corey crushed by a bulldozer.

Driven west by the government, the remnants of The Indians gather with the shreds of other tribes; in a familiar historical parallel, almost all are annihilated. By the end of *Dance the Eagle to Sleep*, only Shawn, a scruffy female named Ginny, and a badly scarred black (Marcus) remain alive. It remains for the pregnant Ginny, who is politically naive, to issue final judgments of her male revolutionaries: "She was gentle with them both and angry with them both. She would not love them, because they had not been willing to escape. She told them they were in love with apocalypse, like all men, more in love with machomyths than any woman" (217). The tale ends on the tiniest of glimmers. Shawn, Ginny, and Marcus have come through the fire with few illusions left. At the end, somewhat sentimentally, they are prepared to make a start. The fiction closes with the difficult birth of Ginny's child: "The baby lived and she lived and it was day for Marcus and for him, it was day for them all" (224).

The political import of Marge Piercy's cautionary tale was seized by most reviewers. Her strongest messages are delivered mainly to her fellow leftists:

> I regard the politics of Apocalypse as dangerous to our success in taking the control of the world away from those who own it

and us, and I was trying to exorcise that fascination with a struggle viewed as final, fatal, sudden, and complete in *Dance*. The end is trying to suggest, So you get your Armageddon, so? What do you do then? You still have to go on, if you survive, trying to change things. The enemy is very real, real as Rockefeller ordering the murders at Attica, but so is the fact that our course is long and slow and this revolution, for all that we win or die, will never be finished.[23]

Praised by left liberal critics in *Nation*, *Commonweal*, and *New Republic* (John Seelye, Linda Kuehl, Todd Gitlin), *Dance the Eagle to Sleep* is politically informed and convincing.[24] The force and detail of Marge Piercy's analyses are valuable—the liberal undermining and cooptation of the radical left, the roots of radical divisiveness, the agonizing self-criticism and dialectical examinations—these are astute observations. But I have basic reservations about the work and dwell on the question of how art may most effectively move people to share or act upon a political belief. More exactly, how can fiction best convey a political vision? How can political concepts, values, and judgments be submerged in fictional forms, be translated into compelling patterns of character in action with which people can identify?

John Updike seems right in suggesting that Piercy's tale is less persuasive than it might have been and therefore politically inefficient. She has a tendency to indulge in "saying" rather than "showing." Individual characters are offered in exposition as case studies rather than as individuals *in actions* with which we can empathize. Although large segments of *Dance the Eagle to Sleep* are told through the viewpoints of Shawn, Corey, Joanna, and Billy, the language and rhythms of their flashbacks, dreams, or monologues are undifferentiated and incessantly editorial. Updike is correct in saying that Piercy is "not fastidious about cliches, resorts to a hurried sociological tone, makes people talk like press handouts, and declines to linger upon sensual details."[25]

"The emphasis is on the significant episodes of a collective action": although Piercy's comment suggests a purposeful lack of individual focus, it cannot excuse the weaknesses of the tale.[26] Adults, parents, indeed most of the human components of "The System" are never seen in action. Rather, they are offered as a vast, monolithic repression-machine, and their corporate heinousness is finally difficult to accept. Psychological aberration forms the nucleus of each of her characters, but neither aberrations nor their causes are accounted for beyond this sort of general rhetorical posturing:

> For years the culture has been telling everybody through every boob tube that only youth was sexual and beautiful, and that all an over-twenty-five schmuck like you could do was buy Brand X to look a little more youthful. Schmuck, schmuck, the boob tube said all evening long, you're powerless, sexless, fumbling, clumsy, mindless, unable to decide. Average man=schmuck. Average woman=bag. Buy our product once, and maybe nobody will notice what a drag you are. . . . Thus is a people conditioned to hate its young and focus its frustrations down upon them in a vast dream of those half-dependent, half-independent children demanding and rebelling and threatening. . . . They were different, alien. You were warned that you could not hope to communicate with them or understand their ways without the guidance of certified experts who had degrees in studying them, like biologists, specializing in tree monkeys or fighting fish. Them Versus Us: the first step in the psychological conditioning for war. [178]

Only later, when Piercy is more patient in depicting the involvements of her characters, especially the sexual ones, and in coiling the springs of their actions, does the fiction engage one's attentions and belief. Although *Dance the Eagle to Sleep* is finally impressive, it only partially fills its promise. Judging from Piercy's other recent writings, she is fully aware of the main requisite of political fiction:

> Now I get coarse when the abstract nouns start flashing.
> I go out to the kitchen to chat about cabbages and habits.
>
> I try hard to remember to watch what people do.
> Yes, keep your eyes on the hands, let the voice go buzzing.

Economy is the bone, politics is the flesh,
Watch who they beat and who they eat,
Watch who they relieve themselves on, watch who they own.

The rest, the rest, the rest is decoration.[27]

Sweet Wine in Place of Life: *The Revenge of the Lawn*

28. He retired when he was sixty-five and became a very careful
sweet wine alcoholic. He liked to drink whiskey but they couldn't
afford to keep him in it. He stayed in the house most of the time
and started drinking about ten o'clock, a few hours after his wife
had gone off to work at the grocery store.
29. He would get quietly drunk during the course of the day. He
always kept his wine bottles hidden in a kitchen cabinet and
would drink secretly from them, though he was alone.

He seldom made any bad scenes and the house was always
clean when his wife got home from work. He did though after a
while take on that meticulous manner of walking that alcoholics
have when they are trying very carefully to act as if they aren't
drunk.
30. He used sweet wine in place of life because he didn't have any
more life to use.—Richard Brautigan

Richard Brautigan's literary fortunes have been directly connected to
the discovery of underground youth culture by private business and
later by the American public. One of the few figures to make the tran-
sition from the West Coast "beat" culture of the late 1950s to the "hip"
of the 1960s, Brautigan was a familiar figure in San Francisco in the
late 1950s. His earliest work was poetry, privately printed by small
presses in volumes like *Please Plant This Book* (no date, poems printed
on packages of flower seeds)—given away to friends and acquain-
tances or proffered for whatever gifts or donations might be offered.
Thereafter, Brautigan's work appeared in a series of small poetry and

prose works published by Donald Allen under the Four Seasons Foundation imprint.[28] In 1969, Brautigan's underground reputation was made official as Delacorte Press acquired national rights to *Trout Fishing in America*, *The Pill Versus the Springhill Mining Disaster*, and *In Watermelon Sugar*.[29] The three works were bound in a single facsimile edition, and Brautigan quickly joined Kurt Vonnegut, Herman Hesse, and Rod McKuen as a popular cult literary figure. Since that time, *The Abortion: An Historical Romance 1966* (1970), *Revenge of the Lawn* (1971), and five prose books (most recently, *June 30th, June 30th*) have sold very strongly.[30]

It has become a popular critical pastime to dismiss Richard Brautigan's writing as merely faddish, a more hip, barely weightier version of Rod McKuen's maunderings. Brautigan's poetry does little to discourage this sort of overreaction. It seems uniformly slight; arch, almost unbearably naive, it is consciously unself-conscious (picture a moronic adolescent friend waving hello from a televised bowling show).

As in the case of Leonard Cohen's poetry, the figure behind the poems is taken with the notion that his every single gesture is an act of art. Consider Brautigan's "Albion Breakfast":

> Last night (here) a long pretty girl
> asked me to write a poem about Albion,
> so she could put it in a black folder
> that has albion printed nicely
> in white on the cover.
>
> I said yes. She's at the store now
> getting something for breakfast.
> I'll surprise her with this poem
> when she gets back.[31]

The problem is that there are two Richard Brautigans. One is commercial property and a created cultural hero; the other, a unique writer of narrow but very distinctive talents. In his worst moments, Brautigan the spokesman is offered to us as a creature of the new consciousness, Mr. Gentleness and Soft Drugs himself, the antigeneral commanding the Green Brigade, a guy nonfighting the un-war against mean Mr. Alcohol Suburbia—as in *In Watermelon Sugar*, where the villainous InBOIL (inwardly boiling perhaps?) and his gang of "trash" threaten the pastoral allegory of the sugar works: "InBOIL came out to greet us. His clothes were all wrinkled and dirty and so was he. He looked like a mess and he was drunk. . . . A couple of other guys came out of the shacks and stared at us. They all looked like InBOIL. They had made the same mess out of themselves by being evil and drinking that whiskey made from forgotten things. One of them, a yellow-haired one, sat down on a pile of disgusting objects and just stared at us like he was an animal" (70). This is the Brautigan who lounges on the covers of his records and books (with successively prettier girls accompanying him), who peers from book advertisements and reviews in underground newspapers and popular magazines: commercial, promoted, annoying. The conversion of whatever extant counterculture there has been to a series of products and images has long been a reality in the world of the youth culture market. Like Kurt Vonnegut and Leonard Cohen, the first Brautigan has been a prime commodity on the "revolution and evolution" market. Mercifully, a second, rather talented Brautigan lingers behind that carefully hustled facade. This second Brautigan, the writer, concerns me here.

Brautigan, Cohen, Vonnegut: the appeal of their works stems from the fact that each offers an imaginative recreation of a hostile world. And like Kurt Vonnegut in particular, Brautigan's appeal results from the sensibility he creates and sustains in his writing. "So it goes" of *Slaughterhouse Five* contains a lingering tone, a distinct way of reporting the world, a personal, original *voice* that suggests to us that, in the face of unspeakable horrors like Dresden and Vietnam, one must resign oneself to laughter and fantasy; one must touch, however briefly, another troubled human being. Similarly, another Richard Brautigan appears in *The Revenge of the Lawn*, where the style is less whimsical and the voice less infantile; he is a writer of more controlled prose in these pages and often approaches the surreal, constantly attended by a sense of the primacy of loss and death.

From the start, Richard Brautigan's characters have been children, recluses, various orders of naïfs, or mildly demented innocents—how they can, and indeed must, imaginatively reconceive the world. In *Trout Fishing in America* his "Kool-Aid wino" mimics a peculiar adult game, creating "his own Kool-Aid reality and . . . illuminat[ing] himself by it": "When I was a child I had a friend who became a Kool-Aid wino as a result of a rupture. He was a member of a very large and poor German family. All the older children in the family had to work in the fields during the summer, picking beans for two-and-one-half cents a pound to keep the family going. Everyone worked except my friend who couldn't because he was ruptured. There was no money for an operation. There wasn't even enough money to buy him a truss. So he stayed home in bed and became a Kool-Aid wino" (8).

This sort of imaginative play—an awareness of the necessity and force of mental leaping that can transform a base external world—suffuses Brautigan's fiction. "Attrition" is the first word of his first prose book, *A Confederate General from Big Sur*; although attrition, the gradual death of the substantial world, is inevitable, it must constantly be resisted.[32] Loss, death, and the destruction of dreams wait at every corner but can be held off by the imagination. An exemplary tale from *Trout Fishing in America* makes the point:

> One spring afternoon as a child in the strange town of Portland, I walked down to a different street corner, and saw a row of old houses, huddled together like seals on a rock. Then there was a long field that came sloping down off a hill. The field was covered with green grass and bushes. On top of the hill there was a grove of tall, dark trees. At a distance I saw a waterfall come pouring down off the hill. It was long and white and I could almost feel its cold spray. . . . The next day I would go trout fishing for the first time. I would get up early and eat my breakfast and go.
>
> The next morning I got up early and ate my breakfast. I took a slice of white bread to use for bait. I planned on making doughballs from the soft center of the bread and putting them on my vaudevillean hook.
>
> I left the place and walked down to the different street corner. How beautiful the field looked and the creek that came pouring down in a waterfall off the hill.
>
> But as I got closer to the creek I could see that something was wrong. The creek did not act right. There was a strangeness to it.

There was a thing about its motion that was wrong. Finally I got close enough to see what the trouble was.

The waterfall was just a flight of white wooden stairs leading up to a house in the trees.

I stood there a long time, looking up and looking down, following the stairs with my eyes, having trouble believing.

Then I knocked on my creek and heard the sound of wood.

I ended up being my own trout and eating the slice of bread myself. [5]

Attrition is a constant menace to Brautigan's various imagined worlds, and it moves gradually to the center stage of his works. By *In Watermelon Sugar*, for example, it is a major concern, but even here Brautigan proceeds indirectly through strained allegory, as the forces of death are aligned with InBOIL's whiskey-guzzling bandit gang. They constitute a first of physical violence, impinging on the misted dreamy world of iDEATH:

In Watermelon Sugar the deeds were done and done again as my life is done in watermelon sugar. I'll tell you about it because I am here and you are distant.

Wherever you are, we must do the best we can. It is so far to travel, and we have nothing here to travel, except watermelon sugar. I hope this works out.

I live in a shack near iDEATH. I can see iDEATH out the window. It is beautiful. I can also see it with my eyes closed and touch it. Right now it is cold and turns like something in the hand of a child. I do not know what that thing could be.

There is a delicate balance in iDEATH. It suits us.

The shack is small but pleasing and comfortable as my life and made from pine, watermelon sugar and stones as just about everything here is.

Our lives we have carefully constructed from watermelon sugar and then travelled to the length of our dreams, along roads lined with pines and stones.

I have a bed, a chair, a table and a large chest that I keep my things in. I have a lantern that burns watermelontrout oil at night.

That is something else. I'll tell you about it later. I have a gentle life. [1]

With *The Abortion: An Historical Romance 1966*, Brautigan seems at once more relaxed and more controlled. The allegorical stiffness that flaws *In Watermelon Sugar* is gone, and Brautigan seems more willing to give his talent the rein it needs. His strengths are in no sense analytical or political, and the allegory of old versus new culture pervading *In Watermelon Sugar* has a forced, puppet-show quality. He also shifts to a more serious tone when death, wasting away, and the impermanence of the physical world occupy his attention. This is a sparer book than his others, more metaphorical and more controlled. The poetic quality of his prose tends to be less indulgent and less filled with strained naiveté; he evokes the surreal with a new authority. Consider the "talisman" the narrator notices on the wing of a plane taking Vida and him to Mexico for her abortion: "I looked down on my wing and saw what looked like a coffee stain as if somebody had put a cup of coffee down on the wing. You could see the ring stain of the cup and then a big splashy sound stain to show that the cup had fallen over. . . . I looked down beyond my coffee stain to see that we were flying now above a half-desolate valley that showed the agricultural designs of man in yellow and in green. But the mountains had no trees in them and were barren and sloped like ancient surgical instruments" (136–39).

In his most recent book of stories, *Revenge of the Lawn*, the second Brautigan emerges more clearly than ever. The book contains sixty-two freshly conceived fictions, in which the main theme is how imagination, especially in children, can directly reconceive and recreate the world. Innocence runs like a stream through this book and is almost always deflected off some modern discomfort or horror. The horrors take many forms. They may appear as the tedium and ennui in the life of Mr. Henly, "a simple American man" who "works in an insurance office keeping the dead separated from the living. They were in filing cabinets. Everybody at the office said that he had a great future" ("The Wild Birds of Heaven," 51). They may emerge as pure senselessness, as in "A Short History of Oregon," which closes on an unexplained gothic country scene and the cryptic notation, "I had no reason to believe that there was anything more to life than this" (107). But whatever forms appear, a note of death and loss pervades. Brautigan's humor is, as always, abundant, but the tone here is bittersweet and elegiac—yearning for the ghosts and pasts of Tacoma and Portland childhoods—or nostalgic—evoking memories of dead friends, lost lovers, tainted innocence. Death: old people are rightly terrified of it, as when the young narrator causes discomfort in "The Old Bus":

> I felt terrible to remind them of their lost youth, their passage through slender years in such a cruel and unusual manner. Why were we tossed this way together as if we were nothing but a weird salad served on the seats of a God-damn bus?
> I got off the bus at the next possibility. Everybody was glad to see me go and none of them were more glad than I.
> I stood there and watched after the bus, its strange cargo now secure, growing distant in the journey of time until the bus was gone from sight. [72]

Death: children bumble happily by it; some creatures, like the dog in "The Rug," would welcome it, should it present itself: "He was so senile that death had become a way of life and he was lost from the act of dying" (58). The skull grins more and more, even through the beautiful faces of ladies that grace the covers of his books. Strangely, Brautigan's fiction has increasingly yielded the taste of more tragic cases: Ambrose Bierce and Ernest Hemingway. This is particularly true if one sees in his style, with its lucid, intentionally simplified landscapes dotted by occasional metaphors, a strategy for filtering insanity and chaos out of the world.

Like many recent writers, Brautigan has moved increasingly toward truncated, highly impressionistic forms. Donald Barthelme expresses amazement that anyone can sustain fiction for longer than twenty-five pages. The reputation of an acknowledged prose master, Jorge Luis Borges, rests on three books of short *ficciones*. Like that of his more prestigious fellows, Brautigan's best work denies a fixed form or genre, as if closed forms (short story, novel, sustained discourse) were rigid cultural projections of totalitarian minds. His work has increasingly abandoned the few pivots of realistic fiction evident in, say, *A*

Confederate General from Big Sur. John Clayton's appraisal strikes me as accurate:

> Part of the magic is in the discontinuity itself. If *Trout Fishing in America* is in part a life-style of freedom and rambling, these qualities are present not only in the metaphorical transformations and illogical connections but in the apparent looseness, casualness, easy rambling of the narrator's talk. Brautigan has no interest in character—in introspection or psychological insight, in interpersonal dynamics; no interest in materiality; no interest in time or causality. The book runs profoundly counter to the bourgeois instincts of the novel. It runs counter to the bourgeois world view of practicality, functionality, rationality.[33]

It becomes apparent that the attraction of a Brautigan or a Vonnegut results from the overall tone of the work, from an entire attitude toward the eccentric worlds laid out in their fictions. More than anything else, what unifies Richard Brautigan's work and gives it appeal is his *sensibility*. With *Revenge of the Lawn*, his sensibility suggests that life is brief and bittersweet, happiness is ephemeral, and fiction, therefore, should bear witness to this condition. Furthermore, fiction should go beyond incorporating this condition; it should strive to resist it and attempt to arrest entropy and the forces of attrition. Thus his fictions become brief capsules in which one, two, or three instants of perception, mental metaphorical leaps, can permit beauty to hold the forces of death temporarily at bay. One of his briefer fictions, "Lint," contents itself simply with offering metaphor as a means of transforming lost bits of innocence:

> I'm haunted a little this evening by feelings that have no vocabulary and events that should be explained in dimensions of lint rather than words.
> I've been examining half-scraps of my childhood. They are pieces of distant life that have no form or meaning. They are things that just happened like lint. [121]

It is exactly this tone and sensibility that make Brautigan a unique writer and one of special attractions for younger readers. His particular contribution to the incipient counterculture is to offer instances of evasion, examples of how a harsh world can be held at a distance or transformed. Unlike Marge Piercy, he shows increasingly less interest in politics as a mode of transformation. Indeed, John Clayton's phrase, "the politics of imagination," is apt.[34] Gurney Norman's comment on the "stoned" quality of his perception seems similarly accurate: "I think your phrase 'yield to it' is important, because Brautigan is not a hard-sell kind of writer. It's not his style to overload the senses. He very softly invites you into his fictional world. But once inside, indeed, your heart may well be broken, because within these apparently delicate pieces are people up against the ultimate issues of love, loneliness, and death."[35]

As already suggested, *Revenge of the Lawn* does demonstrate the wry, antic humor that flavors Brautigan's early prose. But these fictions turn less to humor as a means of masking pain than as an alternative to ugliness; they have much to do with nostalgia, memory, and loss. Such humor is particularly true of the three most effective pieces in the collection: "Revenge of the Lawn," "Blackberry Motorist," and "The World War I Los Angeles Airplane."

The title story, the first of the collection, is also the most humorous. "Revenge of the Lawn" is an amusing remembrance of the narrator's grandmother and her second husband Jack. The actions resemble slapstick as Jack is haunted and later revenged by the front lawn and its conspiratorial fellows. However, the comedy draws up short at the close of the fiction, as Brautigan leaves us with a stark, suggestive scene:

> The first time I remember anything in life occurred in my grandmother's front yard. The year was either 1936 or 1937. I remember a man, probably Jack, cutting down the pear tree and soaking it with kerosene.
> It looked strange, even for a first memory of life, to watch a man pour gallons and gallons of kerosene all over a tree lying stretched out thirty feet or so on the ground, and then to set fire to it while the fruit was still green on the branches. [14]

"Blackberry Motorist" seems thoroughly innocent, refreshing, a simple account of adolescent berry-picking. On second glance, it also bears a richly evocative, almost Biercean image of darkness and waste

at the center of things. Climbing under a bridge, the narrator spies
the hulk of an old Model A sedan tangled deep in the vines:

> Sometimes when I got bored with picking blackberries I used to
> look in the deep shadowy dungeon-like places way down in the
> vines. You could see things that you couldn't make out down
> there and shapes that seemed to change like phantoms. . . . It
> took me about two hours to tunnel my way with ripped clothes
> and many bleeding scratches into the front seat of that car with
> my hands on the steering wheel, a foot on the gas pedal, a foot on
> the brake, surrounded by the smell of castle-like upholstery and
> staring from twilight darkness through the windshield up into
> the sunny green shadows. [82].

"The World War I Los Angeles Airplane" is the final piece in *Revenge of the Lawn*. It is also a recollection: the narrator tells a lover
that her father has died. "I tried to think of the best way to tell her,"
the narrator relates, "with the least amount of pain, but you cannot
camouflage death with words. Always at the end of the words somebody is dead" (170). He offers a fictional cenotaph, thirty-three numbered statements about the father: "He has been dead for almost ten
years," he tells us, "and I've done a lot of thinking about what his
death meant to us" (171). The statements provide a skeletal summary
of loss, disappointment, and disillusionment in the forms of overbearing immigrant parents, ruined marriages, automobile accidents, repeated job failures (banks, sheep ranches, bookkeeping, custodial
work). But in spite of his long decline in fortune, the father remains a
decent man, and his last five years are paid out decorously:

> 28. He retired when he was sixty-five and became a very careful
> sweet wine alcoholic. He liked to drink whiskey but they couldn't
> afford to keep him in it. He stayed in the house most of the time
> and started drinking about ten o'clock, a few hours after his wife
> had gone off to work at the grocery store.
> 29. He would get quietly drunk during the course of the day.
> He always kept his wine bottles hidden in a kitchen cabinet and
> would drink secretly from them, though he was alone.
> He very seldom made any bad scenes and the house was always

clean when his wife got home from work. He did though after a while take on that meticulous manner of walking that alcoholics have when they are trying very carefully to act as if they aren't drunk. [174]

Like one of Brautigan's earliest characters, the Kool-Aid wino in *Trout Fishing in America*, the father chooses to gently ignore an unpleasant existence. Although the ruptured boy has his watery, unsweetened Kool-Aid, he has mainly the dreams it releases for him. This is certainly true of the father in his own way, for Brautigan tells us: "30. He used sweet wine in place of life because he didn't have any more life to use" (174). Kool-Aid and sweet wine, each is a way into dreaming, a way of reconceiving human existence. Brautigan's dreams take shape in words, but he knows finally through the boy and through the father, and we know too, that "always at the end of the words somebody is dead" (170).

The Truth Even If It Didn't Happen:
One Flew Over the Cuckoo's Nest

I been silent so long now it's gonna roar out of me like floodwaters and you think the guy telling this is ranting and raving my *God*; you think this is too horrible to have really happened, this is too awful to be the truth! But, please. It's still hard for me to have a clear mind thinking on it. But it's the truth even if it didn't happen.—Ken Kesey

Along with Norman Mailer and Allen Ginsberg, Ken Kesey represents the familiar unsettling artistic type.[36] For all three of these men, the once comforting borders separating the artist's work from his life are thoroughly dissolved. Mailer's prominence as a public figure, as the personal existential eye of the American hurricane, has dominated our attentions and his as well, and his work has surely suffered for it. But Ginsberg and Kesey are younger breeds and knottier figures: each has sought to transcend the category of poet or novelist by making his life a larger poem or fiction. Both Ginsberg and Kesey have become powerful cultural figures over the last decade, exemplars and proponents of a countercultural life-style, modes of being attractive to millions of young Americans. In the case of Kesey, especially, biographical concerns have overshadowed the writing, a fact demonstrated by the mere existence of Tom Wolfe's pop biography, *The Electric Kool-Aid Acid Test.*

Wolfe's fascination with Kesey is natural. The man has lived at the heart of America, and his path has traced a chain of separations and returns. Born in 1935 in Colorado, Kesey migrated westward with his parents, several generations beyond the desperate vitality of the Okies. As Wolfe recalls, the elder Keseys were less unwilling adventurers than "entrepreneurs, who looked to the West Coast as a land of business opportunity."[37]

Kesey attended the University of Oregon and graduated in 1958. During his years in Eugene, he was a minor campus celebrity, an athlete, and an accomplished actor. In that time span, Kesey also came under the influence of the first of a series of prominent writer-teachers, James B. Hall. By 1958, when he entered Stanford University as a writing student, Kesey had completed a decent body of writing: short stories, one-act plays, poetry, and an unpublished novel about college athletics, *End of Autumn.* The years following (1959–60) were a natural watershed for Kesey. He was fully engaged at Stanford, where he studied writing with Wallace Stegner, Frank O'Connor, and Malcolm Cowley; he lived and worked on Perry Lane, a quasi-bohemian Palo Alto artist's colony that provided a yeasty medium for his energies.[38]

Another unpublished novel, *Zoo* (1960), about San Francisco's North Beach, grew from Stanford's writing seminars, but an unlikely extracurricular experience as a medical volunteer was of far greater import to Kesey's life and writing. By this time Kesey had married and fathered a child and, like the classic graduate student, found his debts exceeding his income. Heeding a friend's tip that a government medical experiment paid human guinea pigs at the rate of seventy-five dollars a day, Kesey presented himself at Menlo Park Veterans Hospital, volunteering for experiments with "psychomimetic" drugs. Between spring of 1960 and spring of 1961, fully two years prior to psychologists Timothy Leary and Richard Alpert and their infamous experiments at Harvard, Kesey ingested a wide variety of psychedelic (mind-altering) drugs: LSD-25, psilocybin, mescaline, peyote, morning glory seeds, IT-290 (a meta-amphetamine)—the list swells to a small pharmacopoeia. Kesey extended the experiments beyond the hospital. Although the singular effects of his drug experiences would have been quite powerful enough, Kesey took a job as night attendant on a psychiatric ward at Menlo Park Hospital to supplement his income. As he recounts vividly in *One Flew Over the Cuckoo's Nest* and later in *Kesey's Garage Sale*, he was fascinated and disgusted by life on the ward; and he often raised his perceptions to a higher power with on-the-job doses of peyote.[39] Out of this experience grew his first and most successful novel, *One Flew Over the Cuckoo's Nest* (1962), and an entire life-style, neither of which the American public will soon forget.

In the years following, Ken Kesey's literary achievements have not matched the power of his first published novel. His second novel, *Sometimes a Great Notion* (1964), is longer and more ambitious but for great stretches nearly impenetrable.[40] Stage versions of *One Flew Over the Cuckoo's Nest* have continued for ten years: one starring Kirk Douglas in New York (1963) ran briefly and with little success; a revised version was well received in New York and San Francisco, where it ran very successfully until 1977. Between 1964 and 1973, Kesey published only letters and occasional fragments, which were riddled frequently by a kind of careless obscurantism, as if he were content to address only himself and a coterie of friends who already knew the language. Cynics have suggested that he may well have lost great sections of his mind to heavy drug use, like many young Americans of the time. More accurately, we can say that Kesey became bored with the possibilities of fiction after *Sometimes a Great Notion*; perhaps he came to believe that the novel was an inadequate form for recording his complex human experience. In the early 1970s, he worked mainly in the visual arts (films and drawings) and made recordings, and also co-edited (with Paul Krassner) *The Last Supplement* to the highly popular *Whole Earth Catalogue*.[41]

Deeply into the drug culture by 1964, Kesey invested much of his royalties in a remarkable coast-to-coast bus trip, documented in lurid detail by Wolfe. In the attendant deluge of legal harassments that followed, he was arrested several times for possession of marijuana and related offenses. Finally, in mid-1966, Kesey melodramatically faked a suicide and fled to Mexico, to avoid persecution by the FBI. In October of that year, he "surrendered" to the authorities and soon thereafter served two concurrent three-month jail sentences in San Mateo, California. Many of Kesey's experiences are recounted in *Kesey's Garage Sale*, an uneven ragbag of memoirs, letters, interviews, and articles woven together by his own illustrations. As the title page very modestly suggests, aesthetic considerations are at least matched by a need for money, the book stemming from "The Ancient Search for AND Subsequent Discovery, Application, Loss and Reappearance of $$$."[42]

Following the acid hijinks that very nearly destroyed him as an artist, Kesey retired to a family dairy farm near Pleasant Hill, Oregon —a move "up to the country" undertaken by a whole generation of young agrarian zealots and in many ways the precursor of the current evolution of interest in ecology and self-supporting communities. Unlike many others, Kesey was successful in building a family and a vocation, often from a blend of intense desire and a willing ignorance.

In 1975 he began writing seriously again and published "Abdul and Ebenezer" in *Esquire*, an essay on his early life among the cows, the first substantial writing in many years. Since that time, Kesey has been hard at work with a small circle of friends, and his renovated literary interest has led to the publishing of a "family" little magazine, *Spit in the Ocean (SITO)*. *SITO* has been a vehicle for his most recent fiction, *Seven Prayers by Grandma Whittier*, a markedly biographical sequence of seven dense interior monologues by a loving grandmother among the crazies. It marks a daring shift in Kesey's art and, as John Clark Pratt notes, "Keseyphiles . . . who appreciate him only for *Cuckoo's Nest* will be at least startled if not openly distressed."[43]

Ken Kesey's overriding passion in the last eighteen years, both personally and artistically, has been the qualities and possibilities of human consciousness and particularly the modes of literary rendering of every sort of mental state. This passion has been a constant element, from the fragments of the unpublished *Zoo* to those in the current *Seven Prayers by Grandma Whittier*. Frankly, one can learn as much in the turnings and tracings of his life as in his fiction, for we can read in the scattered lees of his past a cultural history of underground America in the 1960s. But my main interest here is in the particular artistic uses of those experiences in his single major fiction to date, *One Flew Over the Cuckoo's Nest*. More exactly, I wish to consider the novel as one of the few successful literary treatments of the alteration or expansion of human consciousness.

That the novel was warmly greeted seems indisputable. Critic Malcolm Cowley, teaching at Stanford during Kesey's stay, saw the promise in a rough, semifinished manuscript. He advised Kesey in a letter that the book contained "some of the most brilliant scenes I have ever read" and "passion like I've not seen in you young writers before." Thirteen years later, Cowley seemed to have renewed his estimate by including *One Flew Over the Cuckoo's Nest* in his Viking Critical Library series. Cowley's early appraisals strike me as correct: the novel is vividly and powerfully realized and, though Kesey remembers long scenes as coming "more easily to my hand than anything before or since," it was doggedly written and revised.[44]

His account of the novel's origin is an apocryphal variant among modern underground novelists. Much of Malcolm Lowry's *Under the Volcano* issued from the author's alcoholic deliriums; William Burroughs attributes the surreal qualities of *Naked Lunch* to his use of marijuana; his friend Jack Kerouac wrote much of his fiction—*On the Road* and *Dr. Sax*, for example—with the aid of benzedrine. Kesey's version differs only in detail, the drug of his choice being peyote, "because it was after choking down eight of the little cactus plants that I wrote the first three pages."[45] Actually, before his experiences with peyote, Kesey had been fumbling through the book, mainly because of problems with point of view. With the aid of Wallace Stegner at Stanford, he worked toward a resolution. A letter to Kesey's friend Ken Babbs recalls: "I am beginning to agree with Stegner, that it is truely [sic] the most important problem in writing. The book I have been doing on the lane is a third person work, but something was lacking, I was not free to impose my perception and bizarre eye on the god-author who is supposed to be viewing the scene. . . . I am swinging around to an idea that I objected strongly to at first; that the novelist to be at last true and free must be a diarist."[46]

So, at Stegner's suggestion, he shifted to a first-person narrative and, under the unsubtle pressures of peyote, the first three pages emerged as follows:

I think it way time to let somebody in on it, if they can stand it I can. I think I can. You must read about it in those advances those sheets you get every morning which have what they desire you to know. you got that same part that makes them a dime a sheet. Nothing else. I think it way time one of us tried to tell you and let you see what truely happend.

The basic story is this: one of us is dead, and it don't make much difference which one because you won't even remember and you just read it this morning at the bottom of the last page of that sheet you get. One dead. He dead. A man dead. Died in hospital. Died of Pnemonia. Exhasstion. Recent, once long ago, sometime way back, A Colenel in Europe. Oh yes.

That you get in you sheet and go right on with you business, running a tunge around a coffee cup edge. That much you can digest and puke not back up. But I think it way time somebody, me, told you. I have decided I can stand it if you can.

Let's go back to when he came in.

Let's go back to before he came in, the morning, so you can look around. It's all part of the filthy machinery and combine, anyway.

They out there. Black boys in white suits, up before I am to commit sex acts in the hall and get it moped up before I can get up to catch them. They are mopping when I come out of the dorm and they all look up at me, eyes out of a vacuum tube. They stick a mop at me and motion which way they figure me to go today, and I go. Behind me I can hear them humming hate and other death; they always hum it out loud around me, not because they hate me special, but because I don't talk and can't tell about it.

The big ward door is a funnel's bottom. We keep it locked so all the backlog won't come pouring in on us and sufficate us like ants in the bottom of an hour glass. When the big nurse comes through she close it quick behind her bacause they're out their

pincing at her ass. She locks it with a sigh and swings a load of
clanking bottles off her shoulder; she always keep them their in a
fresh laundried pillow case and is inclined and grab one out at
the tiniest provokation and administer to you right where you
stand. For that reason I try to be on the good side of her and let
the mop push me back to the wall as she goes by. "Home at last," I
hear her say as she drags past and tosses her pillowcase into a
corner where it crashes, mixing everything. "What a night, what
a night." She wipes her face and eyes like she dipping her hands
in cold water. "What a relief to get back home," is what she say
near me, because I don't talk.

Then she sight the colored boys. Wheoo, that's something
different! She goes into a croach and advances on them where
they huddled at the end of the corridor. My god, she gonna tear
them black limb from limb! She swole till her back splitting out
the white uniform, she let her arms get long enough to wrap
around them five six times, like hairy tentacles. I hide behind the
mop and think My god, this time they're gonna tear each other
clean apart and leave us alone. But just she starts mashing them
and they start ripping at her belly with mop handles all the
patients come pouring out of the dorms to check on the
hullabaloo and the colored boys fall in line behind the nurse, and
smiling, they herd the patients down to shave. I hide in the mop
closet and listen to the shriek and grind of shaver as it tears the
hide off one then another; I hide there, but after a while one
colored boy just opens out his nostrils like the big black ends of
two funnells and snuffs me right into his belly. There he hold me
wrapped in black guts while two other black bastards in white in
white go at my face with one of the murder combines. I scream
when they touch my temples. I can control the screaming until
they get to the temples and start screwing the electrodes in, then
I always scream and the last thing I hear that morning is the big
nurse whooping a laughing and scuttling up the hall while she
crash patients out of her way with the pillowcase of broken glass
and pills. They hold me down while she jams pillowcase and all
into my mouth and shoves it down with a mophandle.[47]

Self-disordered states of consciousness may be initially helpful for a writer, but some sort of refining and revision is always necessary. In this case, revisions brought the style and structure of the novel into focus. Comparing the early and final manuscripts, we can note several changes. Primarily, the difference is one of telling and showing. Note that Kesey places emphasis in the original on Chief Bromden's *narration* of events, on the oral qualities of his tale. Kesey is more concerned here with capturing the semiliterate qualities of Bromden's speech, with creating an idiolect replete with intentionally awkward and agrammatical constructions, phonetic spellings, and dropped verbs. His speech is clanging and oddly awkward to the ear, but it is also more metaphorical than the final version ("The big ward door is a funnel's bottom" [334]); this is yet another narrative detail placing the narrator squarely between events and the reader. The early manuscript is generally unfocused: it lacks the detail allowing us to see characters, observe action, overhear dialogue.

By contrast, the final manuscript is more sharply focused and more thoroughly dramatized. Emphasis is properly placed on establishing vividly differentiated characters in a concrete situation. Although the black attendants are phantasms in the pervasive fog of Bromden's tale in the early version, revision focuses them on the stage of the narrator's consciousness. They are described more trenchantly, their actions made specific, they are given idiomatic dialogue: "Here's the Chief, the *soo*-pah Chief, fellas. Ol' Chief Broom. . . . Haw, you look at 'im shag it? Big enough to eat apples off my head an' he mine me like a baby" (3). Because the drama of Bromden's consciousness is Kesey's main interest, he reshapes his narrator into a less obviously mediating character. Much dialect is dropped and metaphor diminished in favor of a more fully dramatized narrative. The final focus early in the novel is on Chief Bromden's acutely heightened but passive *state of consciousness*; his narrative is a distorted, detailed film on which a menacing world leaves its grain and shadow. "They're out there" is buried in the second page of Kesey's first draft. This phrase opens the completed novel, establishing the major emphasis on Bromden as pure receiver: mute for twenty years, he can only receive the world and have it impinge upon his consciousness, and his only weapons are scrambling devices. Hallucinations, nightmares, and fantasies

heighten characters and scenes that press on his mind, and his last
retreat is into the fog that descends regularly to seal him deeper in his
own insanity.

The state of Chief Bromden's consciousness is clinically termed
paranoid schizophrenia. He is insane. He can perceive the world only
in fragments that happen to him, fragments that assume menacing cartoon shapes from which unconsciousness is the only refuge. Terry G.
Sherwood accurately reads *One Flew Over the Cuckoo's Nest* as a kind of
comic strip, the aesthetic of which is "that of the caricaturist, the
cartoonist, the folk artist, the allegorist. Characterization and delinea-
tion of incident are inked in bold, simple, exaggerated patterns."[48]
But this is a recurring mode of perception limited to Bromden's early
consciousness. Things are unreal for him, "like a cartoon world,
where the figures are flat and outlined in black, jerking through some
kind of goofy story that might be really funny if it weren't for the
cartoon figures being real guys" (31). Thus the world of the asylum,
rendered through Bromden's schizoid mind, is a black and white
world, one in which people are dehumanized, represent or embody
qualities, or exist as static states. The Chief's hallucinations and nightmares further define the specific threat of each character. Our first
glimpse of Big Nurse, for example, occurs when she enters the ward
to find the black attendants loafing:

> I can see she's clean out of control She's going to tear the black
> bastards limb from limb, she's so furious. She's swelling up, swells
> till her back's splitting out the white uniform and she's let her
> arms section out long enough to wrap around the three of them
> five, six times. . . . So she really lets herself go and her painted
> smile twists, stretches to an open snarl, and she blows up bigger
> and bigger, big as a tractor, so big I can smell the machinery
> inside the way you smell a motor carrying too big a load. I hold
> my breath and figure, My God this time they're gonna do it! This
> time they gonna let the hate build up too high and overloaded
> and they're gonna tear one another to pieces before they realize
> what they're doing!
>
> But just as she starts crooking those sectioned arms around the
> black boys and they go ripping at her underside with the mop

handles, all the patients start coming out of the dorms to check on what's the hullabaloo, and she has to change back before she's caught in the shape of her hideous real self. [4–5]

Bromden's nightmares caricature truth even more. On the evening of the "vegetable" Blastic's death, he has a terrible premonitory vision. As he enters sleep, he has a vision of the entire ward being lowered into a deep, hellish chamber: "a whole wall slides up, reveals a huge room of endless machines stretching clear out of sight, swarming with sweating, shirtless men running up and down catwalks, faces blank and dreamy in firelight thrown from a hundred blast furnaces. . . . Huge brass tubes disappear upward in the dark. Wires run to transformers out of sight. Grease and cinders catch on everything, straining the couplings and motors and dynamos red and coal black" (83–84). Out of this inferno, a gigantic worker swings a hook toward Blastic, the man's face:

> so handsome and brutal and waxy like a mask, wanting nothing. I've seen a million faces like it.
>
> He goes to the bed and with one hand grabs the old Vegetable Blastic by the heel and lifts him straight up like Blastic don't weigh more'n a few pounds; with the other hand the worker drives the hook through the tendon back of the heel, and the old guy's hanging there upside down, his moldy face blown up big, scared, the eyes scummed with mute fear. He keeps flapping both arms and the free leg till his pajama top falls around his head. . . . The worker takes the scapel and slices up the front of Old Blastic with a clean swing and the old man stops thrashing around. I expect to be sick, but there's no blood or innards falling out like I was looking to see—just a shower of rust and ashes, and now and again a piece of wire or glass. [85]

Chief Bromden's aberrations are a form of peculiarly heightened truth. He *does* foresee Blastic's death accurately. His paranoid vision of Big Nurse, recurringly depicted as a mechanical, domineering figure entombed in ice or glass, is likewise accurate in its symbolism. She oversees this world from a raised glass booth, a doubly threatening figure who is obviously in control and thoroughly shut off from the human consequences of her power: "What she dreams of there in the center of those wires is a world of precision efficiency and tidiness like a pocket watch with a glass back" (27).

When the knowledge of what goes on around him is too intense for his consciousness to transfigure by distortion, the fog descends. The device is effective under Kesey's hand and works in several ways. Because Bromden is both paranoid and passive, he imagines that Big Nurse regularly turns on the fog machine to hide her machinations. And it is here that she is caught up in the web of institutions impinging upon and blinding Bromden's consciousness. The army, Department of Interior, his Anglo mother, Big Nurse—all are aspects of "The Combine," "a huge organization that aims to adjust the Outside as well as she has the Inside" (26). The fog is a paranoid metaphor, a concrete figure of fear and secrecy, of the threat that "they" are systematically deceiving you. But the fog is also a grotesque comfort representing unconsciousness for Bromden. As he recalls his army days, "You had a choice: you could either strain and look at things that appeared in front of you in the fog, painful as it might be, or you could relax and lose yourself" (125).

Briefly then, this is the state of the Chief's consciousness before Randall McMurphy arrives on the ward. Bromden, who was born a half-blooded Columbian Indian of immense stature, has been worn down by life. Evidently, he has been deaf and dumb for the last twenty years, consigned to sweep the floors of this microcosmic ward and unable to perceive people humanly or to leave his imprint on the world. But inmate McMurphy's appearance alters much of this.

Bromden's first impression of Randall McMurphy is that of a vital, protean figure. He strikes the diminished narrator as being like his lost, disgraced father, a full-blooded Columbian Indian chief. But, more than a surrogate father, McMurphy is a cartooned, holy con man: "The way he talks, his wink, his loud talk, his swagger all remind me of a car salesman or a stock auctioneer—or one of those pitchmen you see on a sideshow stage, out there in front of his flapping banners, standing there is a striped shirt with yellow buttons, drawing the faces off the sawdust like a magnet" (12–13). Like the best American con men, McMurphy finally sells himself. He does not offer a product but evokes and embodies a way of life to ponder and desire.

His effect on the patients is electric. They are collectively dominated by Big Nurse and her staff, but he very quickly sets off human responses in them; his impulse runs precisely counter to Big Nurse's. He runs toward vitality, spontaneity, friendship, and warmth—the accumulated detritus that makes a human life and a person. By the midpoint of *One Flew Over the Cuckoo's Nest*, he has propelled his fellow patients into a major act of resistance. Randall Patrick McMurphy (*R*evolutions *P*er *M*inute) is exuberant; through his efforts near the end of a group therapy session, the fog parts for Bromden, and he recognizes that his fellows are also fogged in: "Maybe Billy's hid himself in the fog too. Maybe all the guys finally and forever crowded back into the fog" (128). Billy Bibbit and Colonel Matterson, Old Pete and his own wrecked alcoholic father, their "faces blow past in the fog like confetti" (131).

Bromden has a sudden, insightful hallucination of "that big red hand of McMurphy's . . . reaching out into the fog and dropping down and dragging the men up by their hands, dragging them blinking into the open. First one, then another, then the next. Right on down the line of Acutes, dragging them out of the fog till there they stand, all twenty of them, raising not just for watching TV, but against the Big Nurse, against her trying to send McMurphy to Disturbed, against the way she's talked and acted and beat them down for years" (134). In those hands and faces, Bromden sees a fused image of all that has systematically driven him into the fog. For the first time in twenty years, he can act. With Bromden casting the deciding vote, the ward rebels and turns on the television to watch the World Series (one of the stranger acts of rebellion for our time). They see, appropriately, a cartoon: "A picture swirls into the screen of a parrot out on the field singing razor blade songs" (137). Enraged, Big Nurse turns the set off, "and we're sitting there line-up in front of that blanked-out TV set, watching the gray screen just like we could see the baseball game clear as day, and she's ranting and screaming behind us" (138). As the first part of the novel ends, the group is self-conscious for the first time, watching a small blank screen out of which each man has been dragged into the world, white and shining, by Randall McMurphy.

As their first handshake telegraphs to Bromden, McMurphy's function is to feed his consciousness, to aid in psychic recovery: "My hand commenced to feel peculiar and went to swelling up out there on my stick of an arm, like he was transmitting his own blood into it. It rang with blood and power" (24). Paramount among his influences on Bromden is the recovery of memory. In *One Flew Over the Cuckoo's Nest*, Kesey suggests repeatedly that memory, knowing one's individual and collective pasts, is a key to any sense of present or future. For patients like Ruckly, "memory whispers somewhere in that jumbled machinery" (16). Significantly, the recovery of memory for Bromden is a process of reimagining the sources of his own pain and paralysis. McMurphy triggers him and, as the novel progresses, Bromden experiences vital parts of his past in flashbacks. Flashbacks are a familiar technique for the first-person novelist. They permit him to offer the reader a past for his characters, a sequence of motivation. But in addition, each time Bromden experiences these dreams of key moments in his past, he retrieves a part of himself from the fog and becomes more conscious. His flashbacks are poignant and often painful. They involve reenacting the oppression and destruction of his father by his mother, the wasting of his tribe by various U.S. government agencies, and his own paralysis and emasculation.

Very gradually, as Bromden reclaims his past, his sense of himself and of things beyond himself evolves. He perceives differently. For one thing, he is conscious of himself in relation to a larger world: "I realized I still had my eyes shut. . . . I was scared to look outside. Now I had to open them. I looked out the window and saw for the first time how the hospital was out in the country" (153). For another, he sees a more humanized existence around him. People are no longer cartoons: "For the first time in years I was seeing people with none of that black outline they used to have" (154). In fact, Bromden has almost ceased to see the world as a stream of aberrated and unrelated phenomena. He can form associations; in this context, the purely associative cognition demonstrated by Matterson suddenly becomes sensible: " 'Mexico is . . . the walnut'. . . . I want to yell out to him Yes, I see: Mexico *is* like the walnut; it's brown and hard and you feel it with your eye and it *feels* like the walnut! You're making sense, old man, a sense of your own. You're not crazy the way they think. Yes, I see" (129). He can relate events in the present with his own past. At the ward windows, for instance, Bromden sees that "the stars up close to the moon were pale; they got brighter and braver the farther they got out of the circle of light ruled by the giant moon. It called to mind how I noticed the exact same thing when I was off on a hunt with Papa" (155).

So Randall McMurphy serves as an energy source and an inspiration to Bromden and his fellows. They become less lethargic and more interested in their own sexuality and physical existence. But mainly, they become able and willing to struggle for life. Through McMurphy's prodding and coaxing, they venture into the world outside, the occasion being a deep-sea fishing expedition. By this time, McMurphy has become aware of the paradox of his existence in the asylum. The inmates are voluntary admissions but lack the psychic abilities to sign themselves out; he is *committed* but can be released only on Big Nurse's judgment. What follows is a sequence establishing McMurphy as a kind of holy con man who "sells himself" by giving up his life for the patients on the ward. For if Kesey's protagonist is the true American hero, the confidence man, he is also an avatar, a Christ —the healer, literally a fisher of men. A pattern of Christ-like suffering is carefully wrought in the background of *One Flew Over the Cuckoo's Nest*. Early in his tenure on the ward, while examining the electroshock table, McMurphy is told: "You are strapped to a table, shaped, ironically, like a cross, with a crown of electric thorns" (67). Later, as he is about to receive his first shock treatment on that very table, he regards the graphite conductant: "'Anointest my head with conductant. Do I get a crown of thorns? . . . They put those things like headphones, crown of silver thorns over the graphite at his temples'" (270).

The fishing scene is an extended figure of Christ and his disciples, an instance of McMurphy as fisher of men. Here we see that McMurphy is Kesey's laughing Christ—profane, spontaneous, and above all loving, leading men not to immortality but back into this physical world. After a series of trials, the men are safely at sea on an old fishing craft. They repeatedly request McMurphy's aid in handling the boat and landing fish, but he laughingly refuses them. Imperiled by hostile men, seas, weather, and fish, they survive and flourish as a community. By the end of the trip, Bromden notices that the men have been energized by the trip, but the robust McMurphy looks "beat and worn out" (243). His men are psychically cannibalizing him. Slightly later, the Chief notes "the windshield reflected an expression that was allowed only because he figured it'd be too dark for anybody in the car to see, dreadfully tired and strained and *frantic*, like there wasn't enough time left for something he had to do" (245). And finally, part 4 of the novel concludes as directly as possible: "his relaxed, good-natured voice doled out his life for us to live, a rollicking past full of kid fun and drinking buddies and loving women and barroom battles over meager honors—for all of us to dream ourselves into" (245).

Near the end of the novel, after McMurphy has been quieted by repeated electroshocks and is about to be lobotomized, his purpose has become even clearer to Chief Bromden. By this time the Chief is fully conscious, able to articulate the peculiar insistence that his friend feels to defy Big Nurse and go the full route of consciousness reduction by lobotomy:

> We couldn't stop him because we were the ones making him do it. It wasn't the nurse that was forcing him, it was our need that was making him push himself slowly up from sitting, his big hands driving down on the leather chair arms, pushing him up, rising and standing like one of those moving-picture zombies, obeying orders beamed at him from forty masters. It was us that had been making him go on for weeks, keeping him standing long after his feet and legs had given out, weeks of making him wink and grin and laugh and go on with his act long after his humor had been parched dry between two electrodes. [305]

At this point, Bromden and the entire ward have changed radically. Following McMurphy's attack on Big Nurse and his subsequent lobotomy, many of the Acutes have signed themselves out or otherwise taken control of their lives. Big Nurse's domain is toppled, and Randall McMurphy's mind must be dimmed, extracted as fealty. Bromden performs a final action, the mercy-killing of the burned-out husk that remains of McMurphy. He quickly assimilates his master through a series of ritual actions. Like McMurphy, he becomes protean, a water force that breaks through walls of glass or ice. In a repetition of McMurphy's earlier actions, Bromden seizes the control panel and hurls it through the window—one of the many ritual cleansings and baptisms in the novel: "The glass splashed out in the moon, like a bright cold water baptizing the sleeping earth" (310). Bromden escapes northward, now a con man and storyteller himself, but we recognize at the novel's conclusion that the only certitude is Bromden's new consciousness. What lies ahead is at best tentative, but it is certain that Bromden has come through whole and sound:

> I might go to Canada eventually, but I think I'll stop along the Columbia on the way. I'd like to check around Portland and Hood River and The Dalles to see if there's any of the guy I used to know back in the village who haven't drunk themselves goofy. I'd like to see what they've been doing since the government tried to buy their right to be Indians. I've even heard that some of the tribe have took to building their old ramshackle wood scaffolding all over that big million-dollar hydroelectric dam, and are spearing salmon in the spillway. I'd give something to see that. Mostly, I'd just like to look over the country around the gorge again, just to bring some of it clear in my mind again.
>
> I been away a long time. [311]

Five

The Romance of Terror and Jerzy Kosinski

There is a moving scene near the opening of Joseph Novak's *No Third Path* in which the sociologist-narrator and Zina F., lovers vacationing near Sevastopol, must part. Their weeks began as an idyll, but in the steely Russian world of the 1950s, the sweet lover's kiss is a terrible intimacy. Distraught, Zina strikes a line from the poet Blok: "The frightening world! It's too small for the heart," and attacks him. They seem to have shared much, yet she feels invaded by his presence, his attitude, his analytic tack:

> And yet you are a little egoist, wrapped up in yourself! Your own nose, which you consider too long, your naturalistic remembrances of childhood and the war, your hatred of village life and primitive conditions, your "exercise of intimacy"—*image*. . . . Where will your "philosophy of the distorted image" lead you in the long run? To a manner of life resembling that of medieval monks or the present-day degenerates in the capitalist countries, to intellectual degradation and a spiritual void, to cultivating your wounded ego and the nightmares of your memories to the degree of causing pain to others and the "right" of disregarding others? . . . In the name of what humanism are you fighting against the Soviet humanism, you *the man on the fence*, the worst phenomenon of the coexistence of two social systems?[1]

The man on the fence is a heraldic figure, a shared emblem of the paradoxical life and work of Jerzy Kosinski. He suggests a being posed between two equally tempting but impossible alternatives, an aloneness, a detachment, a separation of the solitary self from any form of social life.

This static image seems passive until we realize that fences do not merely entrap Kosinski's protagonists; they present an antithesis in the constant dialectic underlying his world and offer a fixed perch against which his painted birds push off into flights of freedom and self-definition. The man on the fence seems quiescent, but he is charged with the potential for action. He contains multiple identities: both the stranded, helpless child-self (Jonathan Whalen of *The Devil Tree*) and the aggressive, conquering agent (Tarden and Levanter of *Cockpit* and *Blind Date*). He is metamorphic and self-realizing; indeed, his very watchfulness—his voyeurism, as Zina F. painfully discovers —cloaks action, and thus she rightfully feels violated by his watching eye. As Kosinski's "agent," Novak thus possesses Zina and listens silently to her plaint, taking her again in memory as he records the scene. The unnamed boy of *The Painted Bird* watches almost to his death, straining to read his name in the signatures of fate and society as they press down on him. Like Tarden and Levanter, he grows up to war with the world, projecting his being outward in constant martial action, a spy and a confidence man whose operations brand the lives around him.

Joseph Novak is, of course, the pen name under which Jerzy Kosinski published his first American books, the sociological studies of Russian collective man: *The Future is Ours, Comrade* (1960) and *No Third Path* (1962).[2] The man on the fence is the guiding principle of his fiction, for both the man and the novelist evolve very much from that contradictory and ambivalent sitter. This cryptic figure provides the clue to Kosinski, the romancer of modern terrors. I wish to examine the psychic, philosophical, political, and artistic aspects of his work, for they are often fused into a complex multistranded vision.

The writer's life, his psychic evolution, and his social and philosophic opinions are most certainly of literary interest. Our lexical playfields have lost many of their boundaries since World War II. The roles of writers have become more tangled, more puzzling, and take us increasingly beyond the citadel of the text. The pattern and detail of Kosinski's life—indeed lives—for example, constitute an enviable work of the imagination. Born in Lodz, Poland, of Russian bourgeois parents who had fled the Revolution, Kosinski was separated from them at age six and wandered through the nightmare war years much as the boy of *The Painted Bird*. Adrift from 1939 to 1945, he was stricken mute by the trauma of his experiences, like the boy, and finally recovered speech three years after the end of the war, in 1948. Fiction is a scar, and Kosinski's seven novels forget and remember the violence of his early years incessantly, shedding and holding those dark experiences in an adopted English language.

An excellent postwar student, he attended the University of Lodz, gaining master's degrees in history (1953) and political science (1955). He owes a great debt to his early training, particularly in his exposure to Hegel and the process of the dialectic. A good young communist, Jerzy Kosinski learned his lessons well, particularly Hegel's reading of history and human consciousness as a struggle between Master and Slave, in which each recognizes the Other, and as a process by which each is humanized and yearns to possess the Desire of that Other. The endless dialectic of Master and Slave energizes his fiction, illuminates the grappling embraces of lover and soldier, and is an ironic, unforgettable legacy of a culture left behind.

Kosinski's early research on nineteenth-century Russian life prefigures his later disillusionment with socialism. And in his first publication of 1954, before he is alienated from the State, he nonetheless writes that "the true apotheosis of man, the fight of humanity and the respect for human rights . . . was born in the places of execution, in the prison cells, in the dungeons and casements, in the torture chambers, and amidst the ice of Siberia."[3] We can see his later works in these seeds: a hatred of collective forms, an insistence on the regenerative powers of the single self, the ironic process by which society and the self deny and paradoxically create each other.

During the 1950s, Kosinski also developed two continuing interests. Skiing and photography have been both avocations and professions, and the author early became proficient in each discipline. As a young man, he worked near Lodz during holidays as a ski instructor and he still lives part of the year in European skiing regions. His expertise in photography came a bit later, but he obtained considerable knowledge of chemical processing and printing techniques. By the mid-1950s, he was a prized contributor to central and eastern European exhibitions. Fascinations in one life have often emerged as recurrent fictional metaphors, polar images of the ritual drive to break from the earth in utter freedom and the complementary need to freeze life and stop the entropic slide toward death.

Following research at Lomonosov University in Moscow (1957), out of which focal experience the Novak books developed, Kosinski fled the iron curtain. The epilogue to *No Third Path* records his crisis with a characteristic cold eye:

> His subconscious came into conflict with his conscious self. He began to view his surroundings with a suspicious eye—and perceive suspicion in the eyes of friends. He attempted intensively to "separate himself from his own ego" and to work out a method of becoming a "detached observer of himself." . . . As a consequence he ceased to live in harmony with himself. . . . At some moment during process he understood that, instead of becoming a good citizen and a creative member of the socialist community, he became a bad—because playing unconvincingly—actor who, moreover, was incapable of believing, even for a little while, in the authenticity and relevance of his role. [357]

Attuned to the ways of socialist bureaucracy, he wove an elaborate hoax of documents and interviews, creating a fictitious research project in the United States that was purportedly sponsored by the Chase Manhattan Bank. The Kafkaesque experience was a deadly game and is chillingly reimagined in the opening passages of *Cockpit*. Shortly after the Russian cosmonaut Yuri Gagarin was shot into orbit in December 1957, Kosinski arrived in New York. He recalls himself as a lonely immigrant—a penniless, jobless, friendless, languageless political refugee. Working first as a scab laborer and truck driver (the scenes are again transformed in *Cockpit*), he quickly won a Ford Foundation Fellowship (1958) to continue his scholarly work. Shortly thereafter came the dream of success. The Novak books were hail-fellowed in cold war America, excerpted in *Reader's Digest* and *Saturday Evening Post*. *The Painted Bird*, which was initially rejected by several publishers, appeared with superb notices in 1965. Since that time have come a National Book Award (1969) and similar acknowledgements, as well as six subsequent novels: *Steps* (1968), *Being There* (1971), *The Devil Tree* (1973), *Cockpit* (1975), *Blind Date* (1977), and *Passion Play* (1979).[4] Along with those widely praised and translated works have come prestigious appointments—to the faculties of Wesleyan, Yale, and Princeton, to the boards of several United Nations committees, to the presidency of P.E.N. American Center—and the rewards and distractions of fame, relative wealth, and influence.

This entire scenario would seem at first glance a vignette from the pen of a contemporary Horatio Alger (with a touch of MGM here and there), but, viewed more closely, that life has often been tinged with the infernal. Only by an accident of misplaced baggage, for example, did he miss a 1969 party at the home of Roman Polanski and avoid the grisly fates of Sharon Tate, Jay Sebring, Abigail Folger, Susan Parent, and his schoolboy friend from Poland, Voytek Frykowski. Indeed, one strongly suspects that Kosinski is a historical witness to many brutalizing experiences of contemporary life and that his fiction is the imaginative testimony of a not undamaged survivor. The biographical core of his writing suggests that he has suffered—or more uncomfortably, participated in—the terrors of modern life. His work has a dimension, a realistic resonance that cannot be dispelled by critics who insist we read it as pure fiction of the imagination, any more than the face of memory can vanish under the hand of conscious desire.

The biographical records of Kosinski's life are sufficiently well-preserved that his creation of a historical persona and a public myth was probably a very conscious and successful auctorial undertaking. Although one recent interviewer labels his project "rare" and another solemnly tells us that the author "does not like to talk about his past," such views are not in any sense accurate.[5] Kosinski has been incessantly available, with his "biography" often offered to audiences, and his public persona is fully documented and more thoroughly crafted than that of *any* serious literary figure of recent years. I am interested not merely in a tooth for literary gossip but in the uses of psychobiography, for Kosinski's creation of a historical self by the dissimulation of materials selected from his past mirrors the process of self-creation and invokes the same themes and preoccupations undertaken by the protagonists of his fictions. To create one's life in the minds of others, make history, write a novel, act as a protagonist in a fiction, these are shapes of the same figure. Thus Kosinski describes Lenin, Trotsky, Stalin, and Mao as "great fiction writers of the twentieth century" and draws together the threads of biography, fiction, and history as realizing acts of the existential self.[6]

A compelling performer, Kosinski makes frequent lecture appearances in the United States and abroad—I have seen him captivate audiences in California, New York, and France. He has been a regular, telegenic guest on nighttime "talk shows" since 1968. Though he speaks of himself as an extraordinarily private person, he has made himself available to popular media and serious literary scholars for interviews and probing inquiries. He has spoken and written often of his life: not only the nightmares of World War II but also the darker moments of his first American years; his brief first marriage to the widow of steel magnate Ernest Weir, a vibrant woman almost twenty years his senior; his friendships with the powerful and wealthy of the planet; his teaching of the collegiate "dead souls" in the late 1960s and early 1970s. He has not only doled out "factual material" but has tirelessly supplied and encouraged the recording of instant apocrypha. One story, told with relish to an appreciative "Tonight Show" audience, appears in three other recorded sources. Recalling late night problems with his new language in the Novak books, he sought anonymous aid: "Thus I would call a New York telephone operator and I would describe my predicament. I would tell her that I was a foreigner, that I was writing a scholarly work in a recently adopted tongue, and that since some of the passages of this work described situations not commonly known in the United States, I wanted to make certain that they would be understood, and that she understood them. . . . This was the initial stage of my writing of the book: I looked for an ideal reader. I dialed 'o.'"[7]

Current Biography recounts another titillating anecdote in "the legend of Kosinski": "The first day of his seminar on 'Death and the American Imgaination' at Yale stands out. No more than twenty students were expected—or wanted—but 2,000 showed up. Kosinski whittled the crowd down to twelve by explaining, in the course of his introductory lecture, that the seminar would confront the experience of death as directly as possible, through visits to hospitals, morgues and mortuaries. 'Regrettably,' he solemnly added, 'in order for the experience to be complete, it will be necessary for one member of the seminar to die.' There was a mad, mass rush for the exits."[8]

An examination of biographical materials yields almost forty sources of such information, much of it provided by Kosinski himself. They include his motto (from Descartes, appropriately: *Larvatus prodeo* ["I go forth disguised"]), self-described character assets and weaknesses, his favorite literary characters, authors, color (brown), and bird (owl).[9] Several factors are at work here. First, the infant Boswell naps in every scholar's breast; in venal moments, each of us would be explicator, confessor, friend, Bunny Wilson, and Malcolm Cowley to the next Johnson, Fitzgerald, or Faulkner. Too, the fact is unmistakable; culture is a commodity in the modern capitalist society, and books are sold like pills, cars, and every imaginable consumer item. As Truman Capote sighs in moments of televised honesty, "a boy *does* have to hustle his book."

But beyond the corporate interests of a willing talent, an active agent, and a good publicity department, Kosinski has carefully erected a public self and has made use of that disguise in much the same way as, say, Norman Mailer. Since the whetting of his existential appetite shortly after 1945, Mailer has also fashioned a public self and a series of guises and has worn them into the world like loose skins. One is struck by the symbiotic relationship between Mailer as performer on existential errands (as mayoral candidate for the fifty-first state, as intellectual leader of the antiwar movement, as a baron of the fifth estate in the war for truth, and also as fool: public intoxicant, inmate of Bellevue, common criminal, boorish wrecker of the best parties) and Mailer as writer. Mailer has *acted* in his public guises—the persona of the Irish cop he cherishes even now or the later "Aquarius." Then, after creating a field of tension or outrageously exploring dramatic situations, he has returned to his desk to report his findings. This has been particularly true of his "nonfiction fictions" like *Armies of the Night*. But the relationship has been reflexive, often more than the author would have cared. His Celtic dummies take on an unbidden life of their own, and his writing often serves as a self-manifesto, a bullying voice insisting that he again tread the existential path between literary text and public performance. Thus Mailer and his "white negro" have each had a hand in the creation of the other.

Kosinski, no less personally and artistically compelled, has similarly created a public persona, "a new wall" from "the stones" of his past.[10] This public Kosinski is finally a literal pseudolife, a mythic carapace first hardened in the pseudonymous Joseph Novak. Thus the man on the fence, cherishing his silence and distance, is also an invasive agent. Like the mute Pynchon and the garrulous Castaneda (recall Don Juan's advice to "erase personal history"), he insists that a past, a history, is a trap. Like Castaneda, he straightway proceeds to create a past for us, to link the patterns of his life and his art, and to offer us initially the delights of the voyeur, for the fictive circlings of Kosinski's painted birds are very much his own. We are made uneasy by the simultaneous closeness and distance of the man and his writing, especially with the development of the morally ambiguous operators of *Cockpit* and *Blind Date*. Tarden and Levanter are murderers, punishing a faithless world like a wayward lover, much as Tarden bombards Veronika with hidden radar, "invisible missiles assaulting her body and brain" (236). Irving Howe describes the author of *Steps* as "an astronomer locating dead stars" but continues more uneasily when he traces the line between life and fiction: "There is a trouble making out the relation of the writer and the narrative . . . between what the 'I' registers and how Kosinski would have us respond."[11]

From *The Future Is Ours, Comrade* to *Passion Play*, a distinct vision is unfolded. We are disquieted by the author's insistence on the absolute value of the liberated consciousness coupled with his full awareness of the darker energies of that self. Writing in a time in which the pursuit of the individual has been romanticized as the blossoming of a human flower, Kosinski ritually holds our gaze on the breaking open of lives, revealing a terrible, painful beauty. The sharpness of his visions and the cinematic detachment of their rendering are unnerving, particularly in the sadomasochistic fantasies of torture and revenge from *Steps* onward. There is also a nagging sense—as in the possessed fictions of Yukio Mishima, William Burroughs, and Jean Genet—that we are not merely experiencing a work of literary art but are caught up in a larger, more personal drama, witnesses to the exercise and exorcism of very private demons.

Thus his willingness, his insistence on anchoring his work in personal details of postmodern disaster gives his work a resonance we cannot deny. "It was and it was not": Levanter summarizes the paradox of fiction, the truth of lies. Kosinski's work is a fictional construct, a textual triumph of the imagination, but it is also a literature of moral witness that contains testimonies by those who survive the burning and return, scarred and purified, to insist that we recognize and remember our own darkest potentials.

In America, this literature of moral witness survives most richly in the Afro-American fugitive slave narratives, songs, autobiographies, poetry, and fictions, the written legacy of coffle and yoke. Jerzy Kosinski's work, however, has European roots in the genocide committed by the Nazis and (for Kosinski) by any collective group larger than one, and in other attempted exterminations of Jews, gypsies, and many faces of the scapegoat Other. Kosinski's novels circle back constantly over that dark land and share the memories of others who escaped the Holocaust to create art from their waking nightmares: Tadeusz Borowski, Elie Wiesel, Wolfgang Borchert, Heinrich Böll, André Schwarz-Bart. Like the morally hysterical narrator of Borowski's *This Way to the Gas, Ladies and Gentlemen*, a man who processes countrymen to the gas chambers and crematoria and is at once victim and executioner, Kosinski's fiction underscores the terrible price of survival and relentlessly poses the question: "Are we good people?"[12]

The responses to this central question, couched in the scalding experiences of Kosinski's heroes, are complex and indirect, and their sum finally offers little comfort to readers and critics who require a literature nourished by liberal humanism, who ask of fiction a sense of man's essential decency or his ability, through reason, to improve his moral and social lot by acts of personal or collective integrity. The author works a much more radical, consciously antihumanist, modernist, and postmodernist vein of literature; he is one of a chorus of Artaud's "voices from the flames," writers whose visions of modern social life are essentially pessimistic and devolutionary in experience. He possesses the sight of dark prophets: the Europeans de Sade,

Artaud, Céline, and Genet; the Japanese Mishima; the American William Burroughs; all of whom would view what human civilization has become as "one disaster created to solve another."[13]

Indeed, most alarming in Kosinski's version of the Holocaust is the fact that good and evil are inextricably coiled. The work confronts us regularly with paradoxical scenes, charged with a brutal tension and ambivalence, in which the torturer and the tortured require, even *demand*, each other for human definition. The medieval world of the peasant village is a demonic fairy tale set in an ignorant, superstitious land, but the modern ruthless Nazi counterpart scarcely offers the painted bird any more comfort or humanity.

If the worlds envisioned by Hieronymus Bosch and Leni Reifenstahl are finally synonymously evil and inhospitable, the postwar collective states of Russia and Poland pose the same threat to survival of the self. As one of those interviewed cheerfully notes for us in the first Novak book, "don't forget that our country by-passed the period of genuinely bourgeois culture. . . . In a way, we moved directly from Russian feudalism into Russian socialism . . . and from the feudal to the socialist commune" (32–33). A second informant, linking the past and modern worlds, drives home the point:

> They still raise Czarist generations, though born in the time of socialism. These generations consist of people attached to the soil and to their own customs. For them, the world begins and ends with their own community. It is a world still equipped with ideas of divine power, and magic, and old customs and morals. . . . But at the same time it is a world under socialist authority, with a Communist Party, a socialist radio whose antenna juts high over the hamlet. . . . Common law and socialist law tolerate each other and pass joint verdicts. These are places where supplies of products for daily life, received twice a year, are distributed in the most feudal manner under the sun. But the lords are not only the priest and his suite, but also the Party secretary with his suite, and the commander of the local militia with his suite. . . . You could say that in all these lost, dispersed centers of humanity, Czarist Russia has remained inside a socialist frame. There has also remained the nebulous, enigmatic Russo-Asiatic soul of

these people caught between the orthodox Church and the police post. [148–50]

Here too Kosinski's writing is a witness to modern terror, to the impersonal dystopia of the Stalinist State. Though his vision is at times Kafka's paralytic nightmare of the modern self lost in an endless corridor, he shares a willingness to offer, however grudgingly, testimony to the threat of collective socialism and his escape from it, along with Alexander Solzhenitsyn, Yuri Daniel, Andre Sinyavski. Here again he is the man on the fence. Although they escape and witness the same psychic archipelago, Kosinski does not share Solzhenitsyn's "old fashioned" humanism: his belief in a supreme being, his stubborn faith in man's potential goodness, his fondness for Russian (as opposed to Soviet) culture, his enthusiasms (albeit waning) for democratic capitalism since he settled in America in 1975. Although Kosinski's early success was very much connected with his value as a political prize—the quick winning of a Ford Foundation grant with little proficiency in English and the publication and acclaim of the Novak books were no accidents, coming at the height of the cold war—he has refused to advertise the virtues of his adopted society. As president of American P.E.N. (Poets, Essayists, and Novelists), he emphasized his distrust for all collective causes in a 1973 inaugural address:

> If, in spite of my mistrust and fear of collectivity, I have accepted the presidency of American P.E.N. for the coming year, it is because the aims of P.E.N. match my own: freedom to write, to oppose any form of censorship, to promote the exchange of ideas and the meeting of intellectuals of diverse origins and views, to foster translation of works of merit, always aware that in today's atomized societies, literature—above all—triggers imagination, mobilizes emotions, and ultimately arms its reader to face his very own self and cope with the unknown in his very own existence.[14]

Literature is a defensive weapon because it "triggers," "mobilizes," "ultimately arms" the reader against those forces around him that threaten to diminish or obliterate his consciousness. Thus Kosinski extends the enemy line: the peasant village and the modern socialist commune, nazism, communism, Christianity, capitalism, the aggression of war, and the benign malignance of apparent peace. They are all coconspirators against the self, and he has most recently indicted the mass culture of the United States as "no less indoctrinated by the Polyanna values of popular culture than are, let's say, their Russian counterparts by the decades of dehumanizing ideology of omnipotence of the Party."[15] His most explicitly critical observations on technological America are reserved for sections of *Being There* and *The Devil Tree*, but he has been most vehement and most repelled when we were at the height of social protest against involvement in Asia. He writes then in strained rhetoric about contemporary young Americans as manipulated and unthinking "dead souls," who are as dangerous as his medieval peasants, priests, or Russian bureaucrats, the social herd at its worst:

> The entrapments of collectivism are overwhelming: TV and radio, which permeate our privacy and destroy the aloneness out of which it becomes possible to build a self; drugs which smash the mirror of personal identity; the virtual disappearance of creative self-employment and of professions and opportunities which ask for the use of the self; the terrifying featurelessness of the modern physical environment; the debilitation of the arts; the great gray educational machine; the devaluation and disparaging of the imagination; the "own things" of the eroded self.[16]

In a more recent novel, *Blind Date*, he skips the stone westward from Polish village to suburban Los Angeles, a morphic dreamland in which "strings of invisible sprinklers sent up fine sprays that turned sunlight into rainbows." The narrator Levanter and author Kosinski recall the life and death of their mutual friend Woytek. The memories are painful, an attempt to preserve in text and release from memory the slaughter of Woytek Frykowski at the hands of the Manson Family in 1969. The Cancerous gangs are the "Crabs of Sunset . . . out of balance with the world . . . the missing link between man and robot." Unknowingly speaking of his killers shortly before his murder, Woytek pronounces Kosinski's ultimate unicellular American horror:

"Had California been an independent country, it would have long ago gone fascist—Left or Right, it wouldn't matter. For the Right, Crabs of Sunset would become the fuel for the final draconic measures that would be used to get rid of them; for the Left, they would be the ignition for the revolution that would swallow them later. As it is, the state of California has become the embodiment of their mental state: neither Right nor Left, with no shape or direction, a giant amoeba. Here, everything stretches—nature and people." [174–75]

I suggest that Kosinski's vision is blackly Hegelian, which is fitting given his communist education as a social scientist, and that he constantly struggles in his work between the impinging shapes of society and the dream of the self. Though his writing is firmly rooted in the detail of his own psychic past and is an act of self-definition related to the fiction making of biography and history, it contains its own antithesis, a countermovement. "It was and it was not": projections of the author's will, his works break loose from him. His imaginings have their own life as textual constructs and seek to lure him away, like a bird from its cage.

On the most basic level, Kosinski's fictions are dominated by actors and protagonists, and one may see a strong emphasis on the liberating qualities of the independent self. The nature of his protagonists follows a path of evolution. The boy of *The Painted Bird* discovers the necessity of the self as the only fixed point in a chaotic world; Jonathan Whalen of *The Devil Tree* is a retrograde image of the dangers of the damaged self; and Tarden and Levanter are protean selves, modern confidence men who enact the fullest, ambivalent potential of the free consciousness. The painted bird's most powerful dreams are those of metamorphosis, of release in wind and fire from the earth of the peasant village, of being Levanter—as his name implies, a shifting wind blowing through the lives of others, the realized spirit of change itself.

Against this core of central character, there is an equal pressure exerted by the author wary of containing his fiction's development, of holding Proteus to the rack. The jail of the social body is transferred to the text itself; and there is a desire in seven novels to deny plot and to resist the gradual accumulation of episodes into "lines" intersecting in any causal pattern. At their strongest, his protagonists manifest a fierce desire to create themselves through their selective memory of the past, yet memory hardens like dead skin and restricts the play of the self in the present. Thus the narrators shape themselves like contemporary sculpture, asserting their negative spaces, the uncreated pockets of their existences, and their potentiality. They wrench their memories free from time and place, describing Robbe-Grillet's ideal "double movement of creation and destruction." Kosinski's imagination is visual, almost cinematic, and Robbe-Grillet is an allied spirit:

> It is not rare, as a matter of fact, in these modern novels, to encounter a description that starts from nothing; it does not afford, first of all, a general view, it seems to derive from a tiny fragment without importance—what most resembles a *point*— starting from which it invents lines, planes, an architecture; and such description particularly seems to be inventing its objects when it suddenly contradicts, repeats, corrects itself, bifurcates, etc. Yet we begin to glimpse something, and we suppose that this something will now become clearer. But the lines of the drawing accumulate, grow heavier, cancel one another out, shift, so that the image is jeopardized as it is created. A few paragraphs more and, when the description comes to an end, we realize that it has left nothing behind it: it has instituted a double movement of creation and destruction which, moreover, we also find in the book on all levels and in particular in its total structure.[17]

The protagonists of the works following *The Painted Bird* seek full consciousness, and they embody a world of anxiety in the record of that quest. Recorded language is a confession, a self-indictment, and thus, as Robbe-Grillet declares, they seek an enormous and dialectic present, "which constantly invents itself, as though in the course of the very writing, which repeats, doubles, modifies, denies itself, without ever accumulating in order to constitute a past—hence a 'story,' a 'history' in the traditional sense of the word" (156). Kosinski uses interviews often to establish his poetics of disruption. He writes of *Steps* that it "has no plot in the Aristotelian sense. In Aristotle's terms for the revelation of the action, the end fulfills the beginning and the middle determines the end. But the aim of *Steps* precludes such an ordering of time."[18] Speaking later of *Blind Date*, he continues in a more moral strain: "That's why in fiction I stress an incident, as opposed, let's say, to a popular culture, which stresses a plot. Plot is an artificially imposed notion of preordained 'destiny' that usually dismisses the importance of life's each moment. To bypass that moment, to dilute it in the gray everydayness, is to waste the most precious ingredient of living: the awareness of being alive."[19] Thus in the Novak books, he has sought in the cinematic montage and the literary episode his ideal means of preserving those spurts of experience; he has drawn on the paradox of film, in which the perception of movement issues from the steady progression of fixed frames.

Céline, Burroughs, Kosinski: they are pseudonymous brothers. The works of all three are haunted by the fear of a totalitarian state and a loathing for mass existence. Detroit, Freeland, Poland—these landscapes are hallucinated in paranoia, their citizens repelled by and finally drawn toward the character and nature of *power*. The protagonists are burnished or consumed by it, perhaps even fascist in its self-defense, and they go forth into labyrinths of conspiracy and hatred, as if there were evil inherent in the physical world itself. They are abnormally armored counteragents sealed against the hidden and open corrosives of modern life. But they also share the postmodern anxiety of contemporary fictional characters, sensing that the forms giving them birth will, at every turn, bring on their extermination. Thus the corpus of their work is self-mutilated, as if to dispel a monster with a totem of its own menace. The putrifying corpse of modern life in Céline's *Journey to the End of Night* and *Death on the Installment Plan* is rent repeatedly by ellipsis, "my damned three dots." Burroughs's resonant image of the junkie nodding in "the grey fibrous wooden flesh of terminal addiction" is finally a metaphor for the imprisonment of modern consciousness. The piercing of flesh by the needle, the body by the phallus, the rending of the text, and finally the shattering of the physical cosmos itself, these are transformations. Burroughs's endless cranky experiments with cut-ups, fold-ins, and breakings of sentence, image, and word are his attempts at fiction making as an antidote to corporeal addiction, as an attempt to dismember the text to release the will, turn off the machines, and undo the entire phsycial world. In Kosinski's work we see the same paradox, the narrative yearn for omnipotence and release from the body (depicted in the feats of his protagonists) contradicted by the impermanence of the surrounding world, the skin of the text, the body of meaning.

Working against this structural spirit of disjunction is Kosinski's spare presence in language. Although Irving Howe speaks for many in praising him as a stylist, "a master . . . [who] has few equals among American novelists born to the language," even comparing him with the senior emigres Conrad and Nabokov, we should note more precisely the severe nature of that syle.[20] At its best, it is a ruthlessly disciplined, cold, detached instrument.

Style is a reflex of consciousness, and Kosinski's spartan vision forbids certain indulgences of language. He in no sense shares the comic linguistic exuberance shown by Barth or Barthelme, nor does he fashion the baroque interiors of a John Hawkes or a William Gass. Unlike his countryman Conrad, whose hothouse English grew like a thicket, Kosinski prunes and espaliers his language. The vocabulary is limited, the syntax simplified, the conceits as direct as possible. His strength is in conveying disquieting scenes with absolute lucidity, and his language, to that end, must be transparent as water. "It is the opposite, for instance, of what Nabokov does," he notes; and continues, "his language is made visible . . . like a veil or a transparent curtain with a beautiful design. . . . My aim, though, is to remove the veil. . . . For me the novelist is not a displayer of stylistic bonfires; he is primarily conveying a vision."[21] Thus the language is direct: with its icy mechanical body of nightmares and obsessions, it inscribes many variations on a few deep patterns and, precariously allied with the prose instruments of pornography, becomes a sublime vehicle for freezing, fixing, entombing—and thus preserving—human experience.

Again, Kosinski exhibits a "double movement" of the man on the fence. That man is a body, a protagonist, a text-active and quiescent, declaimed and undone, omnipotent and imprisoned—and is propelled through the buried literary geographies of myth and archetype. Traditional mythic and archetypal forms possess implied unity, growth, order, and evolution, but in this novelist's hands they become plastic molds that are handled ironically, parodied, inverted, and shaped to his own very different ends. *The Painted Bird* is a demonic fairy tale, Jung's child voyager passing from the dark unconscious to the light of self-realization. But Kosinski twists the conventions of folklore and mocks the traditional reconciling assertions of psychic wholeness and social continuity in the conclusion. *Steps* is a contemporary, inverted *Metamorphoses*. *Being There* is a cosmogenic parable, a biblical allegory of the seven days of creation that is used to indict the perversion of the American Eden by mass media and popular consciousness. *The Devil Tree* issues from our dream of success: Horace Whalen, steel magnate, is Horatio Alger, and his son Jonathan is an inversion of that myth, a devolution who takes down empire, father, and self. Tarden is an international agent who has transcended national causes and *Cockpit* is his deceptive contemporary confession. Levanter, his most recent romantic hero, is a wind and a merchant and a mythic place—an archetype of metamorphosis itself—a picaresque god who trades in the essences most tempting to us: youth, beauty, passion, power. *Passion Play* is a failed medieval drama.

Thus we move from Novak to Levanter, and the progression is clear, for Zina F.'s "man on the fence" has already begun the process of shape-shifting to avoid the necessity of impossible choice. If there are two equally entrapping modes beckoning to the man on the fence, there are soon two men, two voices.

I speak of Kosinski as writing within a tradition of antihumanists, aligning him particularly with his pseudonymous brothers Louis-Ferdinand Céline and William Burroughs. All share chthonic visions as well as the kindred paradoxical gestures of pseudonymy: to write under a pen name is at once a disclosure and a hiding. Destouches became Céline only in 1932, with publication of *Journey to the End of Night*. Burroughs assumed the mask of William Lee with *Junkie* in 1953. In this sense, the "Novak" who stands behind the two sociological works of the 1960s is an ambivalent fictive persona, a paradoxical figure at once revealed and cloaked. Though the name "Novak" vanishes with those two works, the voice and consciousness do not. There is a rough art in the early efforts, and Kosinski's imaginative powers seem to undercut the "truths" offered by social science. Noting the deft shuffling of materials in *The Future Is Ours, Comrade,* one reviewer suggests it "should not be read uncritically."[22] Kosinski/ Novak is surrounded by anxious Kremlinologists. They introduce each work with a tentative air and are clearly anxious with their covey, as newsman Richard C. Hottelet's self-assurances betray: "In a book like this . . . everything depends on a reporter's credentials. Joseph Novak . . . is certainly a serious person, and there is nothing to suggest that he has not honestly recorded and summarized the remarkable material on everyday life and opinions in the USSR."[23]

European pedagogue that he is, Novak concludes stiffly that "the fundamental intellectual goal of this study is to reflect through individual human experiences a picture of mass processes, to discover the mechanism of the formation of the distinctive *social yardsticks* by which the people of the USSR measure themselves and others, their criteria of social evaluation."[24] Clinical and dispassionate, he is analytical and conclusive as well, and if his efforts are made suspect by the closet novelist, he has lasting revenge.

The Novak books mark a watershed for Kosinski's novels and are the precursors of his fiction. They offer a detailed picture of the menace of the collective state—the psychic backdrop of the novels— and reveal early techniques of composite, episodic narration. They are a fund of sketched anecdotes and metaphors (the painted bird, the skier), and characters like Gavrila in *The Painted Bird* and Romarkin in *Blind Date* have a first ghostly life in these pages. But Novak does not vanish. He is not fully eclipsed by the novelist Kosinski and occasionally surfaces as a distracting, explanatory presence in the novels. His voice is instructive—drawing conclusions, underscoring "meaning," and undercutting the cinematic power of carefully established scenes. Kosinski's best art is one of understatement, of withheld judgment, of emotion implied in action or image, but Novak is a noisy guest. As Gerald Weales rightly notes, his "greatest weakness as a novelist is his desire to explain things—his symbols, the significance of his scenes, the political and philosophical implications of the action. One corner of his mind seems never to have gotten on that plane that let him escape from a society in which ritual self-examination is the norm."[25] His denials to the contrary ("I never talk about a book"), the author is an incessant, artful critic of his own work. Novak steals only a corner in the novels but takes the center light in orchestrated interviews and the long explanatory essays, *The Art of the Self* and *Notes of the Author*.[26]

Thus our "little egoist," the man on the fence, is an extraordinarily rich figure. We find, while examining his nature, that Kosinski's unique mode of contemporary American fiction is that of philosophical examination. The shapes and energies of his work are generated by a constant dialectical inquiry, an examination of the magnetic tensions between related sets of oppositions: fate and the independent will, collective society and the elected self, history and the renewing existential moment, the tomb of the body and the energetic play of mind, the illusion of myth and the reality of the broken pattern, the permanence of art and the evanescence of experience. His protagonists and their distorted images are created in the posing of these oppositions. Their beings are force fields describing the contradiction, ambivalence, irony, and temporary reconciliation between the polar forces that shape modern life and Jerzy Kosinski's seven romances of modern terror. I consider his first work, *The Painted Bird*, as his essential artistic statement and the ensuing works, from *Steps* to *Passion Play*, as progressive variations.

It is nowhere more evident that America lacks a fully formed "literature of frightfulness," as Wylie Sypher calls it, than the fact that the most successful fiction based on the experience of World War II is written by a naturalized citizen in an adopted tongue. *The Painted Bird* is rivaled only by Kurt Vonnegut, Jr.'s *Slaughterhouse Five* and Joseph Heller's *Catch-22*, but it is denied their healing black laughter and is thus more disturbing. It is also significant that Kosinski's hero is no Frederick Henry, disillusioned by life and war. Nor can Kosinski accept man's way with a weary Vonnegut "so it goes." His protagonist is a six-year-old, who is almost destroyed and then finally nourished by the iron age barbarism around him. This is a novel of dark education, and Kosinski's linking of war and moral development takes a page from Swift. The painted bird's experience teaches him that human life is a struggle, that "man carries in himself his own private war . . . which is his alone to administer" (186–87). What is perhaps most disturbing about *The Painted*

Bird and what certainly resonates in the American consciousness shaped by Viet Nam is the fact that the clear cut borders of morality in war, heroism and villainy, good and evil, and the rightful triumph of one group, ideology, or flag over another are dissolved. Kosinski suggests that any social order holds the seed of nazism and that the experience of evil may not be banal but is certainly normal. As Arthur Miller recognized in a letter to the author, "To me the Nazi experience is the key one of this century. They merely carried to the final extreme what otherwise lies within so-called normal social existence and normal man. You have made the normality of it all apparent, and this is a very important and very difficult thing to have done."[27]

Swiftean, too, is the control with which the retrospective narrator distances and shifts our perspectives on his terrible past. American audiences have problems with the plausibility of his six years in hell, and a class studying *The Painted Bird* always yields one or two innocents who refuse to believe that "a boy that young could survive experiences like that." Certainly the force of the book depends on the coldness of recollection and a peculiar doubleness of vision, so that the boy is alternately fully naive and prematurely aged. Near the end of his adventures, for example, he faces the moment of reconciliation with parents, a bright time in the world of romance and fairy tale. But he is a young Gulliver, at once formed and an innocent: "There was no way out of the situation, no matter how one looked at it," he wearily concludes. "Parents, as Gavrila often told me, had a right to their children. I was not yet grown up: I was only twelve. . . . It was their duty to take me away" (203).

Although the novel is evidently rooted in the war and the author's corrosive experiences, it is quickly clear that Kosinski's purpose is not to characterize the impact of the war on a culture or generation. Indeed, he blurs or omits places and dates—particularly in revising an editorially corrupted first edition—purging the limiting modern details of the boy's experiences.[28] Literal geography has no place here; the boy is unnamed and similarly nationality and locale are unspecified. His purpose is to refine the pattern of action in Polish villages between the years 1939 and 1945; indeed, once cited, the war is not mentioned until a quarter of the way through the novel. It then intrudes by accident, as the boy stumbles across "a military bunker with massive reinforced-concrete walls" on one of his archetypal wanderings into the forests (52). The first paperback edition of *The Painted Bird* was wrapped in a scene from Hieronymus Bosch's "Garden of Earthly Delights," an apt choice because Kosinski's tale is suffused with the elemental stink and color of the medieval village. The boy's experience is timeless, at once ancient and contemporary:

> *The villages in that region had been neglected for centuries. Inaccessible and distant from any urban centers, they were in the most backward parts of Eastern Europe. There were no schools or hospitals, few paved roads or bridges, no electricity. People lived in small settlements in the manner of their great-grandfathers. Villages feuded over rights to rivers, woods, and lakes. The only law was the traditional right of the stronger and wealthier over the weaker and poorer. Divided between the Roman Catholic Church and Orthodox faiths, the people were united only by their extreme superstition and the innumerable diseases plaguing men and animals alike.* [2]

But the world is not strictly the medieval terrain of Bosch and Grimm's tales either; it exists beyond time in a rich alchemical cauldron of fire, water, earth, and air, of warring demons and contrary spirits, of real and symbolic humors and ethers—all the elements that have nourished folk literature and literary transformations from Ovid, through Grimm, to the present day. Kosinski gives us a valuable clue when he suggests that his purpose here was "to peel the gloss off the world," to "strip reality down to material terms," to return us to "the black roots of the fairy tale."[29] So doing, he turns our attentions to the mode of the fairy tale as the fundamental vision for his romance of modern terror.

Certainly myth and fairy tale have been a major source of material and an inspiration for American writers of the 1960s and 1970s. John Barth has been mythically refreshed since his exhausted start. An apprentice work at Johns Hopkins, *Shirt of Nessus*, was an attempt to graft Greek myth and a lurid Dorchester waterman's rumor of murder and incest (as yet unpublished); and *Giles Goat-Boy, Chimera*, and *Lost in the Fun House* rely on highly sophisticated mythic compressions and recyclings. Peter Beagles's *The Last Unicorn* is deceptive in its charm and deft execution and grows from a body of medieval and renaissance legend, much of it captured in ballads and folktales. As *The Crying of Lot 49* opens, Thomas Pynchon's Oedipa Maas thinks of herself as a female quester, like Rapunzel in her dark tower about to let down her hair. Both Donald Barthelme and Robert Coover have used such materials extensively in their recent work: Barthelme's *Snow White* and *The Dead Father* are comic improvisations on the archetypes of the unconscious and our desperate lover's struggles with them. "The Babysitter" and "The Elevator" suggest Coover's fascination with the taboos held in contemporary popular fantasies and myths; however, "The Door" and "The Gingerbread House," also from *Pricksongs and Descants*, deal with the rich threats shown in ancient fairy tales. *The Public Burning*, his fantastic meditation on a twentieth-century witch hunt, brings these two streams together.

From the Novak books on, Kosinski's work shows a strong acquaintance with fairy tales, märchen, fables, bestiaries, and allied folk-rooted forms. Central and eastern European peasant stories pepper the "scientific" studies and recur, transmuted, in the fiction. *The Painted Bird* is a repository for Grimm's tales and may be read as a transformation of the implied treasures of "The Golden Bird," as a relentless definition of the irony and contradiction in each line of that simple cask.[30] The Russian Krylov's fables recur in several works but are of special significance in *Being There*. Kosinski's mature protagonist, the modern spy and confidence man of *Cockpit* and *Blind Date*, is born in the ancient trickster figures and the wraiths of smoke and water found in all cultures: in Coyote and Loki (American Indian), Prometheus and Proteus (Greek), and the many tribal shape-shifters from greater Europe. If anything, judging from a clumsy attack by several Polish journalists who believed their country defamed in his work, Jerzy Kosinski has been *too* cognizant of folk life as a literary source. Writing in "Fun and Games of the Polish People During the Second World War," Hanna Wydzga and Jan Zaborowski accuse him of varied crimes against Poland, concluding that the folk matrix of *The Painted Bird* is stolen whole from "a 400-page work of Professor Biegeleisen, published in 1929 under the title *The Healing Practices of the Polish Peasantry*."[31]

Kosinski cites his special interest in the fairy tale in a long self-glossing essay, *Notes of the Author*. Using Carl Jung's "The Psychology of the Child Archetype" as a touchstone and working with other uncited Jungian materials, he sees in the genre an allegory of the evolution of the conscious mind and the modern self. With Jung and the later Bruno Bettelheim, Kosinski traces a movement from the chaos of the preconscious, through the dark unconscious, toward Jung's "light of higher consciousness." Like the two psychologists, the author uses the tale to articulate the growth of spirit and the full independent self, but his interest soon shifts to more philosophic matters, as does the eye of the book, to explore the double-stranded nature of man's struggle between the forces of fate and free will.[32] As Kosinski indicates, "Jung regards the child motif as representative of the preconscious state of human consciousness, the childhood of the mental processes, of which traces still remain in us all; this he terms the 'Collective Unconscious.' . . . The choosing of the child as conductor of the search can be especially enlightening since only in the growth of the child can we observe an approximation of the mind's evolutionary processes."[33]

We notice several things immediately when entering this world. First, as in all fairy tales, the ritualized, formulaic element is dominant, and the boy's situation is a classic separation archetype: "*A six-year-old boy from a large city in Eastern Europe was sent by his parents, like thousands of other children, to the shelter of a distant village*" (1). His foster parents soon die, and he is left alone to wander from village to village, at his own mindless peril. He is Hansel in the deep wood, the young Prince of "The Golden Bird" lost in the forest, Red Riding Hood before the wolf, and he is by himself. Alone. The iamb thumps in the word like a heartbeat or a deathknell. He is literally and metaphorically totally alone. It is his task to become *aware* of this fact because his life depends upon it. To Kosinski, to be alone is man's precarious and basic state on earth. The unnamed boy moves from nameless village to village, passed from one set of callused hands to another, like a bucket or a hen. There are many masters and mistresses on his six-year quest: Old Marta, Olga the Wise One, Jealous the Miller, Lekh the Birdman, farmers, carpenters, blacksmiths, eleven in all. He learns, finally and ironically, the powers of his own mastery from the collective heroes of the Red Army, Gavrila and Mitka. His owners have in common the traits of ignorance, superstition, and cruelty and are linked literally and figuratively with the animal world in the child's clear eye. Kosinski's working title for the novel was *The Jungle Book*, aptly sardonic.[34] Beasts speak and instruct us in the world of the fairy tale; in the inversion of *The Painted Bird*, characters speak to and mate with their creatures. They imitate the lower world of animals and are just barely "mammals of a different breed," as suggested in the bitter opening epigraph from Mayakovsky.

Kosinski's purpose is truly to lay bare the "dark roots" of his material, the skull looming in a pretty face. The boy's journey is shown at once to be through a poisoned kingdom, a psychic underworld in which dark spirits reign. The world at war is diseased, as we see in first descriptions: *"The soil was poor and climate severe. The rivers largely emptied of fish, frequently flooded the pastures and fields, turning them into swamps. Vast marshlands and bogs cut into the region, while dense forests traditionally sheltered bands of rebels and outlaws"* (2).

Jung and Bettelheim emphasize that Grimm's forest is an ambivalent archetype, a dappled glade by day and a dense, foreboding wood at night, with accompanying suggestions of life and death. It is a place to pass a test, solve a riddle, slay a witch or wolf or fox and release a buried life, by which anxious and crucial experiences Hansel, Red Riding Hood, and the Lost Prince are self-realized and transformed to states of greater awareness. In the process, they traverse the worlds of light and darkness in a full cycle and restore the family of man.

But Kosinski's forest offers only the ironic kind of life-restoring powers and is a grim shelter for the boy's many flights from village civilization. His memories confirm unconscious fears of having fallen into the underworld: "From the black earth that the sun never reached stuck out the trunks of trees cut down long ago. These stumps were now cripples unable to clothe their stunted mutilated bodies. They stood single and alone. Hunched and squat, they lacked the force to reach up toward light and air. . . . Large knotholes low on their boles were like dead eyes staring eternally with unseen pupils. . . . They would never be torn or tossed by the winds, but would rot slowly, the broken victims of the dampness and decay of the forest floor" (126). The landscape writhes with furtive life in the boy's anoetic consciousness, and he hears the living dead unleashed by a storm, as "the forest werewolves would slowly creep forth. Translucent demons would come flying on their beating wings from steaming swamps, and stray graveyard ghouls would collide with a clatter of bones" (50).

Even the most verdant spring mornings, spent mushroom gathering with his village families, reveal an ominous undercurrent: "Bending down to pick the mushrooms, people called to each other in cheerful voices each time they found a rich cluster. . . . Sometimes the sinister cry of an owl was heard, but no one could see it in its deep, hidden hole in some tree trunk. A reddish fox might scurry away into the dense bushes after a feast of partridge eggs. Vipers would crawl nervously, hissing to give themselves courage. A fat hare would bound into the bushes with huge leaps" (88).

He wanders through this real and psychic wasteland in a single large arc, removed from his family and ironically restored to that nest at the end of the Holocaust. He flies, too, in tighter circles, searching repeatedly for his lost parents but is caught in the same pattern of use, entrapment, near-death, reversal, and escape. The bird wheels in flight and the earth turns beneath him, but the pattern continues. He is threatened with extermination as long as he seeks a collective place or yearns to resurrect the lost family in a social body, for his quest does not take place in the life-giving realm of the traditional fairy tale but in an inverted, hellish garden, the dark forest of Wotan in a time of war. He is a lost prince, and his quest to restore the realm of family—at first literally in surrogate parents and later in the abstract authority of ideology—is traditionally a movement toward health and enlightenment. In Kosinski's vision, however, such movement is devolutionary, an unwitting attempt to merge oneself with the powers of evil, death, and self-destruction.

A miasmic haze hangs over the events of this novel, a smoky residue of black magic: the immolation of Jews in crematoria, gypsies on the railway tracks, Old Marta in her hut, groves of trees torched to drive the plague away—constant reminders of the evil trapped in the land, unreleased even in death. Kosinski's forest is the dark eye of a swollen, diseased landscape. The earth is at war with itself, possessed by evil. It becomes a suppurating bitch, its shitty flesh at last breaking open in terrible elemental colors of blood, bile, phlegm, and pus. Would life come from this?

In polar opposition to this diseased world is the innocence and pure receptivity of the lost boy. He is a tabula rasa as the novel opens, and once again Kosinski's intention to invert the shape and substance of the classic fairy tale is clear. *"The Painted Bird,"* he suggests, "can be considered as a fairy tale *experienced* by the child rather than *told* to him."[35] As in the unconscious repository of the dream, the boy will experience the world initially as a sequence of "numina," as Jung termed them, powerful concentrations of unconscious energy. Such figures are ordinarily ambivalent, but in Kosinski's version they are overwhelmingly negative—ogres, witches, and demons associated with entrapment, entombment, and suffocation. The boy's innocence, his presence as "a living incarnation of a motif," taps the deepest springs of the Bosch-like figures he encounters. As the author notes, "He is a child who can lay bare their experiences in terrible and wonderful ways; he provokes their passions."[36] Marta, Lekh, Ludmilla, and Garbos have their deepest beings drawn out by him, and a sick energy radiates in them like the core of a boil. They are creatures associated with the lower quadrants of earth and water, which are linked throughout Kosinski's work to the constraining boundaries of fate, history, and collective existence. This is a land of sores and pestilence, the living social corpse itself, and these lower numina seek, paradoxically, to quench and to be cauterized by the bright flame of the boy's innocence. In their attempts to destroy him, the earth and water create him, sending him on an endless metaphoric cycle toward the upper airs, and, by an inverted alchemy, the airs in turn are made more palpably base.

Wotan's forest is Europe at war. In the crucible of that experience, the boy comes to identify himself, negatively at first, with the upper quadrants of fire and air. His totem is the phoenix, the mythical bird of fire, and in Kosinski's work, his sectors connote free will and the allied unfettered lives of the solitary imagination in a continuous present. If the boy is the Lost Prince, Hansel, Jack, Red Riding Hood, Snow White, the numina are the murdering older brothers, the witch, the giant, the wolf, the gnomes. Victim and torturer, the innocent and the staining world: they make an endless black marriage in Kosinski's fiction and each threatens and requires the other for life.

His first contact is with the crone Marta, an archetypal witch figure, and from this point on, the ironies are painful and constant. A six-year-old sobs for his mother and father, certain that he will meet them "in the next ravine" (11). Though he yearns for and tries to recreate the child self protected by the family, his surrogates can offer neither comfort nor affirmation. His guides are always loners, creatures of the forest periphery barely tolerated by the villagers. Like Jealous the Miller or Olga the Healer, they hold the mob at bay only with special talents or threat of evil magic, their practical values superseding their loathsomeness. Marta is representative, warning him at once that "if they ever caught me they would drown me like a mangy kitten or kill me with an ax" (11). Like Bosch's panels, the boy's young mind is panoramic, undifferentiated, a surface in which the child and the natural background are merged. His first playmate is a squirrel and they share a consciousness. He recalls innocently how it visited "me daily, sitting on my shoulder, kissing my ears, neck, and cheeks, teasing my hair with its light touch" (5). The idyllic tie is soon broken, and the boy's first lesson in this new life is from his human peers. He watches horrified as they trap his little friend, douse him with kerosene and set him afire: "With a squeal that stopped my heart it leapt up as if to escape from the fire. The flames covered it; only the bushy tail still wagged for a second. The small smoking body rolled on the ground and was soon still. The boys looked on, laughing and prodding the tiny body with a stick" (6). Thus he meets his element— the terrible, purging power of the flame.

Very quickly, another lesson comes from his animal mates. He similarly endows Marta's pet snake with mind, noting, "It seemed quite indifferent to the world; I never knew if it noticed me." He watches enthralled as it holes up and sheds its skin, emerging "thinner and younger" (4). He is amazed and moved by this first image of metamorphosis and of physical regeneration, and listens rapt as Marta instructs that "the human soul discards the body in a similar manner and flies up to God's feet" (5). Thus the fiery death of the first friend and the paradoxical regeneration of a second are fused in his mind and become immediately linked with a third image in animal experience, flight.

The Painted Bird is filled with birds; they are Kosinski's totems, and we watch flights of ravens, hawks, sparrows, eagles, pigeons, cuckoos —each with a special character—cross the screen of the boy's mind.

He recalls a living fable, a true parliament of fowls in Marta's back yard, an inverted, prefiguring image of the painted bird itself:

> Strange things happened in the farmyard. Yellow and black chicks hatched out of the eggs, resembling little live eggs on spindly legs. Once a lonely pigeon joined the flock. He was clearly unwelcome. When he made a landing in a flurry of wings and dust amidst the chickens, they scurried away, frightened. When he began to court them, cooing gutturally as he approached them with a mincing step, they stood aloof and looked at him with disdain. . . . One day, when the pigeon was trying as usual to consort with the hens and chicks, a small black shape broke away from the clouds. The hens ran screaming toward the barn and the chicken coop. The black ball fell like a stone on the flock. Only the pigeon had no place to hide. Before he even had time to spread his wings, a powerful bird with a sharp hooked beak pinned him to the ground and struck at him. The pigeon's feathers were speckled with blood. [4]

This is a powerful archetypal pattern in the fiction. It introduces the central picture of the bird, which is continued in a complex of details, images, metaphors, and references of flight, all suggesting the growth and power of the liberated self. The image has a negative, warning aspect as well because it depicts the dangers of lone action and physical separation from the flock.

The precedent for this scene is established in the first appearance of the painted bird, during an episode in *No Third Path* recalled by Vavara:

> I remembered once how a group of us kids caught a sparrow in a trap. He struggled with all his might—tiny heart thumping desperately—but I held on tight. We then painted him purple and I must admit he actually looked much better—more proud and unusual. After the paint had dried we let him go to rejoin his flock. We thought he would be admired for his beautiful and unusual coloring, become a model to all the gray sparrows in the vicinity, and they would make him their king. He rose high and was quickly surrounded by his companions. For a few moments,

their chirping grew much louder and then—a small object began plummeting earthward. We ran to the place where it fell. In a mud puddle lay our purple sparrow dead—his blood mingling with the paint. . . . The water was rapidly turning a brownish-red. [107]

That sparrow is metamorphosed in *The Painted Bird*; though it becomes powerful in flight, the import is the same. The boy's education in the metaphor of flight continues as Lekh the Birdman, possessed by the earthy Ludmilla, plans to invoke her spirit and body. He orders a sacrifice, an act of sympathetic magic which will at once confess her domination and invoke her presence. In the boy's mind, the episode contributes to his sense of the deceptive beauty of the painted bird and its flight and the dangers of headlong, undisguised, unmediated soaring:

> After prolonged scrutiny, he would choose the strongest bird, tie it to his wrist, and prepare the stinking paints of different colors which he mixed together. When the colors satisfied him, Lekh would turn the bird over and paint its wings, head, and breast in rainbow hues until it became more dappled and vivid than a bouquet of wildflowers. . . . Lekh would give me the sign to release the prisoner. It would soar, happy and free, a spot of rainbow against the background of clouds, and then plunge into the waiting brown flock. . . . The painted bird circled from one end of the flock to the other, vainly trying to convince its kin that it was one of them. But, dazzled by its own brilliant colors, they flew around it unconvinced. The painted bird would be forced farther and farther away as it zealously tried to enter the ranks of the flock. We saw soon afterwards how one bird after another would peel off in a fierce attack. Shortly the many-hued shape lost its place in the sky and dropped to the ground. . . . Blood seeped through the colored wings diluting the paint and soiling Lekh's hands. [44]

A triad: pigeon, sparrow, strongest bird. They are real and metaphoric fliers, and their colors and bright actions set them off from the flock, make them individual. Yet each ends in a heap of bloody feathers, a warning about the dangers of explicit flight, the penetration of alien social places, the nakedness of the unconscious self in motion. The second triad of episodes, linking the fates of pigeon, snake, and squirrel, is also a *fabular exemplum* that is burned into the boy's mind. These first lessons are brutal, complex, and unforgettable. In Marta's yard a bird emerges from a shell, a snake from its skin: the acts share a language of release into a larger scheme of rebirth by metamorphosis and speak of the naturalness of changing shape, of futurity. But the squirrel violently and unwillingly leaves a husk of the body and both it and the pigeon are killed for aspiring to natural families beyond their realms, for being conspicuous from the group, for being weak. These are lessons of corporal boundaries and social limits. Birds, squirrel, snake, each distinguishes itself from the pack, creates itself in vivid action, yet each is destroyed. Fate can strike like an unseen hawk or a pack of boys. The lack of consciousness of Kosinski's animal actors suggests that action itself, unmediated flight however soaring, is not enough. The threads of these animal triads are endlessly interwoven from double strands—fate and free will—and that ambivalent skein runs through all of Kosinski's work.

In these first lessons, the boy also senses a saving link between the powers of air (in the figures of flight) and those of fire (in the energy of the flame), but it remains for an encounter with the "higher mammal" to forge that link undeniably. Old Marta dies in the night and the child awakens to find her spiritless, feet soaking in a bucket of dirty water. Her glazed eyes, related in his mind with the time "when the stream threw up the bodies of dead fish," hide a dark secret. She is death, a water witch, an entrapping corporal presence from the offal pit in which the boy is later nearly suffocated. He cannot accept her death—another mother gone—and to his animal mind, she is a creature healing itself: "Marta, I concluded, was waiting for a change of skin, and like the snake, she could not be disturbed at such a time." Cold and frightened, the boy tries to light a lamp, and the ghost of an early burning quickly looms. The room becomes a pyre and the flames are alive, climbing the walls "like clinging vines," crackling "like dry pods underfoot." The fire is strangely attractive, deadly and almost tender; it consumes Marta lovingly, "licking her dangling hands as might an affectionate dog" (8). The hut goes up and the boy's imagination is inflamed. In the glare he sees "a strange oblong shape" rising in clouds of smoke, and he remembers the snake and Marta's human application. In her immolation the boy unconsciously locates a life and mode of being from the flames. She symbolizes a fusion of flight (transcendence) and flame (transformation), a powerful and ambivalent emblem of the upper quadrants. "Could it be Marta's soul making its escape to the heavens?" He is strangely eased by these purifying flames. "Or was it Marta herself, revived by the fire, relieved of her old crusty skin, leaving this earth on a fiery broomstick like the witch in the story my mother told me" (10).

Fire. Water. Earth. Air. Folk-rooted forms like the fairy tale continue an old alchemical magic, and the boy is mesmerized by the quadrant of fire and reads his fate in those flames. He is to be a creature of the upper airs, a phoenix, and his very survival will depend on his ability to sense and define his unconscious empathy. He is the lost golden bird of Grimm's tale, but his mythic origins are much more ancient, antedating even his appearance in Ovid's *Metamorphoses*:

> There is one living thing, a bird, which reproduces and regenerates itself, without any outside aid. The Assyrians call it the phoenix. . . . When it has completed five centuries of its life, it straightaway builds a nest for itself, working with unsullied beak and claw, in the topmost branches of some swaying palm . . . and ends its life amid the perfumes. Then, they say, a little phoenix is born from the father's body, fated to live a like number of years. When the nestling is old enough to carry the weight, it lifts the heavy nest from the high branches, and, like a dutiful son, carries its father's tomb, its own cradle, through the yielding air, till it reaches the city of the sun, where it lays its burden before the sacred doors.[37]

When the boy glimpses rebirth and the possibility of a fresh life in the snake's shedding of skin, Kosinski suggests that metamorphosis in this possessed world implies the continuing entrapment in earthly forms and the accompanying strictures of fate—domination by the group and one's own bestial appetites. The flesh is a symbolic and real sewer in this world, and the line from Marta to the pit is direct. The boy's ironic births from those sewers and pits is rebirth of a kind, a small growth of consciousness, but rebirth also signifies a sentence of domination, threats, potential extermination, and entrapment in a deadly cycle. The boy must somehow break free of this wheel and *internalize* rather than *embody* the figures of flight and transformation. Like Levanter in *Blind Date*, the firebird is a spirit from the East. It represents the eternal power of the imagination, the transformative consciousness, and the liberated, solitary cycle of the self in flight. Thus his model is transformational rather than metamorphic, psychic rather than physical, an articulation of the ethereal dominions of fire and air as opposed to the basic realms of water and earth. His is Heraclitus's flux, the reconciliation of opposites in a tempering and annealing flame, a flame that is at once the force of life and death, a creating and consuming power. Kosinski thus rivets our attentions on the terrible ambivalent potential of the phoenix's flight.

Flight is mind on the wing, and we soon realize that the boy's growth is central to the phenomenology of the fairy tale, that of the spirit or self, Jung's "original wind-nature" that is "always an active, winged, swift-moving being as well as that which vivifies, stimulates, incites, fires and inspires."[38] Thus the boy's quest represents man's movement toward fire and light (consciousness) and the articulations of the strong and chosen self, pushing off from the quadrants of earth and water and their accompanying suggestions of death, stasis, and entrapment in the body and the collective unit. Flight also has a second, closely related meaning, for, like the Russian "Forest King" and Germanic "The Golden Bird," *The Painted Bird* begins as a quest through a mythic kingdom but quickly becomes a flight; the pattern in all three is, as Jung notes, "the boy's repeated attempts to escape from the clutches of the magician."[39]

The peasants are water spirits and mud devils, static gods of the lower depths, and are terrified of the transforming flame. "Fire, they said, is no natural friend of man." They equate the boy's presence as a foreign element with the demonic forces of lightning. He is not merely alone but also helpless and unspeakably dangerous, "olive-skinned, dark-haired, and black-eyed," certainly a Jew or gypsy, the mere discovery of whom will confirm fears of his evil nature by drawing a quick death by German bayonet or bullet. The carpenter and his wife fear their gypsy foundling can draw vengeance from the angry gods. As they curry him one hot night, the evidence crackles in the air as static "bluish-yellow sparks jumped over my head like 'the Devil's lice'" (49). He is tethered in the forest during thunderstorms, where his baseness is certain to bring "great fiery bolts from the heavens." Hiding once unnoticed in a barn, the boy is astonished to find it destroyed around him in a single blinding flash.

Satanic, a threat to the villagers, he is also a god, a young Prometheus, for Kosinski suggests that he is the mythic, egoistic bringer of the gift of fire to man, the powers of human enlightenment. The boy wanders with a comet, a lamp hammered from a tin can, fed with slow fuels and swung by a leather thong. It is a source of warmth and light, a stove and a toy, but also a weapon, an "indispensable protection against dogs and people." With it a boy "can become a fortress" (25). The comet is a psychic transformation, an absorption and outward projection of the social hatred directed at him. Armed with his gift, he is mainly a vanquished god. Bringer of light, reason, and civilization, Prometheus is also a figure of deceit, having lied to Zeus in bringing fire to earth. His gift proves both a boon and a curse, and he is eternally tortured for his transgression. Thus the boy is a demon and a deceiving god. Buried in dirt, his face picked by ravens, he is Prometheus subdued, bound to his fate on a crag in Scythia, his immortal liver devoured by eagles.

Hatred burns with a clear flame, and the element almost destroys him. First he is convinced of his own evil by the sick world around him, then of his worthlessness, until his self-abnegation is virtually complete. Before the utter purity of Nazi hatred and power, he is vermin, "a creature that could not harm anyone yet aroused loathing and disgust. . . . I was genuinely ashamed of my appearance. I had nothing against his killing me" (101). He realizes, however, that he must absorb and somehow convert these terrible energies. Though not precisely in Artaud's terms, we must "become the flames," must incorporate the powers of the phoenix without being consumed by them. Human consciousness, the spirit, and the self are defined only in a human body, and one sees dangerous reminders of literal metamorphosis and unconscious transformation, particularly in the boy's almost fatal flights as a skier and ice skater.

One can appreciate his task by comparing him with another un-named innocent, the narrator of Ralph Ellison's *Invisible Man*. Early in his experience, that young man finds himself grappling blindfolded for coins on an electrified carpet and soon senses that his quest for self, for the elusive "power and light" that lead on his search, will be caught up with his ability to "contain the electricity." He must counter the threat of the Other, seize and turn outward the current of white hatred that makes him twitch like a black puppet. He also sees the danger of going too far in the figures of blacks who have deflected their powers inward and been consumed by them. Ras the Destoyer is impaled by his own rage; the Reverend B. P. Rinehart is submerged, a protean self unable to survive the waters he turns loose. These men teach him to heed his lesson on the carpet as a dynamic of survival: "I discovered I could contain the electricity—a contradiction, but it works."[40]

Similarly, the boy must find the lost golden bird in this forest and, in so doing, transform himself and become aware of the transmuting powers of the flame. He must catch and refract that essence like a gem, for the philosopher's stone in this alchemical quest is the dia-mond of the controlled self. The brilliance of consciousness can be reflected like a gem only in the material body, and the dangers of the self's unwitting destruction of its own physical host are made clear. Such joyous unconscious flights end in death. The boy is warned as an earthly flier, one who skims, skis, and skates across the skin of a dead world.

He is seized by fishermen and tossed overboard with a monstrous fish bladder. He floats with it, terrified by his anxious freedom, "the sun shone straight into [his] eyes and its dazzling reflections danced on the shimmering surfaces." Though he survives, the aural landscape whispers of doom, as "vague voices, human or animal, could be heard in the alder groves and dank swamps" (23). Several years later, he wind skates between villages almost at will, blown across the ice by wind caught in a crude sail. He is elated, freed from the pack: "Flying along that endless white plain I felt free and alone like a starling soaring in the air, tossed by every flurry, following a stream uncon-scious of its speed, drawn into an abandoned dance. Trusting myself to the power of the wind, I spread my sail ever wider. It was hard to believe that the local people regarded the wind as an enemy and closed their windows to it, afraid that it might bring them plague, paralysis and death. They always said that the Devil was master of the winds, which carried out his evil orders" (140).

His bright freedom soon vanishes when the wind extinguishes his comet and blows him into the hands of a pack of boys, who beat and force him through a hole in the ice. He finally escapes into the forest, soaked and freezing, where the upper and lower realms join to teach him a lesson: "Every gust of wind robbed my body of precious remnants of warmth. . . . My skates caught on roots and bushes. I stumbled once and then sat on a tree trunk." His flight ends as he slides into unconsciousness, toward death, "sinking into a hot bed full of soft, smooth, warmed pillows . . . a woman's voice" (144).

The third element of this triad appears in the final scene, which I will examine more extensively later. Let us simply observe that he finds his parents and is sent to the mountains for a rest cure. He skis alone through a deserted, cauterized geography where "the hostels had been burnt down, and the people who had inhabited the valleys had been sent away." Skiing is the perfect metaphor for his psychic and physical state—his aloneness, his precarious freedom in motion, his nearness to death: "The blizzard came suddenly, blocking out the peaks and ridges with swirls of snow. I lost sight of the instructor and started on my own down the steep slope, trying to reach the shelter as quickly as possible. My skis bounced over hardened, icy snow and the speed took my breath away. When I suddenly saw a deep gully it was too late to make a turn" (212).

The pace of these three episodes grows progressively quicker to suggest the boy's growing awareness; he has been here before and sees much more rapidly on each return. He skis down into the dead womb of the postwar world and is again almost destroyed in soaring, mindless flight. Unconscious in the hospital, he is warmed by "April sunshine." He again experiences the world anew in sound, in the ringing of a telephone and a metallic voice that grates in his ear.

The essence of Kosinski's ironic vision is made clear in the pattern of these scenes. He works to pose and temporarily reconcile opposites. Thus the innocent boy and the blighted world, the torturer and the victim, the lower and upper quadrants, are at war but are ironically brought to life, defined, and created in that struggle. Similarly, man's inescapable fate is to be a creature of the body, and the flame of will and consciousness must be held within those bounds. The skier's very literal flights threaten literal death at each turn.

A creature of fire and air, then, a phoenix of the upper spheres, but his self-definition is gradual, ironic, painful: it is a knowledge that accrues by resistance. Fleeing Marta's pyre, he is captured by the crowd, smeared with cow dung, pelted with "moldy potatoes, apple cores, handfuls of earth" (13). He is trapped like a beast in a great sack and thereafter is tried and purified incessantly in rites of containment, through earth and water: buried by Olga, tethered by the Carpenter, hung up by Garbos, penned by Makar, pursued by the mob. Flocks of birds, packs of dogs, mobs of boys, congregations in a church: they are all the same muddy world refracted in the bright colors of Kosinski's peasants.

A short time later, he is to be punished for his escape from the Carpenter, apparently doomed to "a sizable sack he used to drown sick cats." The boy begs for his life, describing a concrete pillbox of war booty in the forest. The Carpenter listens greedily and, after tying the boy to his wrist like a prize cow, they descend to the wood. The scene strikes with the sledge of a hammer as the boy, hysterical in his fight for survival, shoves his master into the rat-filled bunker:

> Horror-stricken, I tugged suddenly at the string, so hard that it cut my wrist to the bone. My abrupt leap pulled the Carpenter forward. He tried to rise, yelled, waved his hand, and dropped into the maw of the pillbox with a dull thud. . . . The man completely disappeared, and the sea of rats churned even more violently. The moving rumps of the rats became stained with brownish red blood. The animals now fought for access to the body—panting, twitching their tales, their teeth gleaming under their half-open snouts. . . . Suddenly the shifting sea of rats parted and slowly, unhurrying, with the stroke of a swimmer, a bony hand with bony spread-eagled fingers rose, followed by a man's entire arm. . . . The corpse sank under renewed thrusts. When it next came to the surface of the blood writhing sludge, it was a completely bare skeleton. [54–56]

The rats symbolize perversion of the life force, "their eyes reflecting daylight as if they were beads of a rosary," a strange religious hint fully expanded in an equally grotesque later scene.

The village observes Corpus Christi, a celebration of the assumption of the Eucharist, a Catholic festival affirming belief in metamorphic magic, the conversion of symbolic wafer to real flesh. He serves as an altar boy. Feverishly sensing that this is a black mass, he drops the missal and the churchgoers erupt in a murderous burst. On this most sacred of days, they are most profane—the rats transformed —and a voice pronounces the innocent a "Gypsy vampire" (123). They swarm from church to offal pit. His struggle to resurrect the lost family and a social place in this world of the living dead has led him down this path to dead matter:

> Its brown wrinkled surface steamed with fetor like horrible skin on the surface of a cup of hot buckwheat soup. Over this surface swarmed a myriad of small white caterpillars, about as long as a fingernail. Above the surface circled clouds of flies, buzzing monotonously, with beautiful and violet bodies glittering in the sun. . . . The peasants swung me by the hands and feet. I was hurled to the very center of the brown filth, which parted under my body to engulf me. Daylight disappeared above me and I began to suffocate. I tossed instinctively in the dense element, lashing out with my arms and legs. A spongy upswell raised me toward the surface. I opened my mouth and caught a dash of air. I was sucked back below the surface and again pushed myself up from the bottom. . . . I fought against the suction of the reluctant maw and pulled myself to the edge of the pit, barely able to see through my slime-obscured eyes. [124]

This is a ritual element, a step in the formula of the boy's quest. The group attempts to bring him into the underworld and to suffocate him; he in turn resists and becomes conscious by that threat, taking flight in resistance. A few scenes later, trapped by the sons of that congregation, he fights bitterly, but they prod him through a frozen lake:

I slid underneath the ice, and it rubbed my head, my shoulders and my bare hands. And then the long pointed pole was bobbing at my fingertips, no longer being jabbed into me, for the boys had let go of it. The cold encased me. My mind was freezing. I was sliding down, choking. . . . I grabbed the pole and it supported me as I moved along underneath the surface of the ice. When my lungs were nearly bursting and I was ready to open my mouth and swallow anything, I found myself near the ice-cut. With one more push my head popped out and I gulped air that felt like a stream of boiling soup. I caught the sharp edges of the ice, holding on to it in such a way as to be able to breathe without emerging too often. [143]

This primal birth scene is central to the boy's psychic development, and again the irony is painful. To be born into this land is to enter a world of death. The boy is not only denied a return to the womb's bliss but finds that the mother is outraged in this time of war, a deranged spirit who consumes her young. Jung calls this archetype ambivalent, "the loving and terrible mother," but in this black time she is a demon, an entwining animal linked with "the grave, the sarcophagus, deep water, death and nightmares."[41] She is Robert Bly's "teeth mother," and she is indeed "naked at last." The pattern in these three scenes is meticulous: the bunker, pit, and lake are "great maws" invested with the crusty skin and sharp teeth of a witch. Kosinski's inversion is nowhere more clear than here; the forces of suffocation and death are in control but ironically serve to create a life in him. Alchemy requires base metal for its magic—these unwitting maws are also unwitting mothers, because the boy is born a little after each immersion and his ensuing resistance. He is a symbolic and literal foetus, "my head popped out". He takes a first sharp breath, trembling and wet, the snake in a new skin, the chick slimy from the old shell.

Each scene takes a clue for his survival from the image of the umbilicus. He is tied to the Carpenter's wrist and nearly pulled under until he breaks that string, a psychic and real bond to a diseased parent. He crawls from the offal pit on a long creeper of weeds, an image in which he "births" himself. In the lake scene, the cord is projected as the long pole used to push him under the ice, a negative force that he seizes and transforms, poling up and out toward light and air.

The terrible power of the "teeth mother" is confirmed and reinforced by the female figures along the boy's way. The pole is also a phallus; his sexual initiation, at age eight, comes at the hands of Stupid Ludmilla, Lekh's conquering temptress. Dressed in a sack, her pendulous breasts hanging to her belly, she wanders along with a dog for a mate, luring peasants into the bush and pleasing them so much "with her voluptuousness that afterwards they could not even look at their fat and stinking wives." She is an earth witch, a forest numen of that realm "where everything was infinitely abundant, wild, blooming, and royal in its perpetual decay, death and rebirth; illicit and clashing with the human world" (42).

She accosts him in the forest, her red pelt burning with the color of dark blood. Forcing him to the earth, the succubus literally and mythically possesses him. His screams attract the villagers, who torture and murder her. Thus, in the boy's awful initiation, sex and death are fused in nightmare: "I sat huddled and chilled, on the cemetery wall, not daring to move. The sky grayed and darkened. The dead were whispering about the wandering soul of Stupid Ludmilla. . . . I slept and woke by turns. The wind raged over the graves, hanging wet leaves on the arms of the crosses. The spirits moaned, and the dogs could be heard howling in the village" (48).

Female figures in *The Painted Bird* are not embodiments of willful feminine evil but are succubi, evil numina from the unconscious. They are themselves possessed, like the offal pit; they are "reluctant maws," as the episode of Rainbow and the Jewess depicts. Rainbow "rescues" an attractive young girl fallen from a crematorium train and he plans her sexual use. He rapes her, but rapist and victim are suddenly terrified by a power that wells from her, clutching them both. They make an inverted, hateful marriage, joined by a cold hand. As the boy watches, Rainbow is held fast: "He tried to detach himself from her crotch, but seemed unable to do so. He was held fast by some strange force inside her, just as a hare or a fox is caught in a snare. . . . An invisible bond held them together. I had often seen the same thing happen to dogs. Sometimes when they coupled violently, starved for release, they could not break loose again" (93). Cries again bring the villagers, but here the victim is killed to break the spell, the ignorant Rainbow babbling for weeks of how "the Jewess had sucked him in and wouldn't let him go." The boy is again haunted by nightmare: "Strange dreams haunted me at night. I heard moans and cries in the barn, an icy hand touched me, black strands of lank hair smelling of gasoline stroked my face" (94).

His own later experiences with Ewka, daughter of Makar the Rabbit Man, offer a small island in a sea of terror. She is pure wheatstraw and introduces him to gentle sexual pleasure. They spend balmy afternoons in a field of grain: "I sank onto her and tried to satisfy all her different whims, while the heavy ears of wheat moved over us like the swells of a tranquil sea. Ewka would fall asleep for a few moments. I scanned this golden ocean of wheat, noticing the bluebottle timidly hovering in the sun's rays. Higher up the swallows promised good weather with their intricate gyrations. Butterflies circled in carefree pursuits and a lonely hawk hung in the sky, like an eternal warning, waiting for some unsuspecting pigeon. I felt secure and happy" (130).

The narrator recalls his idyllic pleasure in that moment of glory in the flower. A tranquil sea, an ocean of wheat, bluebottles and butterflies flitting in the sunlight, swallows, a lonely hawk: in another life they might convey warmth, life, and beauty, but in the boy's dark experiences they have collected associations with death, and a proper anxiety undercuts the scene. His mind resembles the watchful presence of a hawk, and a membrane of memory and conscious reflection congeals over the scene like a shadow.

This is a major moment in the novel. In this sterile world, there is no family for the boy and no regenerating connection by mother, sister, or wife to a past, present, or future. His incestuous dream is destroyed when Ewka's thin legs open to show the same yawning abyss as that of Stupid Ludmilla. He watches her, urged on by father and brother, in an ancient pagan rite: "She slipped under the goat, clinging to it as though it were a man. Now and then Makar pushed her aside and excited the animal still more. Then he let Ewka couple passionately with the buck, gyrating and thrusting, and then embracing it" (135). Another shell of an old self cracks, and his mind takes flight again. "Something collapsed inside me," he recalls, and one sees the receptacle of life so yearned for "shattered into broken fragments like a smashed jar" (135).

To offer the seed of life is to turn loose the sewer in one's being, and the act of love may be transformed into a blind allegiance with dark powers. Love is an invasion, a possession, a cage to be fled. At age ten, the boy becomes a hermit and renounces the flesh. Later he watches Labina couple with a visitor, envisioning his own ritual self-destruction: "She embraced his fleshy buttocks with her legs which resembled the wings of a bird crushed with a stone" (147).

"Now I understood." The words are first Vavara's, reading a moral into the painted bird's initial flight in *No Third Path*. Kosinski puts them in the boy's mouth, and he chants them repeatedly, as if they were a magic formula or a witness that would release the golden bird, let down the bridge, and restore the kingdom to health. Like all words in this world, they are immensely deceptive. He understands very little, very slowly, as he moves through numina to the dummy ideological parents of magic, satanism, and Christianity. But he does learn early that there are no magic words on this quest. Language is the seed, the unconscious semen of fairy tales; the asking and answering of riddles and ritual questions call forth life. Umbilicus, phallus, tongue: they are connections to the outside, but this world is no golden bowl and speech no silver cord. From the start, with the chirps and bleats of animals, the tongue is a duplicitous tie. The boy speaks a dialect other than that of beasts and peasants. He is set off from them by the bright colors of educated speech. No direct dialogue occurs in *The Painted Bird*, and the boy soon learns that language runs with the verbal color of Lekh's paints and that survival depends on blocking that polluted stream. The villagers fear these fertile powers and take in sound with a mystic ear: "They were people of slow, deliberate speech who measured their words carefully. Their custom required them to spare words as one spares salt, and a loose tongue was regarded as man's worst enemy. Fast talkers were thought devious, obviously trained by Jewish or Gypsy fortune tellers. People used to sit in a heavy silence broken only infrequently by some insignificant remark" (72).

Language gives him away, and he learns to close his mouth like the peasants who fear the oral entry of dark spirits. His repressed talents also serve him, like good teeth hidden in a horse's mouth, as an early master shelters him for his ability to perform at feasts: "At such receptions he ordered me to display my urban accent to the guests, and to recite the poems and stories I had learned before the war from my mother and nurses. Compared to the drawling local speech, my city talk, full of hard consonants which rattled like machine-gun fire, sounded like a caricature. . . . Listening to stories about a goat traveling across the world in search of the capital of goatland, about a cat in seven-league boots, the bull Ferdinand, Snow White and the Seven Dwarfs, Mickey Mouse, and Pinocchio, the guests laughed, choking on their food and sputtering vodka" (73). His mind blurred by the vodka forced on him, the boy is again addressed by his unconscious. It speaks in torrents of the threat of unmediated metamorphosis, the self out of control, and also of the dangers of language, the cord tying him to "mother and nurses." "The faces around me began to take on the features of the animals in the stories I recited, like some live illustrations in the children's books which I still remembered. I felt as though I were falling down a deep well with smooth, moist walls coated with spongy moss. At the bottom of the well, instead of water, there was my warm, secure bed where I could safely sleep and forget about everything" (73).

Speech itself is a threat and language a tie, a fatal habit that must be broken, as it is in the boy's baptism in the offal pit. His origins are in the vilest sources of the sick world. Unacceptable as he is, the Christians nevertheless try to destroy him. So he is born in that terrible pit but not until the cord of language is cut, the last tie between the infantile self and the deadly social body. He is stricken mute and, like Burroughs's silenced "language addicts," is puking and terrified, covered with a cold sweat. He cannot comprehend the full, saving function of his muteness but dreams it in an elemental glimpse: "Was my voice escaping with it like a solitary duck call straying across a huge pond?" (215). He then wanders silenced, his voice turned inward in his own consciousness, until the final scene of the book.

The boy is born repeatedly from that deadly maw. As his mind evolves, the substance of the text is transformed; it shifts from the color and vividness of scenes burned slowly into fresh film to the depiction of the abstract stream of mind perceiving, defining, articulating (in metaphor), and finally controlling the exterior world, a process which the loss of language ironically intensifies. He retains one last image of the martial world to carry with him. Nature at war is a devouring mother, a terrible river turned loose. Although the peasants are partially able to divert the first Nazi floods, they are soon overrun. Chaos is let loose, and the teeth mother tries to devour the entire world in a final orgiastic frenzy. Caught between the retreating Germans and advancing Reds, the village erupts in violence: "Brothers fought against brothers, fathers swung axes against fathers in front of their sons. An invisible force divided people, split families, addled brains. Only the elders remained sane, scurrying from one side to the other, begging the combatants to make peace. They cried in their squeaky voices that there was enough war in the world without starting one in the village" (155).

The black sickness invades from the outside as well when the dreaded Kalmuks invade like modern Huns. The Red Army finally intercedes, and Kalmuks soon hang from their hocks in the square, rotting carcasses from a ceremonial hunt. Kosinski draws victim and torturer in another tight infernal circle, as the prey hang "with unblinking eyes, and the veins on their necks swelled monstrously. The peasants lit a bonfire nearby, and whole families watched the hanging Kalmuks, recalling their cruelties and rejoicing over their end" (166).

Nauseous and fevered, the boy wanders to the river, where his entire war life is refracted in a watery lens. There is no sound. The mother is at last sated and throws up a silent torrent of mutilated forms: "Its swift current carried timber, broken branches, strips of sackcloth, bunches of straw in wildly swirling eddies. Now and again the bloated body of a horse floated by. Once I thought I saw a bluish, rotted human body hovering just under the surface. For a moment the waters were clear. Then came a mass of fish killed by the explosion. They rolled over, flowed along upside down, and crowded together, as if there was no longer room for them in this river, to which the rainbow had brought them long ago" (166).

The lost prince collapses one last time. A sick world vomits him forth; he is born once more but nearly dies in the process. Strong beyond imagining, he is never fully healed. Though a youth, he is ancient at twelve, as old as lost innocence. The dream bursts forth one last time as the Red Army nears: "If it was true that women and children might become communal property, then every child would have many mothers and fathers, innumerable brothers and sisters. It seemed to be too much to hope for. To belong to everyone! Wherever I might go, many fathers would stroke my head with warm, reassuring hands, many mothers would hug me to their bosoms, and many others would defend me against dogs" (156).

He is damaged and the Red Army takes him in. Wounded by the *materia mater*, he heals himself as a child celibate in a hermitage of men, where he finds a first, ironic male family in the brotherhood of the Communist party. His teachers, Gavrila and Mitka, are monkish fathers to him, nursing his frail mind and body and preparing the fledgling for the flight back to a changed socialist world. The watery maw that once threatened to absorb him becomes a mirror and is transformed to a bright round world reflecting his single image. He recovers language, at least its mimetic function, by reading his first book at Gavrila's side: "It was *Childhood* and its hero, a small boy like myself, lost his father on the first page. . . . After his mother's death, he was quite alone, and yet despite many difficulties he grew up to be, as Gavrila said, a great man. He was Maxim Gorky" (168).

Once again he becomes a blank slate, but his innocence has been transformed by experience and his lessons are all in the saving actions of the self. Ironically, the patient teachings of socialism shape a young solipsist: "According to Gavrila, people themselves determined the course of their lives and were the only masters of their destinies. That is why every man was important, and why it was crucial that each know what to do and what to aim for. An individual might think his actions were of no importance, but that was an illusion" (168–69).

He takes in the world with a concave eye. It stresses history and the masses, but the boy can see only the solitary actor whose powers carve out a lonely present. He comes to share their god: Stalin. But he peers deeply into the harsh lines of a photograph, seeing first "a loving grandfather or uncle, long unseen," and finally himself. Stalin was no doubt a boy like him, "swarthy, black-haired, with dark, burning eyes. . . . He looked more of a gypsy than I did" (170).

After Gavrila and his book, Stalin and his photograph, the boy is instructed by Mitka the Cuckoo in the actions of a "Hero of the Soviet

Army." Both Gavrila and Mitka first appear as characters in *No Third Path*. Mitka, in particular, has recurred throughout Kosinski's work. He represents the paradox of the solitary hero in collective life, the spirit of man rising from the sodden mass. We see him first as the Stakhanovite shockworker, the famed Soviet worker-hero whose labors double, triple, and quadruple production. He is a bright bird in gray collective life, tolerated as long as his energies can be absorbed by a giant amoebic state able to calculate his "bourgeois egotism" in collective figures. Kosinski is fascinated by the same logical contradiction in Yuri Gagarin, the first Russian cosmonaut of 1957. Kosinski feels an affinity with Gagarin, whose flight coincided with the author's to the United States. Novak writes: "The Party decided for the moment to forget about the dangers of the cult of the individual and make Gagarin an example of individual heroism . . . a new dose of individualism, an attempt to innoculate society with greater dynamism" (352–53).

The boy's movement is now back toward the world, away from the clotted, broken river. Many of his early experiences are refigured and inverted. Mitka, for example, is a transfigured Lekh, the conquered aerial trapper who was possessed by Ludmilla and cuckolded, broken, and purged of humanity by her black alchemy. Lekh's totem is the cuckoo, and he is a ruined reversal of creatures he regarded as people turned "into birds—noblemen begging God in vain to turn them back into humans." But Mitka is a noble, decent figure. Unlike Lekh's cuckoos, who "never undertook the education of their young themselves," he brings the boy into the larger circles of humanity by introducing him to poetry, the making of music, cinema.

But Mitka offers a much more powerful knowledge—the transforming vision of the sniper's eyepiece. He was once a famed sharpshooter but, like Lekh, has been ironically purified by a baser element. A Naxi bullet ended his vengeful career a year ago, and he carries a bullet in his side, as if the war has entered his own flesh. From Mitka the Cuckoo he becomes Mitka the Master, premier instructor of the long rifle and, in his lordly and distant manner, the perfect teacher of revenge.

The war has ended, but the war will never end; the streams of village and camp life again converge, and four soldiers are hacked to death in a fight over women. The Master is enraged. Under cover of night, he had the boy steal to the forest, where the old warrior painfully climbs a tree, camouflaged—no painted bird, he—more than a mile from the village.

Five shots. Five corpses. The boy is thrilled as the episode distances and inverts a similar image from his past. He recalls how he once cowered in a barn, sensing himself a hapless target for lightning bolts hurled by an angry Zeus. Mitka refuses him the binoculars, but he looks forward in imagination and back in memory, sensing himself at long last a master of explosive energies, a dealer of fate, a willing instrument of revenge. Mitka is "the unhappy Demon, spirit of exile, gliding high above the sinful world," and the boy his ready apprentice. The Master's hateful imagination has transformed an entire world war into a secret struggle. He carries it in him like shrapnel, "his own private war, which he has to wage, win or lose, himself—his own justice, which is his alone to administer" (186–87).

We hear the boy's words again, a familiar formula: "I suddenly understood." He speaks to himself of silence, exile, and cunning but also of "a single friend," with whom "one could also reach the summit alone" (187). Having learned more than they dared to teach, he parts from his adopted fathers to join a postwar orphanage established to reunite lost children and parents. The war, however, continues unabated and intensified. The school is a brutal village in the forest, jammed with raging, war-damaged children. Each has internalized the war, each is a second-generation numen of destructive energy, and each is a unique entity named for his dominant element: "Tank because he pummeled with his fists anyone who stood in the way. There was a boy labelled Cannon because he threw heavy objects at people for no particular reason. There were others: the Saber, who slashed his enemy with the edge of his arm; the Airplane, who knocked you down and kicked you in the face; the Sniper, who hurled rocks from a distance; the Flamethrower, who lit slow-burning matches and tossed them into clothing and satchels" (195).

That "single friend," of course, is himself, another boy as much like our wounded prince as a sentient creature can be. The Silent One is also mute, but mute *by will.* He ceased talking because "at some stage of the war he had decided there was no point in doing so" (196). He is a slightly larger psychic double. The two boys spend idyllic afternoons together, "completely blackened by their tragic situation" (197). The Silent One is strong, a bold and active self, and his experience is a mirror for the boy, a pool into which he can finally electively descend. Gorged by fear and diseased affection early in their experience, they hunger for power and revenge. They are delighted to find that once awful instruments like the train are comfortable weapons. While planning an avenging train wreck, they become drunk on unsuspected power: "To be capable of deciding the fate of so many people whom one did not even know was a magnificent sensation. I was not sure whether the pleasure depended on the knowledge of the power one had, or on its use" (200).

Free to contemplate the deepest pleasure of his life, he can finally confront his own death, finds that a willful and strong self can transform even the deepest nightmare. The boys play a game on the tracks that now nourish the villages with food and supplies, just as they once cannibalized them by taking people to the crematoria and gas chambers. Trains are evil emblems in *The Painted Bird*. They collect associations of death and their railbeds frame the real, imagined, and escaped deaths of many Jews and gypsies. They are deliverers of fate, social bullets, mechanized lightning. The boy must master their power and free the victim hidden in his mind. He lies very still between the rails as the train thunders over him, risking a death that can leave broken bodies, "like an overbaked potato . . . a squashed pumpkin" (198). His experience is utterly liberating, and he is galvanized by this ultimate risk: "In the moments between the passing of the locomotive and the last car I felt within me life in a form as pure as milk carefully strained through a cloth. During the short time when the carriages roared over one's body, nothing mattered except being alive. I would forget everything: the orphanage, my speechlessness, Gavrila, the Silent One. I found at the very bottom of this experience the great joy of being unhurt" (198).

He is borne down again, submerged under this mechanical witch by a conscious *act of will*. He is ecstatic, filled with a "greater satisfaction than I had ever experienced in exacting the most vicious revenge from one of my enemies" (198). The boy has all but transformed the psychic sniveler. His great pleasure, that of Jack astride the beanstalk or Hansel basking in the oven's glow, is familiar in fairy tales and in life. Facing his own death, the boy has cracked and mastered the greatest fear and taboo, thereby releasing an ecstatic flow of personal energy that is often explicitly sexual. Kosinski's märchen takes an obviously modernist swerve in these sections, where the tale shares more with Sartre and Camus than the brothers Grimm.

Of course his parents find him because the lost prince is always found. The boy returns, ritually tempered like the child-hero of "The Golden Bird," to a world in which there is "nothing now wanting to their happiness for the rest of their lives" (17). But he is Kosinski's modern self, purged and born in terror, and a once blissful social dream is now suffocating, "cramped like the attic of a peasant's shed" (205). The possibility of a social self is gone because he feels like "Lekh's painted bird, which some unknown force was pulling toward his kind." Then he feels like Makar's fierce hare, so "smothered by love and affection" that his cage could be left open: "He now carried the cage himself; it bound his brain and heart and paralyzed his muscles. Freedom which had set him apart from other resigned, drowsy rabbits, left him like the wind-driven fragrance evaporating from crushed, dried clover" (207). He is identified by the birthmark on his chest but shows it reluctantly, like a Jew his badge. Resigned ("I was not yet grown up; I was only twelve. Even if they did not want to, it was their duty to take me away" [205]), the prodigal son is led away to the ironic postwar ovens of family life.

The transformed self makes a bad Jew. His return to mother and father is a parody of romantic endings and, though once suffocated by the world family at war, he is twice stifled in a cozy apartment with his parents. They have another child, a four-year-old in whom the boy glimpses a reverted, helpless self. He too lost his parents but was "saved by his old nurse, who handed him to my father at some point in their wandering during the third year of the war" (207). A saved body and lost soul, the child is a phlegmatic, whimpering, drowned life who nauseates his "older brother." In "The Golden Bird," Kosinski's borrowed tale from Grimm, the end is an act of apparent torture. The fox, who has repeatedly instructed the Prince in how to find the phoenix (advice always bungled, by the way), pleads for his own release and begs him "to shoot him dead and cut off his head and paws" (17). The horrified Prince refuses but at last agrees, and the fox metamorphoses instantly to his true self, the brother of the Princess, free from an evil spell. The fox is a figure of transformation, the boy's teacher and complementary victim. They are psychic brothers, and their fates are bound together in the successful return of the firebird to the King. In *The Painted Bird*, however, this tale takes a nasty but necessary turn when the boy, disgusted by the mock family and this fallen self before him, snaps the brat's arm as he once broke umbilici attached to the festering social body.

He is unable to endure this dead life and quickly joins a pack of whores and thieves who frequent a local zoological park at night. This is another clearing in the forest where they enact old ceremonies in new ways. The boy has been a good student; he thrives. Kosinski leaves us with a last reminder of the figure of the painted bird. The boy and his older colleagues have been too obvious in their sport. Police attack the quarter in darkness, and he is beaten, his uniform and bright red star dirtied and shredded. After a night in jail, the twelve-year-old comes home where he belongs.

But wait—here is a second happy ending, a coda to this demonic fairy tale, in which truly "there was nothing now wanting to their happiness for the rest of their lives" (17). The Prince of "The Golden Bird" is partially successful, in spite of his mortal blunders; he finds the phoenix, the beautiful maiden, and his patrimony but must still release the poor fox. So the firebird has one last flight to show us; it is stamped like a signet at the novel's end, sealing the contradiction and paradox of the modern self in motion. The boy remains unhealed and is sent to the mountains for rest and exercise in the upper air. He stands "at the summit alone," imagining and acknowledging the polarities fused in his existence. "Every one of us stood alone," he admonishes, regarding the frozen ribbon of trail below. "And the sooner a man realized that all the Gavrilas, Mitkas, the Silent Ones were expendable, the better for him" (212). But the phoenix needs watery depths for life. True, they have tried to extinguish his brightness, but the solitary bird needs the social world just as alchemy requires lead to liberate the magic of gold. "It mattered little that one was mute," he continues; "People did not understand one another anyway." Again he is correct. The gift of speech has almost killed him, but the loss of language turned his voice inward to nourish the egg of a stronger self. He soon is overjoyed to recover that voice, swearing never to relinquish it again. Finally, his instructor, whom he scorns as one "who acted like a simple peasant and could not accept the idea that he was alone in the world," happens to be another master. "I tried to obey him," he tells us, "and was glad when I earned his scant praise" (212).

The bird takes wing again, completing a triad of literal flights across the skin of a cold earth. This flight is more joyous and more short-lived than any other. He misses a turn and almost dies in midair, but awakens in another sun-filled room to a radiant self again burnished by death. The flight is once again destructive and creative, and he finds that his voice has returned like a wandering spirit come home. He breaks into ecstatic song, and his words spill forth "like peas from a split pod." He is *alive*: the wolf is dead, the beanstalk cut down, the grandmother brought to life, the song of the sunny wood restored: "The voice lost in a faraway village church had found me again and filled the whole room. I spoke loudly and incessantly like the peasants and then like the city folk, as fast as I could, enraptured by the sounds that were heavy with meaning, as wet snow is heavy with water, confirming to myself again and again and again that speech was now mine and that it did not intend to escape through the door which opened onto the balcony" (213).

So reads a deceptively happy ending, but there is yet a third reconciliation, appropriate to this alchemical world of contradiction and paradox. "Three-ness according to alchemy denotes polarity," Jung reminds us. "In terms of energy, polarity means a potential, and wherever a potential exists, there is a possibility of a current, a flow of events, for the tension of opposites strives for balance."[42] A third parody of romantic healing was unwittingly appended to the first edition without Kosinski's knowledge; it was bandaged together by an editor from his explanatory letters. It hangs like the other endings, a perfumed pendant to a sulphurous fable, but it cannot hide the pattern of Kosinski's modern fairy tale nor mask the dubious cask of the liberated self that occupies his imagination in the remaining five works. He would say it does not even exist. If it does, it merely extends his journey westward in language, through time and space, into the new world of *Steps*, "across an ocean and beyond the confines where no wings could be spread. In this flight the Painted Bird became himself."[43]

"My purpose is to tell of bodies which have been transformed into shapes of a different kind," the singer promises at the opening of *The Metamorphoses*, "to spin an unbroken thread of verse, from the earliest beginnings of the world, down to my own times."[44] Kosinski's second novel is a postmodern version of that ancient classic, and he notes that "the leit-motif of *Steps* is metamorphosis." But Ovid's work taps a rich river of transforming story in which gods reach from the heavens and chaos becomes restless harmony, animals are turned to stone, men and women are changed to trees or returned to those heavens—like Caesar—as stars; Kosinski purifies these waters, reduces and inverts them. He does away with the colors of name and character so that the protagonist changes "his external appearance and plays all the characters," but he refines plot as well. Thus one is left with ritual scenes and episodes of a distilled self, a montage of the individual's desperate attempts to escape the encumbrances of fate and social control.[45]

Kosinski uses his early experiences in America at several points in *Steps*, but the personal signature is less significant here than in *The Painted Bird*. The novel has been whittled down to quintessential episodic and ritual elements. The unnamed protagonist is an immature adult who is hindered by a stifling world. A static, deathly landscape emerges from a sequence of anonymous interlocking buildings and institutions. These buildings form an endless modern maze in which the individual spirit is trapped, regimented, and finally possessed. Office skyscrapers, churches, universities, hotels, political headquarters, military installations, all are transformed into a single long gray tunnel.

Like that chute, Kosinski's protagonist is relentlessly metamorphic. He plays many roles: student, university lecturer, photographer, businessman, common laborer, unwitting victim, and willing master. He sheds personae like old skins or changes of clothing in an attempt to shore up a constantly eroding self that is sliding toward history and is possessed in time by the consciousness of others. Flight is a dream, and his ideal is a self in eternal motion. The flight begun in the corrupted ending of *The Painted Bird* drifts into these pages. The going, not the arrival at his goal of the United States, is the dream: "Had it been possible for me to fix that plane permanently in the sky, to defy the winds and clouds and all the forces pushing it upward and pulling it earthward, I would have willingly done so. I would have stayed in my seat with my eyes closed, all strength and passion gone, my mind as quiescent as a coat rack under a forgotten hat, and I would have remained there, timeless, unmeasured, unjudged, bothering no one, suspended forever between my past and my future" (107). He is Robbe-Grillet's cinematic hero, dreaming again of the existential self constantly creating itself in the act of writing, but making sure that act—doubling, repeating, modifying—finally denies itself fixity, refuses to permit a story, a past, or history to accumulate.[46]

The text is an expression of the narrator's impossible quest for freedom. It is discontinuous, broken in space and time, ruthlessly and almost randomly fractured into eight parts and forty-eight episodes. Fourteen of the episodes are lovers' conversations between the narrator and a young woman. The structure is Kosinski's attempt to deny plot and to disrupt the accumulation of action, character, and temporal sequence that constitute a fictional pattern, a history, or a prison of the self in society. The narrator's desire is reflected in the title of his fictive journey, *Steps*. It is a collection of self-contained moments wrenched free of time and place, simple steps in an endless alchemical formula for self-conversion, episodes set "in the fissure between past and present."[47] The prose style is pure and all but invisible as the journey begins, as if the narrator seeks a language that will evaporate at the end of each scene, with each death of an old self. But, as suggested earlier, the protagonist's quest for a freedom of bright moments is impossible. Beneath the fractures of the narrative surface, a subterranean tension defines itself. As a mind reveals its interests and articulates them in episode and arrangement, a plot begins to cohere and the story of the narrator gathers, if only in the birth and death of the love relationship. When the plot develops, language grows opaque and mataphorical, forming a film like the first cells of a cataract on a clear eye. Steps are fated to lead *somewhere*. Thus, meaning emerges when the metamorphic desire for a new life in every instant, free of the patterns of other minds, becomes itself a pattern, an inescapable cycle.

We see the narrator first as a metamorphosing figure and as a force that transforms other lives. He is "traveling further south" and turns from the modern highway to a backward village. He meets a shy laundry girl and describes a world of travel, luxury, and fine clothing, assuring her that it can be hers. The fantasy is summoned over the totem of a modern plastic credit card, which she examines while considering his offer, holding it "like a sacramental wafer" (3). She accepts, his first victim in a novel composed of an endless series of ritual life invasions by the narrator. Born through these violations of other lives, he is revived, Dracula-like during each ceremony of possession of the Other. The girl becomes a woman in a frenzy of city shopping (O America!) and turns at last to the narrator: "By then the girl was slightly giddy from the wine we had drunk at lunch, and now, as if trying to impress me with her newly acquired worldliness she must have learned from film and glamour magazines, she stood before me, her hands on her hips, her tongue moistening her lips, and her unsteady gaze seeking out my own" (7).

He is a cannibalizing self, a devourer of other lives, but one who does so in self-defense. An institutional world restricts and represses at every point, and the narrator depicts many scenes in which he exposes or does battle with the stultifying appetites of collective society. Church, the military, business and political agencies—they form a giant cancer, a single craving cell feeding from the host of the individual self. The world is evil and anonymous in its corruption, and one lives in the pack at the expense of his spiritual life. But the narrator and his fellows learn early that a strong self can feed on the social corpse and on the dead or unformed souls in its thrall. One can be nourished like the *hyenidae*, the young ski instructors who take as lovers the dying women of a European consumptive hospital.

The narrator is obsessed with transformation. His presented episodes depict the ceremonies by which single lives are seized by the social beast. They enact a civilization based on possession and describe a ritual debasement rooted in physical desecration and sexual torture.

Like the ancient Ovid, Kosinski's imagination seeks and finds instances in which the metaphoric is made literal. Male circumcision, for example, is not a religious or medical transformation implying the assumption of maturity. It is social maiming, a threat carved in the flesh of each male slave, a warning of castration. Early in the novel, the narrator's young lover fondles him and asks innocently, *"Isn't is possible that as a result of mutilating him, the man becomes less sensitive and responsive?"* (31). Her naiveté bears a greater wisdom than she can know.

We turn endlessly from the lover's bed to the battlefield, for the struggles of love and war share strategies, tactics, and final goals. Groups of men in military costume invade and destroy life, even at play, as they make up a soldier's game of "King Arthur of the Round Table." Twenty men sit at a large table, beneath which they have tied long, cutting strings to their penises. A single "King Arthur" pulls one string, inch by inch; the goal for the tortured soldier is to remain as impassive as his undamaged friends. Circumcision is indeed linked with castration. The game enacts the arbitrary power—indeed, the fate—of social control and the individual's stoic yielding to it, and that force is brought home when cheaters are discovered. A true soldier never leaves the war. The guilty men are therefore blindfolded, stripped, and tied to trees in the forest, their symbolic castration made real: "The knights, one after another, slowly crushed each of the victim's parts between two rocks until the flesh became an unrecognizable pulp" (25).

All institutions are diseased in the narrator's eye. He depicts a conspiracy between the Catholic Church and civil court to shelter and sanctify the caging, torture, impregnation, and murder of a retarded girl by an entire village. The narrator confronts the parish priest, who was as silent as his flock for five long years. Enraged, the priest defends their goodness and his own conscience, concluding, "I won't listen! You understand nothing. . . . They are my people" (92).

In the face of such profane and obscene social conspiracy, the narrator turns to the dimmest part of himself, to the "gypsy vampire" who is antisocial and amoral, an ironic spring of purity and freedom. He defines and cleanses himself in antisocial ritual. Kosinski speaks for Sade, Mishima, and Genet in sketching the redemptive powers of sin and perversion in a profane modern world:

If sin is any act which prevents the self from functioning freely, the greatest sources of sin are those formerly protective agencies like society and religion. The original sense of "creative" becomes completely reversed; now the only possible creative act, the independent act of choice and self-enhancement seems to be the destructive act, as in Sade. . . . Perversion, defined as any act or practice or viewpoint which subverts procreation in the physical sense, is esteemed as of freedom, in that it negates the creative-procreative impulse. In perversion, the negation of "the creative" becomes literal—an acting out of a more fundamental negation. . . ."[48]

Thus his power originates in the inversion of social norms. The narrator explores this darker realm, most obviously in his relationship with his younger Catholic lover. Early in their life together, she is controlled by social and religious taboos; sexual relations during menstruation are forbidden, and she denies him, stressing the destruction of the act: "I feel the blood staining our bodies as if your hardness made me bleed, as if you had flayed my skin, and had eaten me, and I was drained" (54). But he wins her like a battle, and she is transformed by his love; the "vilest act," fellatio, once hideous "like eating living flesh," becomes a creative, purifying ritual gesture of the self: "I loved what was ejected from you: like hot wax, it was suddenly melting all over me, over my neck and breasts and stomach. I felt as though I were being christened, it was so white and pure" (83).

The lovers' fourteen conversations are skeletal but of primary significance in the fiction, as Kosinski's initial working title of *The Two* suggests.[49] Their questioning dialogues refine and articulate the larger struggles between self and society encountered by the narrator during his many battles. Indeed, in an early conversation, she innocently poses the crucial question: *"Could you kill a man?"* (35). The most profane act possible in the social world becomes the most sacred here, according to the murderous creative logic shared by Sade, Burroughs, Genet, Mishima, and even Camus. "Murder," Kosinski continues in *The Art of the Self*, "is the ultimate negation, for it genuinely devolves a thing from a human being."[50] This is Meursault's beach, where people are things already, and one transforms oneself and brings one's life alive by the ritual destruction of an object.

The equation for freedom, then, is a simple one of power: murderer and victim. But it assumes many other disguises in the narrative experience: seducer and seduced, master and servant, photographer and subject, hunter and prey, sniper and victim. The narrator is first a lover, and *Steps* is a record of love as possession, as a ritual cannibalism by which lover and beloved are willingly transformed. Love, however, is not a sharing experience for the narrator and his mates. His being is never lost, or even temporarily dissolved, in seduction or mating. His self is defined, illuminated, and expanded in love. Thus the protagonist pursues his beloved like a scientist after a specimen. He urges her to *"Meet me within your own self,"* explaining that *"It is this vision of myself as your lover I wish to retain and make more real."* She becomes conscious of his need, struggling in his psychic grasp: *"All you need me for is to provide a stage on which you project and view yourself, and see how your discarded experiences become alive again when they affect me. Am I right? All you want is to prolong this impulse, this moment"* (131). He conquers her, as he does most women, but finally becomes bored with his lifeless victim, whose allure *"for such a long time has ceased to be a mystery. Now I could manipulate her: she was in love with me"* (129).

As lover, he also becomes Master to Servant and torturer to the sadomasochistic Slave. I have described Kosinski's fictional technique as incessantly dialectic; the influence of Hegel and his theories of Master, Slave, and Desire, as enunciated in *The Phenomenology of Mind*, is readily apparent in this work.[51] But the shadow falls short in Kosinski's art, for neither the dominant one nor his submissive partner are humanized as Hegel imagined two centuries ago. The Master *can* kill. He murdered a young classmate by rumor when she could not bear to be thought of as his mistress; an old watchman who refused to be cowed by his tricks in the dark was eliminated when he stood still under a rain of bottles from a factory roof. As the narrator's powers evolve, he grows restless, and the little murders of the voyeurs and the photographer cease to please him. He plots the seduction and rape of a haughty office girl. He replaces her lover upon her compliant, blindfolded figure at the last moment but afterward feels restless and trapped in memory. Insomniac, obsessed, he finally realizes that he has had her body but not her mind. He requires her self-awareness as victim because her consciousness creates his dominion over her.

Denied this, he dreams that he is "forever undressing her, forever held back by mounds of blouses, skirts, girdles, stockings, coats, and shoes" (101). There is finally no ease for this devouring self. His quest has a purpose, but his appetite for freedom through mastery is insatiable. His desire is boundless, out of control, and, as the epigraph from *The Bhagavadgita* coldly reminds, "For the uncontrolled there is no wisdom, nor for the uncontrolled is there the power of concentration; and for him without concentration there is no peace. And for the unpeaceful, how can there be happiness?" (i).

His metamorphic hunger is bottomless, and he is desperately aware that he requires the recognition of the conquered Other for his own power and identity. He refuses to be "humanized" in Hegel's dialectic between Master and Slave and feels trapped in this consuming cycle of the renewing self. Shedding old selves like the wolf coat he wore from Europe, he elects to be the opposite member of the equation, to submerge his being in the Slave. He then becomes a drug addict, a willful derelict. Though he wanders dangerously through Harlem, he can find no strength even there, for he notes the paradoxical power of the most extreme social victimhood—life in the ghetto. Ghetto dwellers become one black face in his glazed mind. He envies their freedom in a piss-soaked, burned-out squalor. He admires their lives free from a "world of birth certificates, medical examinations, punch cards and computers, telephones, passports, bank accounts." The old talisman of freedom, movement in the social world, possesses his inverted consciousness and he yearns to live as the blacks do, "unattached, each of them aware only of himself." He grows desperate, hoping again for an impossible conversion: "If I could magically speak their language and change the shade of my skin, the shape of my skull, the texture of my hair, I would transform myself into one of them" (133). He imagines himself an urban guerrilla, warring on the demon life of the city. His grievances, however, go far beyond the social oppressions of race, class, and society; they encompass fate, the cramped universe of the genetic code, the limits of life in the flesh itself. "I would wage war against this city," he speaks, a parasite, "as if it were a living body" (134).

He seeks to shed all old selves—the social body, the physical world —and all of them are bound in language. The narrative invention flags; he repeats himself in frustration, as if he were winding into a tighter obsessive circle of consciousness and language. He remembers times in his life when he elected muteness. As he recalls these periods, his language grows more opaque and settles on his experience like dead cells. It becomes difficult to distinguish action, to separate the lovers' voices, to identify the speaker: *"When I'm gone, I'll be for you just another memory descending upon you uninvited, stirring up thour thoughts, confusing your feelings. And then you'll recognize yourself in this woman"* (146).

His devouring self then turns inward, and his end is caught by one of the strongest images of the novel, an entanked octopus slowly consuming its own tentacles. This is a free rendering of Ovid's Cephalus, a god of combat, an insatiable figure "prophesying defeat when it looked landward and victory when it looked seaward; this particular specimen the natives claimed, had only looked landward when captured. A man jokingly remarked that by eating itself it was presumably acknowledging its own defeat" (22).

"Could you kill a man? I mean: for some important reason," his girlfriend asks in an early meeting. His final memory in *Steps* is that of being trapped in disguise, of being forced to cut a political prisoner's throat. He has posed as a mute to watch a revolution. Action, however, is a silent language, and the unwilling knife slices deep and soundlessly, with "the same precision with which I had felled young trees" (145). Alternately Master and Slave, the murderer and the victim, he is both terms of the equation at once in the final scene. The point of view shifts to third person, as if the text has been released from the narrator's consciousness by his death, and in turn, frees him. His suicide is barely suggested: a made bed, a sheath of registered letters, an anxious clerk; but it is there, the paradoxical suicide of the self released from the metamorphic cycle by self-destruction. His drowning is, as Kosinski suggests, "the last definitive act of defiance and the superiority over the human condition." The narrator escapes the cycle of fate and nature in suicide, for "to defeat Nature with her own weapon, is to bring about death at will (truly, one's *last* will)."

So the narrator is freed by that last act, freed by choosing to break Ixion's wheel of self-transformation. "But even in self-destruction, his shadow outlives him," Kosinski concludes, imposing "on other people the necessity for remembering and judging him, for summarizing him as a character."[52] The poet Ovid's last claim is release from the brevity of life, "the gnawing tooth of time," in an artistic metamorphosis that "shall soar, undying, far above the stars, [where] my name will be imperishable." He modestly imagines himself apotheosized, like his last hero Caesar, a star in the heavens.[53] In Kosinski's modern version, the narrator takes a last step and his body floats in the ocean, creating a shadow of language and act on an historical world that just, like his lover swimming at the bottom, look up "to find its source" (148).

Being There is Jerzy Kosinski's most attentuated work. It is mainly of interest because of his broad use of a mythic concept and because of a turn to more exclusively American subject matter. It is, very loosely, a cosmogonic parable, a satiric creation story about a new sort of telegenic being and generation. Kosinski's hero, Chance, is a divine idiot, quite literally. Born of uncertain parentage and brain-damaged, he devotes his young life to working in the garden and watching television. He lives blissfully for an indeterminate time and is watched over by the Old Man, the first god of the novel (there are two gods, both patriarchs of the houses in which Chance is given refuge); and he is driven from the garden only by his benefactor's death. Unprovided by the Old Man's will and unpossessed of his own (Kosinski's coyness in punning is annoying), Chance takes to the streets for the first time in his life.

He is born on the first day of seven in the novel, in a literal accident during which a limousine bearing his Eve almost drives over him. He thereafter sets camp in the home of the Benjamin Rands, his saving and tempting fates. We watch as his radiant idiocy infects increasingly larger circles of power, most notably politicians, bankers, and media specialists. Chance rests on the seventh day, but not before he is cited as an economic prophet, investigated as a foreign agent by Russian and American service, courted by beautiful women and wealthy businessmen, and almost chosen as vice-presidential candidate, all without his comprehension.

Kosinski uses the novel to satirize and criticize mass media and the rise of a passive television consciousness. Both dangers recur in his nonfiction works written during the widely televised political events of the years 1968 to 1972. I cited a passage from his infamous "Dead

Souls on Campus" earlier, and the jeremiad sounds often in other work as well. Kosinski is fighting a holy war. He speaks of "a nation of videots" in a representative interview, criticizing every sector of American society for "creating weak and vulnerable beings." He goes on to suggest—oddly—that only the wealthy truly know reality in the United States, that only the privileged can neutralize the forces of mass media and can "be involved with real horses, real forests, real mountains, things they can see, touch, experience." In his fractious view, most poor and middle-class children are robots. Society will soon be inherited by "a skid row composed of middle-class, college-educated dropouts, to stopouts, as they often call themselves."[54]

Being There is set in the indefinite "there" of packaged consciousness. Chance's innocence—his simple comments on life in the garden, though bordering on the moronic, are received as *pensées* and oracular pronouncements—and his experience—a profound education in television mannerisms—endow him with a special American magnetism, of which he is barely aware. As his name tells us (there is little subtlety in *Being There*), he is an accident of fate. His mind is virtually incapable of abstract thought. This, coupled with his lack of will and *any* history, offer him the "mysterious" charm of a snowy field. He is literally a television style waiting for a subject, a blank screen to be filled in by a viewer who can provide emotional detail, most of which originates in the clichés of popular culture. As a presidential advisor tells us, "A man's past cripples him. . . . Gardiner has no background! And so he's not and cannot be objectionable to anyone!" (139).

Chance is a modern American Adam fallen from the garden, but he is uncompensated by any "benefits" of that fall, for he possesses neither sexuality, nor consciousness, nor pride, nor independent will. The failure of the passive imagination, at the mercy of every stray cathode, is never more evident than in Chance's "loss" of sexual innocence. About to be seduced by EE (Eve), he brushes her aside, unable to recall a television memory prescribing a suitable course of action (an irrefutable argument for enriched programming). We see him as the novel closes, "Not a thought lifted itself from Chance's brain. Peace filled his chest" (140).

Being There is a minor work in both conception and execution. Kosinski encourages bathos by depicting Chance's evolution as a biblical fable and a creation myth. Novak the moralist is too prominent here, and his point is unredeemed by humor or a more ingenuous irony. One thinks of more skillful treatment of divine idiots like Chance in recent American fiction—Kurt Vonnegut, Jr.'s *Slaughterhouse Five*, James Purdy's *Malcolm*, Walker Percy's *The Last Gentleman*. The language and scenes here are slack, as if lifted for effect from the dead televised world. The problems of mass media and the passive mind are considerable, but Kosinski's fable does not vivify them; they are subtle terrors for man, but *Being There* daydreams them away. The work is of primary interest only because it marks a pivot to the author's dominant concerns and themes since *Steps*. Kosinski now focuses on the centers of contemporary affluence and power (mainly American) and on the movements of actors within those rings to create enduring selves and to reconcile, if possible, those reviving gestures with a moral base in society.

If he was an intellectual minority in criticizing the dangers of mass consciousness and young mindlessness that he saw rampant among his students, Kosinski moves to the dead center of the "Establishment," finding in the bête noire of the age an unlikely hero: the corporate business magnate. The benign paternal features of Benjamin Rand, chairman of the board of First American Finance Corporation in *Being There*, are blackened in the faceless visage of Horace Sumner Whalen of *The Devil Tree*. The experience behind Kosinski's work in this period is personal and unusual and surfaces in an article written for the *American Scholar* in 1972. He writes about Ernest Weir, one of the fathers of modern American steel industry and founder and chairman of the National Steel Corporation. He finds there a curious model for the autonomous self. A multimillionaire who died in 1957, described in his *New York Times* obituary as "a staunch champion of the right of business to operate without government interference" and "a classic embodiment of the rugged individualist," Weir is eulogized as "The Lone Wolf," a sharp voice for a muddled audience.[55]

Ernest Weir came to Pittsburgh a generation after Mellon, Carnegie, and Rockefeller, but his path was identical. Born poor, he began work at Braddock Wire at age fifteen in 1890, taking jobs refused by others for the salary of three dollars a week. He was a doer who worked hard, long, and alone. Kosinski quotes his credo of "practical thinking and practical action of practical men on problems great and small." By 1930 Weir had forged the National Steel Corporation, the sole American heavy industry to thrive in the worst depression years of 1930 to 1934. He became an enormously powerful man, with enviable strength of conviction, and was constantly at odds with President Franklin D. Roosevelt. The two titans loathed each other. Roosevelt sneered at "that feudal lord" and Weir later refused to visit any foreign capital that contained a monument erected to or a street named for FDR.

Weir was a lone wolf in many ways. Kosinski is especially interested in Weir as an old warrior who refused pointless battle, recognized impossible struggles, and contained his powers—like the wolf—in silent movement around the adversary. He quotes *Richard II* in a headnote, the Duke of York's "I do remain as neuter," as Weir's political message to cold war America. Weir was a vital man until his death at age eighty-one in 1957; he was married for a third time in 1942 to a woman forty years younger. He died a very powerful man, with his achievements cited by business and government. Two Eisenhower cabinet members were among those attending his funeral. But mainly, he was borne away as he had lived, alone: he had ordered a bare service with no eulogy and no pallbearers.[56]

Kosinski's interest in him speaks again of the interplay between the facts of a writer's life and the details of his fiction. While Weir was a public figure, Kosinski was a private man. However, the admiration and access to special papers demonstrated in "The Lone Wolf" article suggest a special relationship; and there is one indeed, for Kosinski met Weir's widow on a blind date, not long after arriving in New York in 1957, and married the vivacious older woman in 1962. Mary Hayward Weir and Kosinski were married for four years, during which period *The Painted Bird* was dedicated to her. She is later transformed to Mary Jane Kirkland in *Blind Date*; Levanter's courtship and brief marriage to her, severed by her death, is a rare passage of romantic delight and tenderness in the author's work.

But his interest is finally in Weir, whose life he entered and meditated upon. American industrial empires survive as the long corporate shadows of single driven and driving men—Rockefeller, Mellon, Carnegie, Vanderbilt, Frick—and Kosinski's imagination seized on their patterns. These men lived the myth collected by Horatio Alger, our guileless transcriber of the American dream of a fluid society, unlimited upward mobility, and material success by solitary endeavor. They no doubt read those sagas as boys and repaid him in kind with success stories for his later work. Alger's newsboy fantasies touched people deeply, for they imagined a nation of Weirs. Kosinski reads in that myth of rugged individualism a familiar story: starting as a poor orphan, each boy creates his fate as an existential actor, discovering a life and consciousness innocent of history and social pressure. Ragged Dick, Tattered Tom, Don the Newsboy, the lads of "the luck and pluck series," all transform themselves in action, and the results of wealth and fame are almost secondary. Kosinski looks deep into this American myth and sees, superimposed, the upward flight of his own Polish naïf. This dream of self-creation is the implicit pattern underlying *The Devil Tree*, but again the author inverts the fantasy of success to articulate a contemporary America held in anomic despair between the weight of an achieved past and an unimaginable, threatening future. Jonathan Whalen's New York in 1970 is an eternity removed from Ragged Dick's Gotham of a century earlier.

The father's success is the son's failure. Horace Sumner Whalen is an escapable, paralyzing presence for his only son Jonathan. The steel baron Weir emerges as founder of the aluminum industry in *The Devil Tree*, and the dynamic character and principle of "The Lone Wolf" have become intolerable burdens here. Whalen is dead, only a memory, but his aura is diffused everywhere. He evokes himself in the bullied recollections of his son, former friends, and servants, in letters (to his son at camp, signed "Your Father"), in newspaper clippings. Even in death he looms over Jonathan's life, his being hardened by the granite towers housing the megacorporate "Company," his face literally stamped on that young life, engraved on a postage stamp commemorating a pioneer of American business. He is omnipotent, a paternal master, a creative surge of young consciousness now frozen in glass and concrete. He has become a historical personage and a social force, transformed in death, his body ossified in the walls of factories, his nerves rerouted in the circuits of a computer chip. He is what Alger never gets to. In Kosinski's inverted vision, however, he represents the pinnacle of material success in the capital-

ist state; by implication he suggests all that is devolutionary and profane in the modern world—a static, life-denying manipulating force.

Jonathan James Whalen is the scion of this fatal empire. He is
numbed, pinned helpless beneath the inky face on a postcard stamp.
This is Kosinski's most explicitly social novel, and he uses Whalen to
depict a generation of young Americans, the dead souls oppressed by
a necrotic culture. Whalen's flights from New York are inversely
proportional to his own energies, and he is never revived—like Dean
Moriarty in the 1950s or Randall McMurphy of the 1960s—by women
or drugs or song along the way. Geographically, he moulders like a
sick Adam trapped inside New York, creeping across Europe, Africa,
and finally Asia. In Rangoon, Burma, and Katmandu, he submerges
himself in hashish, opium, psychedelics, and finally heroin. He is
Kosinski's corroded picture of a generation that really did believe (we
must remind ourselves) that transformed consciousness and an expanded self could be won through drugs. Though numb, Whalen is
also more deliberate in his attempts to make himself feel *something*.
Kosinski suggests that his expensive tastes in fine cars, sensory diver-
sions, and glossy and brittle women are technological indulgences;
they add up to a psychic attempt to shortcircuit one nervous system
and simultaneously install another. Jonathan and Karen, their stray
friends, and the extended surrogate family of the encounter group
are all children of a stagnant culture, caught in the upside down
world of the baobab tree. Alger's urban Eden has been perverted and
made a jungle by social darwinists. A similar law operates in Whalen's
life, as he explains to his doomed godparents: "The native calls the
baobab "the devil tree" because he claims that the devil, getting
tangled in its branches, punished the tree by reversing it. To the
native, the roots are branches now, and the branches are roots. To
ensure that there would be no more baobabs, the devil destroyed all
the young ones. That's why, the native says, there are only full-grown
baobab trees left" (199).

If *The Devil Tree* is Kosinski's most directly social novel, it is also his
most superficially psychological. Although we are shuttled between
fragments, scenes, conversations, first and third person, summary
and narration, there is very little energy in the psychic portrait of
Whalen that emerges. Kosinski seems so ambivalent toward him, un-

derstanding but unsympathetic, that the impulses cancel each other. Whalen's split self is a becalmed case study; he drifts into the reader's sight via numerous banal self-analyses and exchanges with his lover Karen and his encounter group. We are told that there is a trapped child in Whalen, "aspects of my personality buried within me that will surface as soon as I know I am completely loved" (31). He confesses his problem in an early cliché: "I see myself divided. My most private, real self is violently antisocial—like a lunatic chained in a basement, grunting and pounding the floor while the rest of the family, the respectable ones sit upstairs, ignoring the tumult. I don't know what to do about the family lunatic: destroy him, keep him locked in the cellar or set him free?" (11).

The child can gain release and Whalen will be freed but only through successful resolution of the hold exerted by the dead father. During psychotherapy on a heroin cure, a doctor suggests that he recreates the master/slave, dead father/lifeless son configuration repeatedly, creating "an artificial system of guilt" with a stream of father figures, "setting myself up to be judged and condemned by a man whom I respected and to whom I felt curiously close" (74). Whalen's juvenile anxiety is rarely released in action; when it is, Kosinski depicts him in scenes like the opening one in which he baits authority and then battens on police apologies afterward, a series of "man-I-showed-those-pigs" fantasies more notable for intent than fictional execution.

The child Jonathan is terrified of discovery. He thus becomes obsessed with evasion and "a master of concealment." His notes and admissions in the text are suitably anonymous, purged of damaging evidence or emotional trails. Sex does not exist in Alger's New York, but Whalen comes to it young. His adolescent relationship with Karen declines to a limp struggle, a bout between her need to dominate and his languid resistance. The language of such episodes similarly loses power. Some reviewers found a poverty of invention in *The Devil Tree*, one quite beyond the author's intent to mimic Whalen's anomie in the blandness of his revelations. Robert Alter, for one, criticizes the style as "a vocabulary of vapid cliches" prone to "the hackneyed formulas of mass journalism and pulp fiction."[57] Either Kosinski's grip on his material (particularly the inner lives of his characters) is tenuous and superficial, or his intent is to depict the emptiness of their lives through their banality of imagination and language. I suspect each is true, but the result is a central moribund expanse in which language is a dead instrument punching up stale perceptions. Consider this intimate moment between Jonathan and Karen:

> "After we make love, a man says, 'Fuck it, I'm not going to worry about being cool. I want to tell you it's never been this good for me before. You don't mind being told, do you?' 'Mind?' I say. 'I love it. Who needs that cool Second Avenue body-exchange pick-up crap in bed?'"
>
> Karen looked at me pensively, then continued. "It isn't a mistake to tell you this, is it Jonathan? I tell myself that it's all right if I don't love you, but I can't stand your not loving me, because then I don't have any power over you. I can dig making it with a man I don't love but not with one who doesn't love me. In a way I didn't want you to be in love with me because it would interfere with my life with Susan and make things awkward for everyone. But I need your love. I'm terrified of being taken lightly." [67]

Karen's fears are well-founded.

At times, Whalen seems little more than a convenient receiver for the novelist's observations on faddish American culture: "This concept of instant intimacy annoys me more than anything else about the encounter group. It breaks down resistance and makes people feel good by allowing them to think that they are really getting to know one another. Yet in the end nothing has happened; we know no more about ourselves and the others than we would after a cocktail party" (101).

Whalen's choices narrow down: to continue as an aging child caught in the baobab branches or to "revert to a father in miniature"; to accept his corporate place as "Horace Whalen fifty years later," which is also a death of sorts, or to choose to be "an anachronistic animal which is going to be destroyed by the jungle" (63). But as the modern extensions of his father's power prove more stultifying, he discerns a third path. Kosinski suggests this path in oddly woolly terms, as if wary of the consequences: "What therefore I think Whalen could pursue would be a pursuit of the new self which could make use of history, but very often by a conscious discarding of it. . . . If there is a value to having a well-defined father, collectively defined, it is that it could force the child to seek a new definition."[58]

Whalen discovers a use of history that is precisely opposite Alger's heroes. Ragged Dick (Richard Hunter) is a literal stalker who he searches for and builds his future on the streets of New York. Whalen, in a terrible pun, is fated to be a deep fisher. His tasks are to recognize his submerged condition and to explore the powers of the surrounding waters. Here again aquatic references suggest death and entrapment. The senior Whalen drowns. His distraught wife then submerges her anxiety on long yacht trips and ends her life drugged by the Atlantic in Palm Beach. But gradually, Jonathan senses a potential freedom in those waters. He is released by skin diving into a "world of serenity and calm," but he is also excited by the danger and thinks of "running out of oxygen and the idea of sharks darting out at you" (48). He envies a deep water snake "spiralling effortlessly through the water" its freedom, "its ability to control its heartbeat, to slow its pulse even as it attacked" (127).

Jonathan Whalen's freedom lies in his willingness to reimagine those waters as an ally and to cast deeply there for a new life. His liberty consists in being an anti-Alger, a decidedly nonheroic Dick Hunter. He must free himself in water, severing the dead roots of history, father, empire, self. Old Macauley, the corporate father, is the final impossible image; he sits behind a media computer console, the nerve center for the octopoid "Company" that now consists of forty worldwide subsidiaries. From there Whalen moves to his father's former best friends, his own godparents, the Howmets, and carefully plans their murder. Playing the charming host, he decides to accept the full responsibility for Whalenhood and invites the Howmets to an Indian Ocean villa for a heart-to-heart talk. He soothes them, leaves them picnicking on a sand bar, and pointedly explains that "I think there are sea snakes around and I want to catch one" (203). His godparents are inundated by the tide and drown, after which Whalen feels "energy flowing into him from outside as if he were a starving man being nourished from an unknown source." Patricide and corporate destruction are liberating acts, and Jonathan feels released as "deep within himself he [hears] a child's laughter provoking urges that [cannot] be satisfied by physical movement" (204).

The end of the novel is ambiguous. Whalen is in Geneva, very ill with an undiagnosed disease and pressed down by physical existence —"he lay like a stone on the shore." Kosinski continues the marine metaphor, depicting him "unmoved by the waves of spring air washing over him." He is enervated and drowning, but one night, as he walks from the clinic to Lake Geneva, he senses himself emerging from a long stupor like a beast from the water, clarified: "The smell of moss spread through the air. He sniffed the dew, listened to the lapping of the water against the stone and felt the skin on the back of his neck prickle. The fog began to lift. He stared across the lake and saw the blinking lights of the villas and hotels of Geneva" (211).

Thus we last see Jonathan Whalen. His flight has taken him from the dead centers of power to the neutral geography of Lake Geneva; during his journey he has canceled the nightmarish grips of history, family, empire, and the achieved world. There is a stillness at the center of *The Devil Tree*; the dialectic between dead father and wounded son—and the contiguous ghostly struggles between root and branch, history and freedom, fate and autonomous action—take place in slow motion, like the last fight of underwater beasts. But we see in Kosinski's ironic American hero the buds of his future protagonists. As the last scenes tell us, Whalen's new active powers are founded in ruthlessness: murder, sadism, industrial sabotage, the technological self. Ragged Dick Hunter is a pure moral force in his dewy American society, but Whalen, who evokes Tarden and Levanter, finds moral complicity in the jungle of the baobab impossible, finds indeed that destruction is the only affirming path.

"*Who will understand the true reasons for the confession?*" ask the closing words of *Cockpit* (249). Kosinski quotes Dostoevski's *The Possessed* and points to the use of still another classic genre, the confession, as the ordering shape of his fifth novel. The confession dates back to the fifth century and St. Augustine's concern for his humble soul, but Kosinski's modern version forms around the agent Tarden and his unburdening of a godlike past. *Cockpit* is a debriefing that is much more an assertion of strength and liberation than an admission of man's weakness or a self-indictment. Confession requires a confessor; the reader serves that function here, as the author stretches the fictive skin to make literal the "you" ordinarily implied in first-person narration. "You probably do not recall," Tarden begins on the first page, continuing in an easy lover's voice, but he remembers more deviously than we can imagine and by his final memories he has possessed us. Recollection is not a passive act; memory is a weapon. By the novel's close, he has invaded our consciousness, emerging fresh from the wreckage of a past in which we are trapped.

Tarden is an undercover agent, retired from the American "Service." He has been a character of great appeal to the literary imagination since World War II, particularly since the cold war and the rise of the CIA. He appears in serious fiction—in raincoat in Graham Greene's "entertainments," in cassock in Anthony Burgess's eschatological spy novel, *The Tremor of Intent,* and as the sinister Hollingsworth in Norman Mailer's *The Barbary Shore.* He has been extraordinarily popular in paperback because of Ian Fleming's James Bond fantasies and John Le Carré's accomplished thrillers, and imitators have rushed with him to the bank, supported by a mass taste for intrigue and escape. Sex, violence, elaborate plots involving empires, gorgeous women, the power brokers of the planet, and foreign intrigue are the substances of mass fiction, and Kosinski has been accused of seeking the sensational. His intent, however, is not to exploit but to reclaim certain territory and experience as the rightful terrain for serious fiction concerned with morality in contemporary life. He uses the spy novel, like Anthony Burgess, as a means of reflection on spiritual matters, on the vagaries of personal morality and social responsibility, on the conflicting obligations to a pure self and a corrupt modern world.

Kosinski is a mature flier and accepts the full conditions of his existence, as the epigraph from Saint Exupéry opening the novel suggests. He is in control of his flight and alert to its turnings. In retrospect he sees his pattern as "*a child* [who] is not frightened at the thought of being patiently turned into an old man" (i). The surname Tarden echoes that of an earlier unseen hero, the Norden who invented the precision bombsight that reversed the second air war to Allied favor. Historical and fictive, they are both visionary bombers, but, in place of a mechanism calibrated by a uniformed officer, Tarden catches his victims in the crosshairs of memory and imagination. "*I too play my games*," he continues from the cockpit, echoing Saint Exupéry: "*I count the dials, the levers, the buttons, the knobs of my kingdom*" (i). Older and retired, the aging warrior summons forth his most intense memories. He affirms life, instead of being passively resigned to it, and embraces the dialectics of body and soul, fate and free will, blind chance and imaginative action, death and life, that torment his younger alter egos in *Steps* and *The Devil Tree*.

Tarden's confession is a seamless expanse of anecdotal memory that is divided arbitrarily into seventeen unnumbered sections, broken only by a capital at the head of each section. The breaks are random, sometimes opening or closing a story but more often serving as brief interruptions or pauses for breath in a continuing tale. Beneath this deceptive drift of mind is a broad pattern, for Tarden's memory is cyclic and contains the oppositions reconciled in his life. As a child he believed that "the wheel was animated by a powerful spirit," and this image continues as the dominant figure in *Cockpit*. But one may be constantly freed within its turnings, not broken endlessly like Ixion or Whalen. As a creative agent, Tarden renews the dead languages of political and military science: circles of power, spheres of influence, rounds of negotiations, global security. An early, warming memory is that of playing with a hoop, and it rolls into his adult life. "Now I have devised a new kind of wheel game. . . . Confronted with hundreds of anonymous faces, hundreds of human wheels, I choose one and let it take me where it will. Each person is a wheel to follow, and at any moment, my manner, my language, my being, like the stick I used as a boy, will drive the wheel where I urge it" (148).

His own freedom is purified in movement through expanding circles of personal power. A precocious child and a credit to the communist State, he outwits family and cell and comes to the United States and the Service. He has passed beyond that time in his life and is now retired, an agent employed by that most generous and demanding of agencies, the self. His duties have lead him around the world through city and country, wealthy and poor, conventional and bizarre, but he attends now to the "urban remains, deserted glass and steel structures," the corpse of modern society. Landscape is character, and

Tarden redeems the droning world by invading "real estate firms, insurance or employment agencies, collection services, marketing research firms, publishing houses or magazine offices" (152). Character is landscape, and he sees the detritus of modern life in the millions of "flaccid bodies" in the city around him, noting how "soon they will grope toward narrow doors and shuffle into the dirty streets" (236).

The novel wheels from Tarden's childhood toward death, and his carefully edited past suggests that the child is father to the man. His strong character is defined from birth, and the lessons of the active self learned in child's play are refined in later life. His earliest memory establishes familiar terms. At age two, he is a sleepwalker, climbing nightly from a tall crib to the warmth of his nanny's bed. He is "cured"; wet towels soon drape the sides of his crib and "their chilly dampness would send me back to the warmth of my own blankets" (110). The sketch would be innocuous elsewhere, an interlude in every child's life, but it contains the first hint of an oblivious desire by the unformed self to thwart its own growth, to return to the impossible womb of the past.

The motif of entrapment painstakingly established in *The Painted Bird* is more deftly sketched in *Cockpit*. Young Tarden is born aware of the forces of human mortality, of death. His flesh is the first prison and he is provoked by his juvenile body. His own fluids circulate independent of his control, and even weeping cuts pose a challenge: "Although I often tried to keep a wound open and bleeding, it always sealed itself overnight, challenging my power over myself. I hated the sense of an autonomous force in my body, determining what would happen to me" (13). To live in the flesh is to be sealed in; sexuality, the second cell, is a blind turning downward toward the animal world and death. A local skier, the Flying Gnome, becomes a national hero. He is a cretinous boy, stuttering and gross-featured, but brilliant and graceful in flights from the snowy skin of the earth. Envious, Tarden finds the secret of his success and the cause of his death. The Gnome was trained and seduced by a German temptress, the Red Whore, a Stupid Ludmilla in furs. Though her sexual attentions coax great performance from the potter's son, he is finally conquered by her flesh and his desire. He soils himself aloft, crashing to an awful end, "his body appearing to have given up, refusing to complete the jump at all." The Red Whore also lures Tarden, but he is repelled by her explanation of the Gnome's death: "The jumper had grown up surrounded by snow and ice, she said, and he could love only when his bones and his body were frozen like stored meat. He saw rot in everything hot and wet and would touch her warmth only when he was drunk. And there she had been, hot and wet, inviting his touch all the time. She said he felt soiled by her love" (126).

The small circle of his child consciousness defines the first meaning of cockpit, a fatal ring for the fights of animals. He and his mountain friends celebrate the last November season of the Ruh, "the wet wind from the warm lakes . . . keeping the snow and the skiers away." It is a watery dead world. Tarden is hydrophobic, recalling how they rush to a swampy pond to appease the spirit of the Ruh and to summon the complementary wind, the dry, cold, life-giving Thule. "Each child brought a canvas bag or a box containing a live animal—a rat, a dog, a cat, a duck, a goose or a muskrat. . . . Attaching stones or iron bars to each animal's underbelly to slow it down in the water, we released the creatures, throwing them into the pond." The animals are blinded and pushed from the shore by the child handlers and their long poles. This is a grotesque cockfight, slogged out in water by dying spirits that fight against the deadening force that drives the blood downward. A cold front sweeps in and the Thule turns the pond "to a platter of thin ice, its glaze broken only by the trapped animals." The wind is overbearing, and they are caught in the cycle of life as it pitches over: life to death, water to ice, blood slowing, thickening, and freezing. The winning animal is the last to die, but they all succumb, "their heads cocked to one side as though listening, their eyes frozen open" (119).

Although the motif of this scene resembles that of *The Painted Bird*, where life in the body is linked with the cages of lower consciousness, social man, sexuality, and the great entropic slide toward death, Tarden's experience has a very different timbre than the painted bird's. Though this young flier is disturbed by the inertia of the blood, we should note that in his world these powers are regenerative and healing. The watery Ruh evokes the Thule, bringer of the cauterizing ice and the flight of the skiing spirit. His young consciousness is seasonal and he soon finds that the apparent enemies of life are joined with, even create, the freedom he desires. Thus the wheel turns or is turned by an active hand to all things in their own time: the Ruh brings the Thule, death yields life, a pained memory of animals trapped like people in a crowd triggers the liberating acts of the individual.

Tarden's first weapons are his most enduring: his memory and a complementing ability to manipulate life in the present. At age ten, his mnemonic genius is confirmed by tests and from that point he enjoys his talent immensely. He is not oppressed by his personal history and takes pleasure in circling back through images of the past. Memory and action, fantasy and desire, they exist in an exponential relationship: each acknowledges and expands the other. Like the process of healing, the autonomy of remembering disturbs the young man: "If I evoke a single memory picture, others will spring up automatically to join it and soon the montage of a past self will emerge" (13). Later, however, the free dynamic of recollection excites the mature man. Our young gunner is uneasy in the presence of the accidental, but the older Tarden has an appetite for those instants in which existence is permuted again, instants when the spontaneous is released and his own potential is made kinetic in the world.

Tarden is the shape-shifter in *Cockpit*, a master of active disguise who delights in cosmetic changes of voice, face, costume, and bearing. In these adjustments, he transforms the boundaries of flesh and is paradoxically released by them. He delights in the free movement of the actor behind a painted face.

A self is a mask and there are endless Tardens. As a ten-year-old, he finds in disguise an exhilarating power. The State telephones. A steely voice instructs that the family will move at once to a distant relocation settlement. A choice deceit revels in truth; the boy's miming voice creates havoc by telephone, cleverly reaching into other lives, multiplying himself in an army of victims the State did not create, does not wish, cannot assimilate. As a mature agent, Tarden is born each time he metamorphoses himself with each new job, new victim, or new lover. But in maturity, as in chidhood, he is a morally ambiguous agent. Though he wars on fraudulent and repressive forces, he is not necessarily an operator on behalf of familiar personal or social ethics, because the moralities of the purging self and the dozing Other—individual or collective—do not rest easily together.

He can be a monstrous hero, even as a young boy. At three, resting in a nanny's lap, he stabs her deeply with a pair of scissors. A year later, incensed at a young friend, the precocious agent tosses a flower pot at him from a high building.

Tarden grows older and moves from the family to the State into a second circle of power. "The State was a vicious enemy," he recalls, and his memory evokes an incident in which he almost dies from anaphylactic shock brought on by a simple dental anesthetic. His mind binds together the strangulation of collective life, the numbness of the drug, and the death of the self, but it also acknowledges again the ironic creative powers therein. He is physically and psychically revived: "Like the elusive substance that had once healed my wound, now the State had saved me without consent" (15). Thus if the State tries to devour him, it also creates an appetite in him—what Hegel calls Desire, the will to know, to master, and to assimilate the world that characterizes self-consciousness and gives rise to the Master self.

We see young Tarden's Desire first as a photographer for the labyrinthine State Academy of Science. His job is to document "an endless bureaucratic jungle," to produce images of a fixed and certi- fied political reality. Photography for the State is scarcely an act of consciousness; it is a deadly interaction, and Tarden in communist Europe is a collector of dead souls. But he uses his talents to create an elaborate hoax, "to turn that confusion back on itself." In the most autobiographical segment of *Cockpit*, Tarden creates a brilliant, lib- erating fiction from the holds of the octopoid State and flees to the United States. Thus he masters the State and transforms his own image in the process. Tarden continues as a photographer, first as an operator for the Service and then for the self. He uses every sort of camera to seize people, to create deception and expose the next layers of human behavior. He peels lives like onions. Photography becomes an extension of memory that makes visible the electricity of the brain and freezes the moment in a scar of chemicals on microfilm and studio paper. Furthermore, the metaphor is a mode of being in Kosinski's work; like Novak's sitting, metaphor is at once active and passive. The lens of the camera is a voyeur's eye that reaches into a scene, a life, a brutal or tender moment, but it also preserves and creates a record. For Tarden, photographs make it possible to relive the excitement of the moment at a later time, when he pricks his imagination by holding those prints in hand and mind. As photographic accountant for the State, he becomes a dealer in lives. Picture taking is transformed into a complex act of desire: an unfelt touch, a slap, a lover's caress.

His special Desire is to photograph the women in his life. Here we note the second graphic significance of the title *Cockpit*, for Tarden is above all a cocksman. His sexual potence is a willed extension of the strong and conscious self but also, paradoxically, a blind pulse of the blood that courses beyond the mind's grasp. He is excited by women, first by their psychic and physical attractions, then by the process of imagining them and photographing them—clandestine and exposed —as if the lens were a phallus or a needle mounting a biologic specimen. He is even further moved by the reactions of his women when they confront their images in the double mirror of his skill and their photographs: their curiosity, their outrage, their desperate need to enter the chemical fantasies he creates, their compulsion to release the worm of daily life to the lepid beauty he traps in paper and stain.

Tarden is not only an occupier of other selves—note again the shared language of love and war—but also a liberator, for his attentions evoke spontaneous actions, hidden aspects of personality, and the Desire of the Other. His special taste is for unformed souls, particularly young women and children. Their armor is readily pierced, their substance released more suddenly, because the shell of the self has not yet hardened. His own protean being is released by the presence of youth. He delights in ventriloquism and storytelling, drawing children into fictions that are serious play. The lover's lingering touch is a tale told to a child, an open self whose response is unpredictable and often passionate. He "seduces" a young skiing student with his stories, fantasizing the time when they will see the world together: "She hung on every word as I described the strange animals we would see in jungles and the parties we would attend on the roof-top terraces of skyscrapers" (49). She lives in these stories and, when he leaves at season's end, she leaps from a roof like an abandoned lover. Later Tomek, a Ruthenian boy, annoys Tarden on an airplane. He wraps the boy in a devious threat, terrifying the child and provoking him to rail uncontrollably at his parents.

But Desire is mainly sexual, and Tarden is a relentless priapic lover. "Some must break/Upon the wheel of love," Stanley Kunitz writes, "But not the strange,/The secret lords, whom only death can change."[59] The wheel is a literal sign in some scenes from *The Painted Bird* and *Steps*, where peasant men sprawl, spokelike, an old woman circulating from one to the next, relieving them like animals. But here the wheel is unstated, turning through Tarden's life from sexual maturity toward death. He is indeed "a secret lord," unbroken but tested endlessly on that great round. His memory turns, sealing one lover's experience to that of another, and in the process, we can see, radiant in his life, a complex meditation on the dialectic of modern life. The dualities that spring from the paradox of the spirit in the flesh are illuminated by sexual life, which is experienced, acknowledged, and recorded as a rich shuttle that creates life and ebbs for a time in a single death.

His being—the current and potential self—is defined and refined by sexual performance. What starts as juvenile fear and repulsion for sex in the Red Whore's story, becomes a necessary aspect of a full existence. Sex is a threat, a stream of blood that seeks another in a second body. Although the young Tarden first senses sex at a distance as forbidden, dangerous, and repressed, the adolescent knows it as an ecstatic revelation, a liberating action. The mature Tarden embraces the full realm of sex as both totem and taboo. He takes up the psychic knots of moral restraint, social taboo, psychological repression, and orgasmic denial; he finds delight in manipulating these strands, himself, and his partners to release a transforming flow of psychic and sexual energy. Thus the political spy is a sexual agent; his disguises are the protean self made substantial, and his own freedom emerges from that deceiving process. The male self is also an impulse held in check, and Tarden sustains and creates sexual energy, in fantasy and action, by manipulating what were once the hardened spasms of moral and social convention.

His memory weaves together many sexual experiences: the Swiss child seduced by his stories (he recalls her leaping from a building as he parts); his lover Theodora, first weaver of the cloth of master and slave (her body collapses from cancer as he leaves the hospital); a psychiatrist's wife taken ruthlessly and anonymously, in which time both partners discover buried selves (she fades as a memory, sleeping in her husband's arms); an elegant French woman with whom he is a rare victim—a slave to his failing body, his image of her, and her power (a time he would like to forget); a village of Italian whores, all offering to satisfy him, "but not inside," saving their aging virginity for marriage (a vivid scene, exciting as yesterday). He is many men: a skier, translator, an agent posing as anthropologist and industrial representative, a tourist, always a lover.

Kosinski has been severely criticized for the sexual morality of his protagonists. The common assumption is that novelist and central character are identical, especially in the destructive creators of *Steps, Cockpit, Blind Date*. The author's vision shuttles us constantly between the lover's bed and the field of battle, and he uses that dual metaphor as a means of exploring an essentially profane modern life. What starts as a military patrol reveals that the righteous and the enemy are one. An ambush breaks the self open, revealing dark and terrible potentials, surprising actions, hidden fears, and false strengths. Sade, Mishima, Genet, Kosinski: they share the common view of a band of warriors, inverted heroes whose antisocial, immoral, illegal, and often murderous gestures are the last purging and cauterizing hope of waking the body of modern life. The struggle on a killing ground may become a lover's shared embrace, a violent rape, the choking of a victim, or a slave's mutilating revenge. Genet's "miracle of the rose" breaks forth in a prison pit—there are many such transformations in the works of these authors, but underlying them all is an unwillingness to accept human sexuality as a predictable exercise. Kosinski denies both the repressions of the past, sex deadened by social code and religious cant, and the false liberation of the present, the consummate act made banal by "immediacy," "honesty," "openness." His agents, like Sade's priests, Genet's thieves and murderers, and Mishima's samurai, refuse sex as a genuflection or a handshake but instead explore it as a ceremony (often incompatible with social norm), a mysterious, deadly, life-giving ritual in which the antinomies of contemporary existence are illuminated, shared, and temporarily reconciled.

Tarden escapes, and the third and fourth circles of power, the

Service and the self, fan out imperceptibly and inseparably. One can only say that his investigations gradually abandon explicit political purpose. They are of two kinds: (1) actions taken against domestic and foreign agencies and groups that hold individuals hostage; (2) invasions of single lives by which the Other is created, consumed, reborn, and devoured again in an endless cycle, all under Tarden's gaze. His work is unified, however, by a profound moral intention, as the author notes. Speaking of Tarden and Levanter, impatient with a popular culture that he despises and with increasingly hostile critics who see his work as sensational, Kosinski concludes angrily that "my characters are all agents in the service of counteracting the emotional suppression."[60]

If the State finally offers him freedom and makes him its highest agent (an unclassified "hummingbird" and a wealthy man), it also destroys him as a social being. He survives by his wits beyond the usual early death of operators and is released to face the world, a conspiracy of enemies. Freer than ever, he is also more alone, for "as a result of the circumstances under which I left the Service, I cannot join any professional, social or political group." He travels from secret apartment to apartment, anonymous in the major cities of the earth. It is a mixed life, sweet and tart: "Yet to live alone, depending on no one, and to keep up no lasting associations, is like living in a cell; and I have never lost my desire to be free as I was as a child, almost flying, drawn on by my wheel" (148).

But the mature Tarden does not despair. Many of the anxieties and obsessions of childhood and young manhood are finally dissolved. He is no longer plagued by accident or blind fate; indeed, he invites chance and is animated by coincidence, the breaking of pattern. He achieves new perspectives on past absorptions, photography for instance, and is almost amused to discover, once again, the primacy of the memory over literal images: "When I think about the energy expended during the past decades in picking up these women, and in taking, developing and enlarging these photographs, I am overcome by its pointlessness." The voyeur's clearest eye is in memory, and he becomes aware of the strength and impermanence of his own human consciousness: "When I die and my memories die with me, all that will remain will be thousands of yellowing photographs and 35 mm. negatives locked in my filing cabinets" (180).

But one should not be deceived by the wistful tone. For all his sense of living within a harmonious cycle, for all his acceptance of failure, illness, accident, disaster, and even death as part of the human condition, Tarden remains a profoundly unsettling figure. He is pleased with his life in large cities and goes for long walks at night "like a solitary visitor in a vast, private museum." But he has no use for his fellow citizens, noting disdainfully that at four a.m., "one can easily imagine that mankind is nearly extinct" (236). He is a negating hero, as Hegel would have it, because the proper function of consciousness is negation rather than pure destruction, and his hand is always on that wheel.

The third significance of the title *Cockpit* is made clear in one of Tarden's final efforts for the Service, the most disturbing scene in the novel. He meets Veronika, a woman of flawed beauty and marred past, and offers to stake her to a new life on the condition that she be available for his pleasure.

They strike a Mephistophelian bargain, and her life blossoms in the soil of a new identity. She becomes wealthy and desired; she moves in the company of an international elite. She tries to avoid Tarden, but he brings her to heel several times, once by a grotesque "blind date" during which she is drugged and sexually tortured by four derelicts. Still she grows anew, beyond his needs, each time. He begs a final meeting at an Air Force open house, pleading for a last set of sentimental photographs. She poses before the newest jet fighter, alluring and impatient, tossing her black hair in the sunlight as he shoots from ground zero:

> I sat back, and tripped the switch. Instantly, the hazard light began flashing. The silvery radar display indicator brightened and the luminescent dots at the center of its screen began to coalesce into a blurred shape, like rapidly multiplying cells. I glanced at Veronika through the jet's open canopy. Posed against the peaceful green field veined with runways, she had no idea that invisible missiles were assaulting her body and brain. I turned

> to the pilot. His face was flushed. He stared at the screen's dim glow as though it reflected something horrible. I switched the radar off, and the screen darkened, then went black. [235–36]

Thus Tarden punishes an act of bad faith with murder. She is cool and indifferent as they part; he basks in his pleasure behind a sad face: "I could bear the thought of never seeing her again only because I knew a part of me would always be with her. Nothing would please me more, I said, than to know there would be days and nights when, unable to sleep, she would recall our arrangement and how it had ended" (236).

The agent's last memories speak of the element of disaster that lurks unknown in every future. While photographing one of his women, he leaves on a quick trip for fresh film and is suddenly trapped in a malfunctioning elevator. He runs through his entire emotional life in several minutes, panicked in fear of a plot, but settles stoically to await his fate. After eight hours, he is rescued and goes home exhausted, his girl friend having grown bored and departed. Looking out his window, he watches ice skaters in a city park, "moving smoothly in their circle of light." His tired mind transforms that placid scene. First the skaters become an afterimage of the childhood animals frozen in the Thule pond, standing "like frozen sculptures growing out of ice." Then, in the last picture, they are transmuted into a "great old army tank, hit decades ago by an enemy shell, sunken in a shallow lagoon." In the pale light of morning memory, he imagines it "washed over by the waves; its corroded gun defiantly trains on trenches and machine-gun nests, long buried in the sands of a deserted beach" (248).

Thus the mind turns from memories in the distant past to the present, exhausted and accepting, weary and godlike. From frozen animals, rusting tanks, and gliding skaters, all lost in dormant pools, the mind wheels to the present of the confessor's debriefing. This triad suggests and reconciles many old oppositions, but the final martial image of the tank held forever in battle is the truest one. Tarden's last victory as agent is precisely in the terms of his confession, for the "true reasons" are not so much to surrender, to ease his soul and share his burden, but to take another victim, to imprint his experience on yet another consciousness. As he warns us, his lover and confessor, very early, "I did not want to just tell you about my past. I wanted you to relive it" (2).

Mediterraneans know the levanter as a damp seasonal wind that returns with the flight of birds each spring and fall. As the name suggests, it blows from the east, usually gathering itself from the hot eye of the Anatolian doldrums. It is a confluence of opposing autumnal pressure systems. It is the Ruh, a mixed spirit, bringing a season of fog and drizzle to the sere underside of Spain; later, less balmy, it whistles through the Venturi Straits, past Ceuta and Tangier and Gibraltar, with sufficient chilling force to hold small planes flying eastward motionless in the sky.

George Levanter of *Blind Date* contains the spirit of that healing and killing wind. He is prompted to unpredictable and disquieting motion again and again. This motion ultimately subsides in his inevitable death and in his return to cold and snow, sand and sea, during the final scene. His name also implies his occupation, for he is another capitalist hero, a merchant, an independent businessman who trades in the rarified spice markets of investment ideas. Levanter has a third connotation, as mythic go-between, for he has been blown from east to west. Like Jerzy Kosinski, he has been set free on an endless seasonal cycle of renewal-decline-renewal. Life in the United States has not met the dream of freedom (how could it?) that the young Kosinski sought twenty years ago, but there is little rancor reflected in *Blind Date*. Levanter is truly international. His experiences weave East and West together in a long skein of accident and irony, fate and absurdity; against these elements plays the woof of his own active radical humanism. Svetlana Stalin is magically transported from Moscow to Princeton, New Jersey, Voytek Frykowski from Warsaw to the Hollywood Hills. Jacques Monod, Charles Lindberg, Leopold Senghor, and many other more anonymous presences, are taken back and forth across oceans and national boundaries, between cities and small towns and villages. East and West are interchangeable in Levanter's mind; they form mass geographic consciousnesses to be redeemed by a single action. "I have found people to be good everywhere," he tells us. "They turn bad only when they fall for little bits of power tossed to them by the state or by a political party, by a union or a company, or a wealthy mate. They forget that their power is nothing more than a temporary camouflage of mortality" (83).

The form of *Blind Date* owes a great deal to the picaresque romance. Indeed, as Kosinski tells us in recent self-commentaries, most of his protagonists are picaros, characters who are constantly in a stage of becoming. They live their lives rather than merely ponder their condition. Kosinski would have us see the picaro as the last champion of self-hood. As always, the author gives the genre a contemporary twist, but the similarities are very clear. The baggy, episodic character of the picaresque romance is convenient for Kosinski's own rambling habits, and *Blind Date* is his most structurally relaxed book to date. Too, Levanter is a rogue-quester. If his origins and stature are several degrees higher than those of Quixote or Gil Blas or Moll Flanders, his moral acuity is also heightened. The picaro is always roguish, at worst a petty criminal, but Levanter can be a demon: an incestuous son, an arsonist, a murderer, an extortionist, a guerrilla against the moral and psychic emptiness of contemporary life, always confronting the forces and institutions that hold the self in thrall. Though ribald comedy and satire have traditionally been central to the picaresque romance, Kosinski is not a comic novelist. The infrequent satire inherent in Levanter's experience is expressed by indignant protests against the philistinism and narrow-mindedness of contemporary middle American life (read Impton), as one of the opening quotations from Swift suggests:

> Remove me from this land of slaves,
> Where all are fools and all are knaves,
> Where every knave and fool is bought,
> Yet kindly sells himself for nought. [i]

The most explicitly shared feature of the picaresque tale and *Blind Date* is the role of accident and chance in the life of the protagonist. Indeed, the central metaphor of the blind date suggests Kosinski's purpose, for the novel is an examination of the creative and destructive potentials of blind chance in contemporary life. As a businessman and scholar (he "creates" accidents in his investing life and writes a long article for *Investor's Quarterly* on "the role of chance in creative investment," which in turn generates another cycle of chance encounters [207]), sportsman and lover, he conceives of life as a series of personal, often amorous, appointments through which his consciousness is renewed, refreshed, and endlessly altered. The force of chance so disparagingly conceived in *Being There* is treated with respect here. Chance is reimagined as a fruitful philosophical principle, as the ideal ethical father of the novel, biochemist Jacques Monod, suggests in *Chance and Necessity*. A philosopher and scientist, Monod suggests that the molecular operations of DNA and RNA are not physical or psychic sentences to a life of limitations on earth, that man is an "accident" based on *chance*, and that accident is perpetuated by the *necessity* of chemical law. Monod goes on further to suggest that only by turning to a "scientific social humanism" can modern man transform what he perceives as the "uncaring emptiness of the universe" to a valuable life. Kosinski's unlikely capitalist picaro is the biochemist's modern "gypsy, [who] lives on the boundary of an alien world." Only by examining his "total solitude, his fundamental isolation," and the ethical structures that have blinded him to his condition, can he redeem a meaningful place in the world.[61] Thus Levanter lives by the second epigraph to the novel (from Monod's *Chance and Necessity*), examining repeatedly in his blind dates the received, moribund, and deadening moral center of postmodern life: "But henceforth who is to define crime? Who shall decide what is good and what is evil? All the traditional social systems have placed ethics and values beyond man's reach. Values did not belong to him; he belonged to them. He now knows that they are his and his alone" (i).

Levanter is less a fixed character than a spirit and pressure against the lives in the novel, including his own. His quest is both social and psychological: to neutralize the many impingements of the social world and to liberate the single self as fully as possible. Thus a new note of radical humanism sounds in Kosinski's fiction, for *Blind Date*, because of the constant stress of human experience commonly held "perverse" or "immoral," implies a willingness to accept man in his full imperfect condition. This chord, distant at best in the early work, reaches major proportions here, and Kosinski is correct when he says of Levanter, that he leads us to accept "one's inevitable deformities—physical and psychological—as a normal part of life. After all, each of us is deformed; nobody is 'perfectly average.' Sickness, social condition, employment, accidents deform us; age destroys. And all this on a blind date that might end at any time."[62]

Like the heroes of *Steps* and *Cockpit*, our wealthy picaro transforms himself and those he touches by going to the most repressed and forbidden centers of human experience. His blind dates are often sexual; Kosinski develops them carefully, at first shocking his reader, then gradually leading him—by an auctorial refusal to judge—to simultaneously weigh his own initial response and the content of the scene before him. *Blind Date* is a human freak show, a mortal bestiary. Levanter goes through every sort of heterosexual experience—incest, bondage and discipline, rape—with every sort of female partner: much older and younger women, nymphomaniacs, transsexuals, dwarfs, an alluring torso nymph.

His first blind date is brought about by a friendship with Oscar, a kindred spirit at a summer youth camp. The boy is a compulsive rapist, an artist of what he calls "blind dates," on which he violently "breaks the eye" of his unfortunate victims. He stalks them, records their movements, plans every detail of their conquest. He speaks of blind dating in an entire surrogate language that distances his actions, an effect not unlike that evoking Alex and his droogs in Anthony Burgess's *A Clockwork Orange*. The disquieting power and irony of Levanter's gradual fascination and willingness to create his own blind date lies in the withholding of value judgment. Kosinski refuses to judge the violence pervading the rape scene. On this first blind date, Levanter finds himself suddenly trapped in his own affection for the victim, in his desire to know her more fully, and in the misdirected accusations that hold Oscar responsible.

To go on a blind date implies a willingness to open one's self to the full spectrum of possibility, but such experience can be unpleasant and surprising, even to Levanter. In a chilling and consummate scene, Kosinski develops his unexpected incestuous relationship, thrust upon him as his father lies dying in a hospital. He and his mother are genital lovers, bound more psychically than physically. Each of them is terrified and attracted in their meeting on this blind date, for they rend the ultimate taboo. They are lovers beyond the decade, and over the years, "Her bed was like a silent physical confessional," undiscussed between them, undeveloped beyond narrative description (10). For an initial jarring moment, the reader is forced to confront his own attitudes toward these players, because Kosinski has expunged every trace of moral judgment in a brilliantly conceived and executed passage. Sex for Levanter is a polymorphous force for discovery, liberation, or revelation; it often frees this self and the other, propelling them into unsuspected realms. He finds repeatedly that his preconceptions about life cannot apply to his experiences in the moment, and, like the classic picaro, discovers that the accidents of life take him through the same experiences with the same people, under wildly different circumstances many years later. Thus the stumbling Arab skier, mocked and resented by everyone at the alpine resort in the opening scene, may well be the transsexual Foxy Lady, a voluptuary who entices Levanter later in the action. The concert pianist Pauline, who flirts gently with him early, is freed later in a very explicit bondage and fist-fucking episode; and his best friend Voytek's European lover, once despising him, is later a beautiful nude sunbather, arching to the oiling hand that led her mate to his bloody death in America. Similarly, the Serena who seemed an attractive coed is really a high-class whore. Mary Jane Kirkland, in an uncharacteristic and welcome tender passage, deceives Levanter by first pretending to be the young secretary of an aging widow (herself) who cannot meet with him, a ruse which enchants and captivates our capitalist player. Man and woman, father and daughter, mother and son, stranger and lover, master and slave, the veils are pierced repeatedly and unsuspectedly. In this sense Levanter is a healing wind, examining the conditions of social convention, beauty, and taboo, and finding them invalid. An early discussion with Pauline, just before the incest scene, outlines Levanter's sense of the common bond of flesh and desire that binds us and seals the human condition. He finds that Pauline's Russian piano teacher has been his mother's some thirty years earlier and that Pauline, like his mother, has been the amorous master's mistress. Again, accident blows through these lives, joining them for a time:

"It must be the same man. He was probably about thirty when he taught your mother in Russia, and he was in his sixties when I studied with him in England. If he were my lover, too, would I be linked to your lover?"

"Yes, and if I had been my mother's lover," said Levanter, "I then would be linked to you." [8]

Healing and healed sexually, he is punishing and avenged politically. He often acts as an independent agent, at times on behalf of rescue organizations like Amnesty International, to arrange the release of ideological prisoners and the violent deaths of their captors. In one scene, a ski gondola containing the heinous deputy minister of internal affairs of Indostan is blown up over a ravine. Later, in a terrible episode, an agent responsible for a European friend's blackmail and imprisonment is literally hoisted on his own petard, drugged and murdered in an act of sword-sodomy. At every point, Levanter learns that if the superficial values and morality of the everyday world can be transformed or redeemed through the introduction of blind dates, there is no guarantee that such unrequested moral action will be recognized or welcomed. Hence an intellectual freed from the notorious PERSAUD prisons in Indostan (Iran) is enraged that he has been released for the "wrong" reasons, by violence and deceit. "I have never been a violent man. . . . Violence does not advance the human condition. Ideas do," he complains. Levanter is curt: "Ideas don't perish in prison cells. People do" (36). Indeed, it is part of the constant risk of blind dating that one may be misconceived or misunderstood, as the acting Levanter often is. After his rape of Nameless, he attempts to confess but is brushed aside, kindly "understood" as trying to protect Oscar. Later, as a young military attaché, he secretly softens the brutal treatments of his contemporaries by his superiors and is rewarded by their contempt and belief that he curries military favor. Thus moral gestures can have no popular sanction and must be extracted and treasured in private. He is quietly pleased at having blown up the Indostan torturer, "elated about having finally helped the execution of justice." He takes solace as the avenging spirit, the ethical potential in man that rages "each time he read[s] a newspaper account of Stalin's henchmen who lived unscathed in the safety of retirement, fearing nobody but old age. And he thought of the Nazis, how justice had waited a decade before meting out its impersonal revenge" (38).

Nor is there any guarantee that action will bring the sought result. There is some clue in the curious colloidal nature of *Blind Date*. As stressed throughout this commentary, Kosinski often works closely with the materials of his own life, but there is a raw vein running through this book, a sequence of characters lifted whole from public life, as if to suggest that fiction and reality are contiguous shapes. This paradox is caught in the recurrent "it was and it was not" of the protagonist's experience. Svetlana Stalin, Jacques Monod, Leopold Senghor, Voytek Frykowski, and Charles Lindbergh are all transported to this world and appear beside their thinly fictionalized counterparts, Mary Jane Kirkland, Romarkin, and Levanter. These historical personages are all witnesses to the necessity of opening one's self to the unknown in life. Through this bold action they have felt the freshening winds of chance; as a result, they have experienced both fame and tragedy and are made whole in suffering, humanized by loss. As his own life progresses, Levanter similarly suspects that the nature of chance often thwarts one's most humane plans and aspirations. He brings Voytek from Poland to Los Angeles. Seeking to transplant his friend in a new home, he unwittingly places him in the hands of the Manson pack. This scene was carefully and grimly imagined by the author; the episode is both thematically significant, because it attests to the potential cruelty of accident and to Kosinski's attempt to exorcise, through the distancing of fiction, his own pained responsibility for Voytek's death. Levanter suffers like his more famous friends and draws back from opening himself to further pain, fearful of accepting Mary Jane Kirkland's proposal because "chance might turn from a benefactor to the ultimate terrorist, punishing both of them for trying to control their own lives, trying to create a life plot" (220).

But he accepts. What are the alternatives? A life of consciousness in action must confront change and loss, but Levanter is a melancholy picaro after Mary Jane's sudden death. He wanders, finds Serena, loses her as well, at the very moment he desires her most and needs to live forever in a timeless moment: "His past was a matter of regret, his future was haunted by premonitions; only the present still gave value to time" (201). With Paula, his last lover, he admits frankly, "Somehow

I think you're my last chance. . . . To have a fresh emotion, a sensation that isn't just a ricocheted memory. To be part of that spontaneous magic" (228). In the penultimate episode, a brilliantly controlled and disquieting image of their mutual release in bondage and discipline, he is freed from past and future for one last time, released from the guilt of incest and from the impinging aspects of other selves and institutions, free one last instant even from "the feeling of his own shape" (231). The furious social and sexual motions at last come to rest and are held suspended in the "No!" and then "Yes!" of shared orgasm. They are dissolved selves, a twoness made one, and Levanter is prepared.

The levanter come up, rages, and subsides. Our last image of the true picaro is the dust from his steps, the cells of the self dispersed again in motion. So this spent human wind blows through one last flight into winter. Finding himself cold and exhausted on a white hillside, he freezes to death as the novel closes. But the last chord is not tragic. Actions of the free self embrace the random, love implies great risk, living with others is to risk losing something, the body slides to death—all these human truths Levanter has experienced. Even as his blood thickens and his heart slows, his mind generates still another image. From the quietude of the Alps and a child held in story, he comes full circle to this temporary waning, dreaming in another season, of another child. We die, we are born, alone, together, every instant.

With his most recent book, *Passion Play*, Jerzy Kosinski seems to have recovered yet another ancient vessel, passion plays, that genre of medieval drama serving as prologue to the cycle culminating in the Resurrection, the ritual celebration of the final freeing of Christ from mortal flesh. Kosinski rams this parallel home early and late in the novel, emphasizing that his picaro hero, Fabian, is not merely a player of world-class polo but an actor on the stage of modern being, "the setting for a striking drama" (12).

But the true source of this tangled novel may be found in an epigraph from Cervantes' *Don Quixote*. The epigraph states that there is a difference "between some knights and others . . . there have been some amongst them who have been the salvation, not only of one kingdom but of many" (i). Fabian is another Kosinski picaro figure, perhaps the most literal. In this novel he is a fused "existential cowboy," a knight errant, and a modern grail quester. His "field of play" —the author insists upon parallels throughout the narrative—is one-on-one polo, the modern dueling field, and his "goal" is to free himself from the familiar traps of collective society: possession by the Other and entombment in the physical body.

Fabian is almost an itinerant polo player. He failed as a world-class player because, while playing on a team of four, "the spirit of the collective" proved intolerable. Thus, at the height of an elite and dangerous sport open only to the select, he disdains team play and becomes a "head-hunter." He finally is blackballed and enters a state of "self-imposed impotence" (30). His cautious strategy, as his name signifies, is one of avoidance. He evades direct confrontation with any group. But, like his mythic progenitor Quintus Fabius Maximus, the Roman general famed for defeating Hannibal by evasive strategy and tactics, he cannot elude his own inevitable mortality. Fabius died circa 203 B.C. As *Passion Play* opens, Fabian is obsessed with his own "documentary of aging," having just undergone a serious medical examination. He rails against "the bad faith of the balding patch, the descent of graying hair, the betrayal of the lashless eye . . . the reflections that debauched the spirit" (11).

His escape from collective society in its many aspects has finally entrapped him. The very means of his freedom—the mobile Van-Home in which he tours and hauls his thoroughbreds—hardens around him and holds him prisoner in its aluminum skin, as surely as sagging flesh and muscle will bind him in final triumph. He has imagined this life as one of the modern picaro, the sexual adventurer sweeping the interstates with his steeds in tow. In the Kosinski mythology, he is familiar: "Man astride his mount . . . the original passenger through air, the traveler borne by winds" (6). A *van* may be poetic, but the mobility and freedom of the VanHome prove illusory, the prospect unintentionally comic. The American camper promises a last vulgar dream of escape from an aging mass. Fabian awakens to see his quest is to rid himself of such delusions: he is a sort of grail hero through these pages, replete with perils, wounds, temptresses, and a rejuvenation by water. In short, he begins as an empty chalice of the self.

Like many of Kosinski's earlier heroes, Fabian is a sexual dueller, a collector of young women, but this passion cools as his body ages. Though in possession of a string of pubescent young southern thoroughbreds, he finds himself a prisoner of his own sexual appetite, and he must witness this obsessive need in order to liberate himself. The vehicle for this recognition and transformation is a wealthy young woman unfortunately named Vanessa. He comes back to her in many guises: as teacher, polo duellist, lover, horseman, writer —each time finding himself more enmeshed in her life, a captor made captive.

This is all well enough. Kosinski knows polo and horsemanship thoroughly, but *Passion Play* is his most misguided and self-indulgent work to date. He has sustained a prose style and the concerns of the modern romancer since *The Painted Bird*, but the scenic drive compelling the reader through that work, and through *Cockpit* and *Blind Date* as well, is seriously diminished in this novel. Kosinski has shown an increasing tendency to intrude in his novels, certainly a legitimate technique if used wittingly, but he is incessantly editorial in *Passion Play*. Long sections of early narrative are composed of chunks of auctorial opinion, most of them thoroughly familiar to his reading and lecture audiences: television viewers, the uneducated young, mass American culture, collective society in any form. The disquisitions are relentless, and we are told, told, told, as if we were a lecture circuit audience. Entire sections on polo and horsemanship are virtually undigested in the narrative, as are expanses of memoir, autobiography, and what appear to be personal psychological obsessions.

When Kosinski does resort to his most effective narrative style, loosely joined episodes, he repeatedly insists that we perceive Fabian as metaphor—as failed Apollo, picaro, wounded grail hero healing himself in singles bars and sex clubs, polo player on the field of being, or self-redemptive Christ. The shaping metaphors of the city, urban highway, and sheltering woods are similarly forced upon us, and thus the reader finds little escape from the artist's unrefracted sensibilities and intentions in the novel. But Fabian survives, as will Kosinski's large reading audience. After refusing Vanessa Stanhope's offer of a fortune to marry her, Fabian leaves Totemfield (!) realizing that he does indeed need others, if only to tell them his stories in person or convey those tales through his art as a writer.

Frantic to say a final "something" to Vanessa, he fails to reach her by telephone and van. He retrieves Big Lick, his prime Tennessee walking horse, from the vehicle, and gallops through the woods along an abandoned railway, clattering past the hulks of barrels, appliances, and rusting car bodies. His destination is the airport, but he arrives in time to see Vanessa's jet ascending. He has been healed and freed by his race and the events leading to it, at least for a time. He has taken flight from his metal cage but Vanessa, soaring ironically overhead in her own, has not. Her final vision is ours: "the sight of a man on a horse, streaming along the black strip of runway . . . the rider tilting, as if charging with a lance, in combat with an enemy only he could see" (271).

This commentary on *Passion Play* may seem harsh, but I believe that work by a serious writer of accomplishment deserves incisive and honest criticism. Many of our classic American writers—Melville, Faulkner, Fitzgerald, and Wright, to be sure—have had a bad book or two among their accumulated works. A poor book does not deaden or negate their artistic achievements; in many cases, it has freed them to find new techniques and imaginative lives. *Passion Play* may only constitute a pause; if so, Kosinski may still be regarded as our finest contemporary romancer of disturbing modern experience.

Six

Postscript: Singer, Temple, Song

The dismembered body of Orpheus is an emblem for the postmodern American character, the divided waters of contemporary writing, the broken texts and tales and selves of many postwar prose fictions. A metamorphic figure of "new buildings,/signals, and changes," the singer beckons even from death to promise new shapes of life.[1] This transmutation is not a progession upward and has no end.

Orpheus broke silence with songs fashioned from the primal chords and tones of the natural world. He held that realm rapt, as Rilke continues, "in a temple for them deep inside their ears."[2] His body and stories blended many separate energies. When, inevitably, flesh and word lost their powers, his healing art failed and men broke back toward refreshing silence and stasis. Torn to pieces, singer, temple, and song returned to their origins in elemental water, rocky soil, darkness. Again, our "silent friend of many distances" is not a dead god but a figure of metamorphosis. His myth is a great wheel reconciling the apparent breaches of rough life and divine art, chaos and harmony, comic sense and tragic spirit, the private self and the greater world.[3]

I make the image of Orpheus a national one, for the singer's body is the American soul, a fragile harmony born of many rough songs, an order often fractured to bring these separate chords to fullest life. Ralph Ellison, like his Afro-American compatriots James Baldwin and Ernest Gaines, writes often of the roads intersecting inside us and speaks of the heart of the American experience as "the puzzle of the one-and-the-many." It dwells in "the mystery of how each of us," he continues, "despite his origins in diverse regions, with our diverse racial, cultural, religious backgrounds, speaking his own diverse idiom of the American in his own accent, is, nevertheless, American."[4] Certainly our history since World War II has been one of absorption with racial, cultural, historical origins that make us different, establish our personal songs in the American chorus.

As suggested throughout *In the Singer's Temple*, fiction is a reflexive phenomenon. We can read our obsession with national pluralism in the divided waters of contemporary fiction, particularly in works by writers who have come to prominence since 1965. Following the paths laid out by Afro-American writers, more recent Third World artists have meditated on the unique pasts and presents that set them apart: native Americans like James Welch; Asian-Americans such as Frank Chin and Maxine Hong Kingston; Latins Tomas Rivera and Thomas Sanchez; Appalachian whites like Wendell Berry. In this study, I suggest that American fiction has fractionated into its primary ingredients, and further, that four distinct elements can be crystallized: metafiction, the fiction of postmodern consciousness, as seen in Donald Barthelme's work; recent Afro-American prose, our most resonant folk stories in historical memory, as represented in Ernest Gaines's writing; the dreaming tales of Richard Brautigan, Marge Piercy, and Ken Kesey, countercultural fables that envision alternatives to mainstream American life; and finally, the contemporary meditations on public power and private terrors, as witnessed in Jerzy Kosinski's keloid romances.

Like the singer's body, dispersed and cast like bread on the Hebrus to serve the larger world, contemporary American fiction has frequently been disruptive and discontinuous: in the gassy fictive psyches prevalent in Barthelme, Sukenick, and Kosinski, and in the more familiar devastations of flesh found in the bullet-riddled bodies of Ernest Gaines's heroes or in Kerouac's consumed Dean, Kesey's Christ McMurphy, Piercy's Billy Batson, all are sacramentally divided and eaten by a larger beast in search of spirit. As we have seen, the American fictive body is broken in style and text as well, because our more avant-garde writers have shattered their orphic vessels repeatedly in the hope of releasing a new song, a new truth.

Perhaps these very separations make us a people, perhaps we are healed in our common search for a whole. Ralph Ellison suggests that the quest is "a property and a witness," that the "small share of reality which each of our diverse groups is able to snatch from the whirling chaos of history belongs not to the group alone, but to all of us." I have a few more reservations than Ellison, but finally agree that this property and witness "can be ignored only to the danger of the entire nation."[5]

Bear with me one last time as I raze my critical temple and take down my tent. Critical commentary requires, momentarily devours, good fiction. Though I suggest that this age and place may well make the titans Faulkner, Hemingway, and Fitzgerald a long time in returning, I do not for a moment imagine fiction obsolete or the novel dead. Such sledgehammer jeremiads as John Gardner's *On Moral Fiction* may shout to us, may "deny, even publicly, that any first-rate American novelists now exist," and may claim that "our serious fiction is not much good" and that "most art these days is either trivial or false," a case attributable to an ominous condition in which "a culture's general world view and aesthetic theory have gone awry."[6] I prefer to close on a truer, less fractious note, with Rilke and his "silent friend of many distances," modern and ancient. The poet's final sonnet to the singer tells us—writers, critics, readers—that art lives, that strange tales grow a harmony in the careful ear, that water springs eternally from dead rock. The singer's tales are not solely his own but are nourished by the cries and murmurs of the natural world, and he can merely shape and harbor them for a time. Rilke urges us to "know transformation through and through," to hold and meditate on the volatile sediment of experience, finding in memory and reflection the elemental harmonies that are there always. Transforming, we are transformed in the crucible of each moment, a pained and ecstatic process that makes our literal and imagined lives ready for these last still and raging lines:

> And if the earthly has forgotten
> you, say to the still earth: I flow.
> To the rushing water speak: I am.[7]

Notes

Chapter 1

1. Rainer Maria Rilke, "Sonnet III," in *Ten Sonnets to Orpheus*, trans. Robert Bly (Berkeley: Mudra/Zephyrus Image, 1976). Sonnets I, III, VI, and IX are available more widely in *Leaping Poetry*, ed. Robert Bly (Boston: Beacon Press, 1975), pp. 75–78.

2. Harvey Swados, ed., *The American Writer and the Great Depression* (New York: Bobbs-Merrill, 1966), p. xvi.

3. Tom Kromer, *Waiting for Nothing* (New York: Alfred A. Knopf, 1935).

4. Tom Wolfe, *The Electric Kool-Aid Acid Test* (New York: Farrar, Straus & Giroux, 1968).

5. Wylie Sypher, "Existence and Entropy," in *Loss of Self in Modern Literature and Art* (New York: Random House, 1962), p. 70.

6. Raymond H. Olderman, *Beyond the Wasteland: A Study of the American Novel in the Nineteen-Sixties* (New Haven: Yale University Press, 1972), p. 1.

7. Ibid., p. 5.

8. Robert Scholes, *The Fabulators* (New York: Oxford University Press, 1967).

9. James D. Houston, *Continental Drift* (New York: Alfred A. Knopf, 1978); Thomas Sanchez, *Rabbit Boss* (New York: Alfred A. Knopf, 1975); Diane Johnson, *Lying Low* (New York: Alfred A. Knopf, 1978).

10. Sol Yurick, *The Bag* (New York: Trident Press, 1968); E. L. Doctorow, *The Book of Daniel* (New York: Random House, 1971); Norman Mailer, *Of a Fire on the Moon* (Boston: Little, Brown, 1970).

11. Alvin Toffler, "Future Shock," *Horizon* 12 (Spring 1970): 82.

12. Philip Roth, *Our Gang* (New York: Random House, 1971); Ken Kesey, *Kesey's Garage Sale* (New York: Viking Press, 1973).

13. Tom Wolfe, ed., *The New Journalism* (New York: Harper and Row, 1973), p. 29.

14. Ken Kesey, *One Flew Over the Cuckoo's Nest* (New York: Viking Press, 1962).

15. Marge Piercy, *Dance the Eagle to Sleep* (Garden City: Doubleday, 1970).

16. Kesey, *One Flew Over the Cuckoo's Nest*, p. 1.

17. Robert Stone, *Hall of Mirrors* (Boston: Houghton Mifflin, 1967). I refer to all of Burroughs's fiction but especially *Naked Lunch* (New York: Grove Press, 1959). John Barth's *The Floating Opera* (New York: Appleton-Century-Crofts, 1956) and *The Sot-Weed Factor* (Garden City: Doubleday, 1960) are his most pertinent works in this regard. All three of Thomas Pynchon's books are directly concerned with plots and conspiracies: *V.* (Philadelphia: J. B. Lippincott, 1963); *The Crying of Lot 49* (Philadelphia: J. B. Lippincott, 1966); and *Gravity's Rainbow* (New York: Viking Press, 1973).

18. Marge Piercy, "In the Men's Room(s)," *Aphra* 3 (Spring 1970): 15.

19. Rudolph Wurlitzer, *Flats* (New York: E. P. Dutton, 1970), p. 157.

20. Olderman, *Beyond the Wasteland*, pp. 28–29.

21. Carlos Castaneda, *The Teachings of Don Juan: A Yaqui Way of Knowledge* (Berkeley: University of California Press, 1968), p. 195.

22. See *William Styron's Nat Turner: Ten Black Writers Respond*, ed. John Henrik Clarke (Boston: Beacon Press, 1968).

23. Ishmael Reed, ed., *19 Necromancers from Now* (Garden City: Doubleday, 1970), p. xvii.

24. John A. Williams, *Captain Blackman* (Garden City: Doubleday, 1972).

25. Ishmael Reed, *Yellow Back Radio Broke-Down* (Garden City: Doubleday, 1969).

26. LeRoi Jones, "The Modern Scene," in *Blues People* (New York: William Morrow, 1963), p. 228.

27. William Melvin Kelley, *Dunfords Travels Everywheres* (Garden City: Doubleday, 1970).

28. Alphabetically, recent fiction of note by women authors includes: Margaret Atwood, *Edible Woman* (Toronto: McClelland and Stewart, 1969), *Surfacing* (New York: Simon and Schuster, 1973), *Lady Oracle* (New York: Simon and Schuster, 1976), and *Dancing Girls and Other Stories* (Toronto: McClelland and Stewart, 1977); Rita Mae Brown, *Rubyfruit Jungle* (New York: Daughters Press, 1973); Rosellen Brown, *Street Games* (Garden City: Doubleday, 1974) and *Cora Fry* (New York: Norton, 1977); Marilyn French, *The Women's Room* (New York: Summit Books, 1977); Diane Johnson, *Loving Hands at Home* (New York: Harcourt, Brace and World, 1968), *Fair Game* (New York: Harcourt, Brace and World, 1965), *Burning* (New York: Harcourt Brace Jovanovich, 1971), *The Shadow Knows* (New York: Alfred A. Knopf, 1974), and *Lying Low* (New York: Alfred A. Knopf, 1978); Erica Jong, *Fear of Flying* (New York: Holt, Rinehart and Winston, 1973) and *How to Save Your Own Life* (New York: Alfred A. Knopf, 1977); Maxine Hong Kingston, *Warrior Woman* (New York: Alfred A. Knopf, 1976); Tillie Olsen, *Tell Me a Riddle* (Philadelphia: Lippin-

cott, 1961) and *Yonnondio* (New York: Delacorte, 1974); Grace Paley, *The Little Disturbances of Man* (New York: Viking Press, 1959) and *Enormous Changes at the Last Minute* (New York: Farrar, Straus & Giroux, 1974); for Marge Piercy's bibliography, see chapter 4 and accompanying notes; Alix Kates Shulman, *Memoirs of an Ex-Prom Queen* (New York: Alfred A. Knopf, 1972). The informed reader may also wish to consult the shelf of fiction by Joyce Carol Oates.

29. Rudolph Wurlitzer, *Nog* (New York: Random House, 1969).

30. Richard Brautigan, "Lint," in *Revenge of the Lawn* (New York: Simon and Schuster, 1971), p. 121.

31. Donald Barthelme, "See the Moon?," in *Unspeakable Practices, Unnatural Acts* (New York: Farrar, Straus & Giroux, 1968), pp. 152, 164.

32. Richard Gilman, "Fiction: Donald Barthelme," in *The Confusion of Realms* (New York: Random House, 1969), p. 43.

33. Don L. Lee, *Black Pride* (Detroit: Broadside Press, 1968).

34. Dudley Randall, ed., *The Black Poets* (New York: Bantam Books, 1971).

35. Ishmael Reed and Al Young have edited six book-length issues of *Yardbird* and *Y'Bird* to date.

36. At this writing, Theodore Solotaroff has taken *New American Review*, now *American Review*, through twenty-two issues and three publishers. The series was initially released by the New American Library, later through Simon and Schuster, finally through Bantam Books. The series has been halted indefinitely by financial demands and Solotaroff fears it may well be impossible to revive. *Fiction*, a tabloid review of contemporary fiction, has appeared through eight issues from New York City. *The American Poetry Review* appeared in November, 1972, and has continued strongly to this time. Edited by Stephen Berg and associates, the review is published bimonthly from Philadelphia and has become the most significant journal of contemporary poetry available.

37. Mark Mirsky, "Introducing *Fiction*," *New York Times Book Review*, 16 April 1972, p. 47.

38. Sukenick's comments were made at a meeting of the Centre de Recherche sur la Litterature Americaine Contemporaine (CRLAC) in Paris at the Sorbonne on 28 April 1978.

39. Ibid.

Chapter 2

1. William H. Gass, "Philosophy and the Form of Fiction," in *Fiction and the*

Figures of Life (New York: Alfred A. Knopf, 1970), p. 25. See also Gass, *The World Within the Word* (New York: Alfred A. Knopf, 1978).

2. Wylie Sypher, "Existence and Entropy," in *Loss of Self in Modern Literature and Art* (New York: Random House, 1962), p. 70.

3. Richard Poirier, "A Literature of Law and Order," in *The Performing Self* (New York: Oxford University Press, 1971), p. 10.

4. John Barth, "The Literature of Exhaustion," in *The American Novel Since World War II*, ed. Marcus Klein (New York: Fawcett, 1969), p. 227.

5. John Barth, *Lost in the Funhouse* (Garden City: Doubleday, 1968) and *Chimera* (Garden City: Doubleday, 1972); Italo Calvino, *t zero* (New York: Harcourt, Brace and World, 1969) and *Cosmi-Comics* (New York: Harcourt, Brace and World, 1968); Robert Coover, *Pricksongs and Descants* (New York: E. P. Dutton, 1969); William Gass, *In the Heart of the Heart of the Country* (New York: Harper and Row, 1968); Jorge Luis Borges, *Labyrinths*, ed. Donald A. Yates and James E. Irby (New York: New Directions, 1964); Ronald Sukenick, *Death of the Novel and Other Stories* (New York: Dial Press, 1969); Ishmael Reed, *Yellow Back Radio Broke-Down* (Garden City: Doubleday, 1969) and *Mumbo Jumbo* (Garden City: Doubleday, 1972); Steve Katz, *The Exaggerations of Peter Prince* (New York: Holt, Rinehart and Winston, 1968); and Leonard Michaels, *Going Places* (New York: Farrar, Straus & Giroux, 1969) and *I Would Have Saved Them If I Could* (New York: Farrar, Straus & Giroux, 1973).

6. Georges Poulet, *The Interior Distance* (Ann Arbor: University of Michigan Press, 1964), p. 28.

7. Donald Barthelme, "The Indian Uprising," in *Unspeakable Practices, Unnatural Acts* (New York: Farrar, Straus & Giroux, 1968), p. 4.

8. Robert Scholes, "Metafiction," *Iowa Review* 1 (Fall 1970): 101.

9. Reed, *Yellow Back Radio Broke-Down*, p. 36.

10. Sukenick, "The Birds," in *Death of the Novel*, p. 165.

11. Donald Barthelme, "After Joyce," *Location* 1 (Summer 1964): 14.

12. John Gardner, *On Moral Fiction* (New York: Basic Books, 1978), p. 69.

13. Barthelme, "After Joyce," p. 15.

14. Alain Robbe-Grillet, *Notes for a New Novel* (New York: Grove Press, 1965), p. 156.

15. Gass, "Philosophy and the Form of Fiction," p. 25.

16. Robbe-Grillet, *Notes for a New Novel*, p. 156.

17. Donald Barthelme's works to date are: *Come Back, Dr. Caligari* (Boston: Little, Brown, 1964); *Snow White* (New York: Atheneum, 1967); *Unspeakable Practices, Unnatural Acts* (New York: Farrar, Straus & Giroux, 1968); *City Life* (New York: Farrar, Straus & Giroux, 1970); *Sadness* (New York: Farrar, Straus & Giroux, 1972); *The Dead Father* (New York: Farrar, Straus & Giroux, 1975);

Amateurs (New York: Farrar, Straus & Giroux, 1976); and *Great Days* (New York: Farrar, Straus & Giroux, 1979). I do not treat a child's book, *The Slightly Irregular Fire Engine* (New York: Farrar, Straus & Giroux, 1972), nor do I consider *Guilty Pleasures* (New York: Farrar, Straus & Giroux, 1974), a work of nonfiction. All subsequent page references are to these editions and are found in the text in parentheses.

18. Gabriel Marcel, *Being and Having* (Boston: Beacon Press, 1951).

19. Poulet, *The Interior Distance*, p. vii.

20. Barthelme, "Brain Damage," in *City Life*, p. 156.

21. Richard Gilman, "Fiction: Donald Barthelme," in *The Confusion of Realms* (New York: Random House, 1969), p. 43.

22. Norman Mailer, "The White Negro," in *Advertisements for Myself* (New York: G. P. Putnam's Sons, 1960), p. 304.

23. Walker Percy, *The Last Gentleman* (New York: Farrar, Straus & Giroux, 1966).

24. Scholes, "Metafiction," p. 101.

25. Poirier, "Introduction," in *The Performing Self*, p. xv.

26. Mailer, "The White Negro," pp. 304, 308.

27. Robbe-Grillet, *Notes for a New Novel*, p. 9.

28. Ibid., pp. 147-48.

29. Ibid., p. 156.

30. Ibid., p. 156.

31. Gass, "Even If, By All the Oxen in the World," in *Fiction and the Figures of Life*, pp. 271-72.

32. Robert Scholes, *The Fabulators* (New York: Oxford University Press, 1967), p. 173.

33. Ibid., p. 171.

34. Poulet, *The Interior Distance*, p. 28.

35. Poirier, "Introduction," in *The Performing Self*, p. xv.

36. Edith Kern, *Existential Thought and Fictional Technique* (New Haven: Yale University Press, 1970), p. 10.

37. Ibid., p. 26.

38. Barth, "The Menelaiad," in *Lost in the Funhouse*, pp. 130-67.

39. Borges, "Tlön, Uqbar, Orbis Tertius," in *Labyrinths*, pp. 3-19; and "The Aleph," in *The Aleph and Other Stories 1933-1969* (New York: E. P. Dutton, 1970), pp. 3-17.

40. Scholes, "Metafiction," p. 101.

41. Diane Johnson, "Possibly Parables," *New York Times Book Review*, 4 February 1979, p. 1.

Chapter 3

1. W. E. B. DuBois, "Of Our Spiritual Strivings," in *The Souls of Black Folk* (New York: New American Library, 1969), p. 45.

2. Ralph Ellison, "Twentieth-Century Fiction and the Black Mask of Humanity," in *Shadow and Act* (New York: New American Library, 1966), pp. 59–60.

3. Ellison, "Hidden Name and Complex Fate," in *Shadow and Act*, p. 166.

4. See especially Frantz Fanon, *The Wretched of the Earth* (New York: Grove Press, 1965).

5. Nathan Glazer and Daniel Moynihan, *Beyond the Melting Pot* (Cambridge: Harvard University Press, 1963), p. 54.

6. Glazer and Moynihan, *Beyond the Melting Pot*, 2d ed. (Cambridge: M.I.T. Press), p. xii.

7. David Littlejohn, *Black on White* (New York: Viking Press, 1966), pp. 3–4.

8. In the case of Bone's book, see Darwin T. Turner, "*The Negro Novel in America*: In Rebuttal," *CLA Journal* 10 (December 1966): 122–34.

9. Ellison, "The World and the Jug," in *Shadow and Act*, pp. 115–47. See also Irving Howe, *A World More Attractive* (New York: Horizon Press, 1963).

10. Ishmael Reed, *Yellow Back Radio Broke-Down* (Garden City: Doubleday, 1969), pp. 34–36.

11. Richard Gilman, "Black Writing and White Criticism," in *The Confusion of Realms* (New York: Random House, 1969), pp. 20–21.

12. Addison Gayle, Jr., ed., *Black Expression* (New York: Weybright and Talley, 1969) and *The Black Aesthetic* (Garden City: Doubleday, 1971).

13. Gayle, "Cultural Strangulation: Black Literature and the White Aesthetic," pp. 39–46 and "The Function of Black Literature at the Present Time," pp. 407–19, both in *The Black Aesthetic*.

14. Addison Gayle, Jr., *The Way of the New World* (Garden City: Doubleday, 1975).

15. Carolyn F. Gerald, "The Black Writer and His Role," in *The Black Aesthetic*, pp. 370–78.

16. Larry Neal, "Some Reflections on the Black Aesthetic," pp. 13–16 and Ishmael Reed, "Can a Metronome Know the Thunder or Summon a God?," pp. 405–6, both in *The Black Aesthetic*, ed. Gayle.

17. Gayle, "Introduction," in *The Black Aesthetic*, p. xxiii.

18. Herbert Aptheker, quoted by John Henrik Clarke in the "Introduction," *William Styron's Nat Turner: Ten Black Writers Respond*, ed. John Henrik Clarke (Boston: Beacon Books, 1968), p. vii.

19. Ibid.

20. "The Uses of History in Fiction," a panel discussion between Ralph Ellison, William Styron, Robert Penn Warren, and C. Vann Woodward, at the Southern Historical Association annual meeting in 1968. The exchange quoted here is found on pages 73–75 of an edited transcript appearing in *The Southern Literary Journal* 1 (Spring 1969): 57–90.

21. Alex Haley, *Roots* (Garden City: Doubleday, 1976).

22. Carolyn Rodgers, works-in-progress cited by Gayle, *The Black Aesthetic*, p. 345.

23. Julius Lester, ed., *To Be a Slave* (New York: Dial Press, 1968).

24. Toni Cade Bambara, ed., *Tales and Stories for Black Folks* (Garden City: Doubleday, 1971).

25. Ishmael Reed, ed., *19 Necromancers from Now* (Garden City: Doubleday, 1970), p. xvii.

26. Ishmael Reed, *Shrovetide in Old New Orleans* (Garden City: Doubleday, 1978), p. 9.

27. Reed, *Shrovetide*, p. 117.

28. William Melvin Kelley, "The Ivy League Negro," *Esquire* (August 1963), p. 55.

29. William Melvin Kelley, "Preface," in *Dancers on the Shore* (Garden City: Doubleday, 1964), p. ii.

30. William Melvin Kelley, quoted by Jervis Anderson in "Black Writing: The Other Side," *Dissent* 15 (May-June 1968): 236–37.

31. William Melvin Kelley, quoted in an interview with Gordon Lish on the recording of "A Reading of William Melvin Kelley's 'Not Exactly Lena Horne,'" New Sounds in American Fiction (Menlo Park, California: Cummings Publishing Company, 1968).

32. William Melvin Kelley, *Dunfords Travels Everywheres* (Garden City: Doubleday, 1970), p. 201.

33. Kelley, quoted in an interview with Gordon Lish on the recording of "Not Exactly Lena Horne."

34. Novels by John A. Williams include: *The Angry Ones* (New York: Ace, 1960), *Night Song* (New York: Farrar, Straus, 1961), *Sissie* (New York: Farrar, Straus, 1963), *The Man Who Cried I Am* (Boston: Little, Brown, 1967), and *Captain Blackman* (Garden City: Doubleday, 1972).

35. Williams, *Captain Blackman*, p. 302.

36. Works by Ernest J. Gaines include: *Catherine Carmier* (New York: Atheneum, 1964), *Of Love and Dust* (New York: Dial Press, 1967), *Bloodline* (New York: Dial Press, 1968), *The Autobiography of Miss Jane Pittman* (New York: Dial Press, 1971), and *In My Father's House* (New York: Alfred A. Knopf,

1978). All page references are to these editions and are found in the text in parentheses.

37. Richard Wright, "Blueprint for Negro Literature," in *Amistad* 2, ed. John A. Williams and Charles F. Harris (New York: Vintage, 1971), p. 8. The editors note that "a shorter version of this essay appeared in the fall issue of a magazine called *New Challenge* in 1937. This version is a much longer development of the original one and it is being published [here] for the first time."

38. Ernest J. Gaines, conversation with Jack Hicks in Davis, California on 18 May 1976.

39. Ibid.

40. Ibid.

41. Michel Fabre, conversation with Jack Hicks in Paris, France on 20 February 1978.

42. "Chapter One of *The House and The Field*," *Iowa Review* 3 (Winter 1972): 121–25.

43. Ernest J. Gaines in a letter to Jack Hicks, San Francisco, California, 26 April 1972.

44. Fred Beauford, "A Conversation with Ernest Gaines," *Black Creation* 2 (Fall 1972): 16–18.

45. Ernest J. Gaines, quoted in *Cutting Edges: Young American Fiction for the '70s*, ed. Jack Hicks (New York: Holt, Rinehart and Winston, 1973), p. 535.

46. Beauford, "A Conversation with Ernest Gaines," p. 18.

47. Kelley, quoted in an interview with Gordon Lish on the recording of "Not Exactly Lena Horne."

48. DuBois, "The Coming of John," in *The Souls of Black Folk*, pp. 245–63.

49. Hoyt W. Fuller, "Books Noted," *Negro Digest* 16 (November 1967): 51.

50. Gaines, conversation with Hicks, 18 May 1976.

51. Ernest J. Gaines, quoted by Hoyt Fuller in "Black Writers' Views on Literary Lions and Values," *Negro Digest* 17 (January 1968): 27.

52. Kelley, quoted by Jervis Anderson in "Black Writing: The Other Side," p. 237.

53. DuBois, "Of the Sorrow Songs," in *The Souls of Black Folk*, p. 267.

54. Gaines, conversation with Hicks, 18 May 1976.

Chapter 4

1. Tom Wolfe, ed., *The New Journalism* (New York: Harper and Row, 1973), p. 30.

2. Ibid., p. 31.

3. Rudolph Wurlitzer, *Nog* (New York: Random House, 1969); *Flats* (New York: E. P. Dutton, 1970); *Quake* (New York: E. P. Dutton, 1972).

4. Tom Robbins, *Another Roadside Attraction* (New York: Ballantine, 1975) and *Even Cowgirls Get the Blues* (Boston: Houghton Mifflin, 1976); Robert Pirsig, *Zen and the Art of Motorcycle Maintenance* (New York: William Morrow, 1974).

5. Elia Katz, *Armed Love* (New York: Holt, Rinehart and Winston, 1971); Michael Rossman, *The Wedding Within the War* (Garden City: Doubleday, 1971); Richard Mungo, *Total Loss Farm* (New York: E. P. Dutton, 1970); Ernst Callenbach, *Ecotopia* (New York: Bantam, 1977).

6. Carlos Castaneda, *The Teachings of Don Juan* (Berkeley: University of California Press); *A Separate Reality* (New York: Simon and Schuster, 1971); *Journey to Ixtlan* (New York: Simon and Schuster, 1972); *Tales of Power* (New York: Simon and Schuster, 1974); *The Second Ring of Power* (New York: Simon and Schuster, 1977).

7. Hunter S. Thompson, *Fear and Loathing in Las Vegas* (New York: Random House, 1974); *Fear and Loathing on the Campaign Trail '72* (New York: Popular Library, 1974); *The Great Shark Hunt* (New York: Summit Books, 1979).

8. Michael Herr, *Dispatches* (New York: Alfred A. Knopf, 1977).

9. Edward Abbey, *The Monkey Wrench Gang* (New York: Lippincott, 1975); *Desert Solitaire* (New York: Ballantine, 1970); *Abbey's Road* (New York: E. P. Dutton, 1979).

10. Todd Gitlin, "Bringing Back the Buffalo," *The Nation*, 7 December 1970, p. 601.

11. Sol Yurick, *The Bag* (New York: Trident Press, 1968).

12. Norman Fruchter, *Single File* (New York: Alfred A. Knopf, 1970); E. L. Doctorow, *The Book of Daniel* (New York: Random House, 1971).

13. M. F. Beal, *Amazon One* (Boston: Little, Brown, 1971).

14. Thomas Sanchez, *Rabbit Boss* (New York: Alfred A. Knopf, 1973).

15. Epigraph on page 143 is taken from a poem by Marge Piercy, "The Aim, The Best That Can Be Hoped For: The Magician," in *To Be of Use* (Garden City: Doubleday, 1973), p. 82. Marge Piercy, "From Maude Awake," in *The Bold New Women*, ed. Barbara Alson (Greenwich, New York: Gold Medal Books, 1966), pp. 23–31.

16. Marge Piercy's novels are *Going Down Fast* (New York: Simon and Schuster, 1969); *Dance the Eagle to Sleep* (Garden City: Doubleday, 1970); *Small Changes* (New York: Fawcett, 1975); *Woman on the Edge of Time* (New York: Alfred A. Knopf, 1976); *The High Cost of Living* (New York: Harper and Row, 1978). All page references are to these editions and are found in the text in parentheses.

17. Marge Piercy, quoted in *Cutting Edges: Young American Fiction for the '70s*, ed. Jack Hicks (New York: Holt, Rinehart and Winston, 1973), pp. 543-44.

18. "Marge Piercy," *Contemporary Poets of the English Language*, ed. Rosalie Murphy (New York: St. James Press, 1970), p. 854.

19. Piercy, quoted in *Cutting Edges*, ed. Jack Hicks, pp. 543-44.

20. Ibid.

21. Ibid.

22. Ibid.

23. Ibid.

24. John Seelye, "The Greening Grows Dark," *New Republic*, 12 December 1970, pp. 24-25. Linda Kuehl, *"Dance the Eagle to Sleep," Commonweal*, 7 April 1971, pp. 92-94. Gitlin, "Bringing Back the Buffalo," pp. 601-2.

25. John Updike, "If at First You Do Succeed, Try, Try Again," *New Yorker*, 10 April 1971, pp. 143-53.

26. Piercy, quoted in *Cutting Edges*, ed. Jack Hicks, pp. 543-44.

27. Marge Piercy, "In the Men's Room(s)," in *To Be of Use* (Garden City: Doubleday, 1973), p. 8.

28. Epigraph on page 151 is taken from Richard Brautigan's "The World War I Los Angeles Airplane," in *Revenge of the Lawn* (New York: Simon and Schuster, 1971), p. 174. Richard Brautigan, *The Pill Versus the Springhill Mine Disaster* (San Francisco: Four Seasons Foundation, 1968); *In Watermelon Sugar* (San Francisco: Four Seasons Foundation, 1968).

29. Richard Brautigan, *Trout Fishing in America*, *The Pill Versus the Springhill Mine Disaster*, and *In Watermelon Sugar* (New York: Delacorte Press, 1969).

30. Richard Brautigan, *The Abortion: An Historical Romance 1966* (New York: Simon and Schuster, 1970); *Revenge of the Lawn* (New York: Simon and Schuster, 1971); *The Hawkline Monster: A Gothic Western* (New York: Simon and Schuster, 1974); *Willard and His Bowling Trophies: A Perverse Mystery* (New York: Simon and Schuster, 1975); *Sombrero Fallout: A Japanese Novel* (New York: Simon and Schuster, 1976); *Dreaming of Babylon* (New York: Delacorte Press, 1977); *June 30th, June 30th* (New York: Delacorte, 1978). All page references are to these editions and are found in the text in parentheses.

31. Brautigan, "Albion Breakfast," in *The Pill Versus the Springhill Mine Disaster*, p. 77.

32. Richard Brautigan, *A Confederate General from Big Sur* (New York: Grove Press, 1968), p. 3.

33. John Clayton, "Richard Brautigan: The Politics of Woodstock," in *New American Review*, ed. Ted Solotaroff (New York: Simon and Schuster, 1971), p. 59.

34. Ibid., p. 68.

35. Gurney Norman and Ed McLanahan, *"Revenge of the Lawn,"* *Rolling Stone*, 9 December 1971, p. 66.

36. The epigraph on page 161 is taken from Ken Kesey's *One Flew Over the Cuckoo's Nest* (New York: Viking Press, 1962), p. 8.

37. Tom Wolfe, *The Electric Kool-Aid Acid Test* (New York: Farrar, Straus & Giroux, 1968), p. 88.

38. John C. Pratt's introduction and chronology in Ken Kesey, *One Flew Over the Cuckoo's Nest: Text and Criticism*, ed. John C. Pratt (New York: Viking Press, 1973), provide much of the available biographical information on Kesey. See also the special Ken Kesey issue of *Northwest Review*, published in book form as *Kesey*, ed. Michael Strelow (Eugene: Northwest Review Books, 1977).

39. Ken Kesey, *Kesey's Garage Sale* (New York: Viking Press, 1973), p. 7.

40. Ken Kesey, *Sometimes a Great Notion* (New York: Viking Press, 1964).

41. Ken Kesey and Paul Krassner, eds., *The Last Supplement to the Whole Earth Catalogue* (San Francisco: Portola Institute, 1971).

42. Kesey, *Kesey's Garage Sale*, p. iii.

43. Two "prayers" appear in *Kesey*, ed. Michael Strelow, pp. 99–166; John Pratt's comments are also in "On Editing Kesey: Confessions of a Straight Man," in *Kesey*, p. 10. "Abdul and Ebenezer" appeared in *Esquire* (March 1976), pp. 55–59.

44. Ken Kesey, "Letter to Ken Babbs," in *One Flew Over the Cuckoo's Nest*, ed. John C. Pratt, p. 337. See also Malcolm Cowley's article, "Ken Kesey at Stanford," in *Kesey*, ed. Michael Strelow, pp. 1–4.

45. Kesey, *Kesey's Garage Sale*, p. 7.

46. Kesey, "Letter to Ken Babbs," quoted in *One Flew Over the Cuckoo's Nest*, ed. John C. Pratt, p. 338.

47. Kesey, "An Early Draft of the Opening Scene of *One Flew Over the Cuckoo's Nest*," in *One Flew Over the Cuckoo's Nest*, ed. John C. Pratt, pp. 333–35.

48. Terry G. Sherwood, *"One Flew Over the Cuckoo's Nest* and the Comic Strip," *Critique* 13 (Winter 1971):97.

Chapter 5

1. Joseph Novak, *No Third Path* (Garden City: Doubleday, 1962), pp. 58–60. Subsequent page references are to this edition and are found in the text in parentheses.

2. Joseph Novak, *The Future Is Ours, Comrade* (Garden City: Doubleday, 1960).

Subsequent page references are to this edition and are found in the text in parentheses.

3. Jerzy Kosinski, "Documents Concerning the Struggle of Man: Reminiscences of the Members of 'The Proletariat,'" *Review of Social and Historical Sciences* (Lodz) 4 (1954):412; translated and cited by Jerome Klinkowitz in *Literary Disruptions* (Urbana: University of Illinois Press, 1975), pp. 86–87.

4. Jerzy Kosinski, *The Painted Bird* (Boston: Houghton Mifflin, 1965 and New York: Bantam, 1972); *Steps* (New York: Random House, 1968); *Being There* (New York: Harcourt Brace Jovanovich, 1971); *The Devil Tree* (New York: Harcourt Brace Jovanovich, 1973); *Cockpit* (Boston: Houghton Mifflin, 1975); *Blind Date* (Boston: Houghton Mifflin, 1977); *Passion Play* (New York: St. Martin's Press, 1979). All subsequent page references are to these editions and are found in the text in parentheses.

5. Daniel J. Cahill, "*The Devil Tree*: An Interview With Jerzy Kosinski," *North American Review* 258 (Spring 1973):56; and George Plimpton, "The Art of Fiction: Jerzy Kosinski," *Paris Review* 54 (Summer 1972):183.

6. Jerome Klinkowitz, "Jerzy Kosinski: An Interview," *Fiction International* 1 (Fall 1973):41.

7. Ibid., pp. 36–37.

8. "Jerzy Kosinski," *Current Biography 1974* (New York: H. W. Wilson, 1974), p. 214.

9. Klinkowitz notes almost twenty in a thorough bibliographical appendix to *Literary Disruptions*. As of this writing in June 1978, I have located almost an equal additional number. I rely mainly on sources listed by Klinkowitz, pp. 218–21, unless otherwise noted.

10. "Jerzy Kosinski," *Current Biography 1974*, p. 213.

11. Irving Howe, "The Other Side of the Moon," *Harper's*, March 1969, p. 104.

12. Tadeusz Borowski, *This Way to the Gas, Ladies and Gentlemen* (New York: Viking Press, 1967).

13. "Jerzy Kosinski," *Current Biography 1974*, p. 215.

14. Jerzy Kosinski, "Presidential Papers," *American P.E.N. Newsletter*, Summer 1973, p. 1.

15. Gail Sheehy, "The Psychological Novelist as Portable Man: An Interview with Jerzy Kosinski," *Psychology Today*, December 1977, p. 128.

16. Jerzy Kosinski, "Dead Souls On Campus," *New York Times*, 13 October 1970, p. 48.

17. Alain Robbe-Grillet, *Notes For A New Novel* (New York: Grove Press, 1965), p. 148. Subsequent page references appear in the text in parentheses.

18. Jerzy Kosinski, *The Art of the Self* (New York: Scientia-Factum, 1968), p. 13.

19. Ron Nowicki, "An Interview with Jerzy Kosinski," *San Francisco Review of Books*, 3 (March 1978):11.

20. Howe, "The Other Side of the Moon," p. 102.

21. Plimpton, "The Art of Fiction," p. 196.

22. "*The Future Is Ours, Comrade*," *Library Journal*, 15 April 1960, p. 1585.

23. Richard C. Hottelet, "*No Third Path*," *New York Times Book Review*, 22 May 1960, p. 3.

24. Hottelet, "*No Third Path*," p. 20.

25. Gerald Weales, "Jerzy Kosinski: *The Painted Bird* and Other Disguises," *Hollins Critic* 14 (October 1972):9.

26. See Kosinski, *The Art of the Self*; also see Jerzy Kosinski, *Notes of the Author* (New York: Scientia-Factum, 1965).

27. Arthur Miller, quoted by Jerzy Kosinski in prefatory comments on *The Painted Bird*, in *Notes of the Author*, p. i.

28. For a discussion of the textual history of *The Painted Bird*, see David H. Richter, "The Three Denouements of Jerzy Kosinski's *The Painted Bird*," *Contemporary Literature* 15 (Summer 1974): 370–85; see also Jerome Klinkowitz, "Two Bibliographical Questions in Kosinski's *The Painted Bird*," *Contemporary Literature* 16 (Fall 1974): 126–29.

29. Kosinski, *Notes of the Author*, p. 19.

30. E. V. Lucas, trans., *From Grimm's Fairy Tales* (New York: Grosset and Dunlap, 1945), pp. 7–17. Subsequent page references are to this edition and are found in the text in parentheses.

31. Cited in Klinkowitz, *Literary Disruptions*, p. 101.

32. C. G. Jung, *The Archetypes and the Collective Unconscious* (New York: Pantheon Books, 1959). See three essays in particular: "Concerning Rebirth," pp. 113–50; "The Psychology of the Child Archetype," pp. 151–81; and "The Phenomenology of the Spirit in the Fairytale," pp. 207–54. See also Bruno Bettelheim, *The Uses of Enchantment* (New York: Alfred A. Knopf, 1976).

33. Kosinski, *Notes of the Author*, p. 13.

34. Plimpton, "The Art of Fiction," p. 200.

35. Kosinski, *Notes of the Author*, p. 19.

36. Ibid., p. 24.

37. *The Metamorphoses of Ovid*, trans. Mary M. Innes (London: Penguin Books, 1955), p. 345.

38. Jung, "The Phenomenology of the Spirit in the Fairytale," p. 210.

39. Ibid., p. 229.

40. Ralph Ellison, *Invisible Man* (New York: Random House, 1952), p. 22.

41. Jung, "Psychological Aspects of the Mother Archetype," in *The Archetypes and the Collective Unconscious*, p. 82.

42. Jung, "The Phenomenology of the Spirit in the Fairytale," p. 234.

43. Kosinski, *The Painted Bird* (Boston: Houghton Mifflin, 1965), p. 217.

44. *The Metamorphoses of Ovid*, trans. Mary M. Innes, p. 29.

45. Kosinski, *The Art of the Self*, p. 17.

46. Robbe-Grillet, *Notes For A New Novel*, p. 148.

47. Kosinski, *The Art of the Self*, p. 15.

48. Ibid., p. 22.

49. Plimpton, "The Art of Fiction," p. 200.

50. Kosinski, *The Art of the Self*, p. 22.

51. I find Alexandre Kojeve's *Introduction to the Reading of Hegel* (New York: Basic Books, 1969) an excellent introduction to Hegel's thought.

52. Kosinski, *The Art of the Self*, p. 23.

53. *The Metamorphoses of Ovid*, trans. Mary M. Innes, p. 357.

54. David Sohn, "A Nation of Videots," *Media and Methods* (April 1975): 56.

55. Jerzy Kosinski, "The Lone Wolf," *American Scholar* 41 (Autumn 1972): 513–19.

56. See Weir's obituary in *New York Times*, 27 June 1957, p. 25; see also the Ernest T. Weir entry in *Who Was Who in America, 1951–1960* (Chicago: A. N. Marquis, 1963), vol. 3, p. 900.

57. Robert Alter, "*The Devil Tree*," *New York Times Book Review*, 11 February 1973, p. 2.

58. Cahill, "*The Devil Tree*," p. 63.

59. Stanley Kunitz, "Lovers Relentlessly," in *Selected Poems 1928–1958* (Boston: Little, Brown, 1958), p. 20.

60. Nowicki, "An Interview with Jerzy Kosinski," p. 13.

61. Jacques Monod, *Chance and Necessity* (London: William Collins Sons, 1972), pp. 160–61.

62. Nowicki, "An Interview with Jerzy Kosinski," p. 13.

Chapter 6

1. Rainer Maria Rilke, "Sonnet I," *Ten Sonnets to Orpheus*, trans. Robert Bly (Berkeley: Mudra/Zephyrus Image, 1976), p. 2; this sonnet also available in *Leaping Poetry*, ed. Robert Bly (Boston: Beacon Press, 1975), p. 75.

2. Ibid.

3. Rainer Maria Rilke, "Sonnet 29," *The Sonnets to Orpheus: Second Series*, trans. A. Poulin, Jr. (Boston: Houghton Mifflin, 1977), p. 195.

4. Ralph Ellison, "Hidden Name and Complex Fate," in *Shadow and Act* (New York: New American Library, 1966), p. 166.

5. Ibid.

6. John Gardner, *On Moral Fiction* (New York: Basic Books, 1978), pp. 57, 16.

7. Rilke, "Sonnet 29," p. 195.

Acknowledgments

Donald Barthelme. Excerpts from *City Life*, copyright © 1968, 1969 by Donald Barthelme; this material first appeared in *The New Yorker*. Excerpts from *The Dead Father*, copyright © 1975 by Donald Barthelme. Excerpts from *Great Days*, copyright © 1977, 1978 by Donald Barthelme. Excerpts from *Unspeakable Practices, Unnatural Acts*, copyright © 1967, 1968 by Donald Barthelme. Reprinted by permission of Farrar, Straus and Giroux, Inc.

Robert Bly. "Sonnet III" from *Ten Sonnets to Orpheus*, by Rainer Maria Rilke, translated by Robert Bly. Mudra/Zephyrus Image Magazine, 1972. Copyright © 1972 by Robert Bly. Reprinted by permission of Robert Bly.

Richard Brautigan. "Albion Breakfast" excerpted from *The Pill Versus the Springhill Mine Disaster*. Copyright © 1968 by Richard Brautigan. Reprinted by permission of Delacorte Press/Seymour Lawrence. Excerpts from "Blackberry Motorist," "The Old Bus," "Revenge of the Lawn," and "The World War I Los Angeles Airplane," in *Revenge of the Lawn*. Copyright © 1963, 1964, 1965, 1966, 1967, 1969, 1970, 1971 by Richard Brautigan. Reprinted by permission of Simon and Schuster, a division of Gulf and Western Corporation. Excerpts from *Trout Fishing in America*. Copyright © 1967 by Richard Brautigan. Reprinted by permission of Delacorte Press/Seymour Lawrence. Excerpts from *In Watermelon Sugar*. Copyright © 1968 by Richard Brautigan. Reprinted with permission of Delacorte Press/Seymour Lawrence.

John Gardner. Excerpt from *On Moral Fiction*. New York: Basic Books, Inc., 1978. Copyright © 1978 by Basic Books, Inc. Reprinted by permission of the publisher.

Mary Innes. Excerpt from *The Metamorphoses of Ovid*, translated by Mary M. Innes. New York: Penguin Classics, 1955. Copyright © 1955 by Mary M. Innes. Reprinted by permission of Penguin Books Ltd.

Ken Kesey. Excerpts from *Ken Kesey, One Flew Over the Cuckoo's Nest: Text and Criticism*, edited by John C. Pratt. New York: Viking Penguin Inc., 1973. Copyright © 1973 by Viking Critical Library. Reprinted by permission of Ken Kesey and Viking Penguin Inc.

Jerzy Kosinski. Excerpt from *The Art of the Self*. New York: Scientia-Factum, Inc., 1968. Copyright © 1968 by Jerzy Kosinski. Reprinted by permission of Jerzy Kosinski. Excerpts from *Blind Date*, a novel by Jerzy Kosinski. Boston: Houghton Mifflin Company, 1977. New York: Bantam Books (paper edition), 1978. Copyright © 1977 by Jerzy Kosinski. Reprinted by permission of Jerzy Kosinski. Excerpt from *Cockpit*, a novel by Jerzy Kosinski. Boston: Houghton Mifflin Company, 1975. New York: Bantam Books (paper edition), 1976. Copyright © 1975 by Jerzy Kosinski. Reprinted by permission of Jerzy Kosinski. Excerpt from *The Devil Tree*. New York: Harcourt Brace Jovanovich, Inc., 1973. Copyright © 1973 by Jerzy Kosinski. Reprinted by permission of Harcourt Brace Jovanovich, Inc. Excerpt from *The Future Is Ours, Comrade*, by Jerzy Kosinski under the pen name Joseph Novak. Garden City: Doubleday and Company, Inc., 1960. Copyright © 1960 by Doubleday and Company, Inc. Reprinted by permission of Doubleday and Company, Inc. Excerpts from *No Third Path*, by Jerzy Kosinski under the pen name Joseph Novak. Garden City: Doubleday and Company, Inc., 1962. Copyright © 1962 by Doubleday and Company, Inc. Reprinted by permission of Jerzy Kosinski. Excerpts from *The Painted Bird*. Boston: Houghton Mifflin Company (2d edition), 1976. New York: Bantam Books (paper edition), 1978. Copyright © 1965, 1976 by Jerzy N. Kosinski. Reprinted by permission of Houghton Mifflin Company.

David Littlejohn. Excerpt from *Black on White*. New York: Viking Penguin Inc., 1966. Copyright © 1966 by David Littlejohn. Reprinted by permission of Viking Penguin Inc.

Marge Piercy. Excerpts from *Dance The Eagle To Sleep*. Garden City: Doubleday and Company, Inc., 1970. Copyright © 1970 by Marge Piercy. Reprinted by permission of Marge Piercy. "In the Men's Room(s)," and "The Magician," from *To Be of Use*. Garden City: Doubleday and Company, Inc., 1973. Copyright © 1969, 1971, 1973 by Marge Piercy. Reprinted by permission of Marge Piercy.

Ishmael Reed. Excerpt from *Yellow Back Radio Broke-Down*. Garden City:

Doubleday and Company, Inc., 1969. Copyright © 1969 by Ishmael Reed. Reprinted by permission of Doubleday and Company, Inc.

Alain Robbe-Grillet. Excerpts from *For a New Novel*. New York: Grove Press, Inc., 1965. Copyright © 1965 by Grove Press, Inc. Reprinted by permission of Grove Press, Inc.

Tom Wolfe. Excerpts (on pp. 8 and 138–39 of this volume) from *The New Journalism*. New York: Harper and Row, Publishers, Inc., 1973. Copyright © 1973 by Tom Wolfe and E. W. Johnson. Reprinted by permission of Harper and Row, Publishers, Inc.

Index